THE POWERFUL NORM FOR CLIMATE CHANGE ACTION

How International Organizations Legitimate Themselves Amid Contestation

Laura von Allwörden

First published in Great Britain in 2026 by

Bristol University Press
University of Bristol
1–9 Old Park Hill
Bristol
BS2 8BB
UK
t: +44 (0)117 374 6645
e: bup-info@bristol.ac.uk

Details of international sales and distribution partners are available at bristoluniversitypress.co.uk

© Laura von Allwörden 2026

The digital PDF and ePub versions of this title are available open access and distributed under the terms of the Creative Commons Attribution-NonCommercial-NoDerivatives 4.0 International licence (https://creativecommons.org/licenses/by-nc-nd/4.0/) which permits reproduction and distribution for non-commercial use without further permission provided the original work is attributed.

DOI: 10.51952/9781529252415

British Library Cataloguing in Publication Data
A catalogue record for this book is available from the British Library

ISBN 978-1-5292-5239-2 paperback
ISBN 978-1-5292-5240-8 ePub
ISBN 978-1-5292-5241-5 OA PDF

The right of Laura von Allwörden to be identified as author of this work has been asserted by her in accordance with the Copyright, Designs and Patents Act 1988.

All rights reserved: no part of this publication may be reproduced, stored in a retrieval system, or transmitted in any form or by any means, electronic, mechanical, photocopying, recording, or otherwise without the prior permission of Bristol University Press.

Every reasonable effort has been made to obtain permission to reproduce copyrighted material. If, however, anyone knows of an oversight, please contact the publisher.

The statements and opinions contained within this publication are solely those of the author and not of the University of Bristol or Bristol University Press. The University of Bristol and Bristol University Press disclaim responsibility for any injury to persons or property resulting from any material published in this publication.

Bristol University Press works to counter discrimination on grounds of gender, race, disability, age and sexuality.

Cover design: Clifford Hayes
Front cover image: iStock/Toa55

Contents

List of Figures and Tables		iv
List of Abbreviations		v
About the Author		vii
Acknowledgements		viii
1	Introduction: Contested International Organizations in Climate and Energy	1
2	Understanding Norms as Guiding Frames in Contestation–Legitimation Processes	17
3	Emergence of the Norm for Climate Change Action: The UNFCCC and Contestation of Global South	47
4	The UNFCCC, US Contestation and Guidance by the Norm for Climate Change Action	62
5	Contestation Along the North–South Divide: The International Energy Agency Turning to Collective Action	78
6	Frozen in Time: The International Energy Agency Moving Towards Climate Change Action	92
7	Comparing Cases: Climate Change Action Across the Climate–Energy Nexus	104
8	Conclusion: Contestation and Legitimation of IOs in the Global Climate Regime	121
Appendix A: List of Interviews		133
Appendix B: Questions to the Interviewees		135
Appendix C: Ethics – Consensual and Safe Research with Participants and Data		139
Notes		142
References		144
Index		164

List of Figures and Tables

Figures

2.1	Conceptual connection contestation–legitimation processes	21
3.1	UNFCCC: Process of G77 walkout	53
4.1	UNFCCC: Process of US contestation of the Paris Agreement	66
5.1	IEA: Process of OECD-only membership	82
6.1	IEA: Process of oil-only approach	93

Tables

1.1	Key issues in the global climate regime North–South divide and institutional format and cases	10
2.1	Markers in practices to deconstruct guiding frame, here: norm for CCA	44
3.1	Timeline of G77 walkout and loss and damage debate	51
4.1	Timeline of US contestation of the Paris Agreement	64
5.1	Timeline milestones of processes IEA	80
7.1	Norm for CCA in contestation and legitimation practices of processes by case and issue area	105
7.2	Summary of contestation and legitimation practices by case and major key issue in global climate governance, North–South divide	117
7.3	Summary of contestation and legitimation practices by case and major key issue in global climate governance, institutional format	119

List of Abbreviations

ADB	Asian Development Bank
APEC	Asia-Pacific Economic Cooperation
ASEAN	Association of Southeast Asian Nations
AU	African Union
BRICS	informal organization of economically emerging states
CBDR	Common But Differentiated Responsibilities
CCA	Norm for Climate Change Action
CEM	Clean Energy Ministerial
COP/COPs	Conference/s of the Parties
ECT	Energy Charter Treaty
EU	European Union
EUROSTAT	European Statistical Office
GCF	Global Climate Fund
GECF	Gas Exporting Countries Forum
GEF	Global Environmental Fund
G7	coalition of 7 countries from the Global North
G20	coalition of 19 countries plus the EU and AU
G77	coalition of 134 developing/of the Global South countries plus China in the UN
IEA	International Energy Agency
IEF	International Energy Forum
IISD	International Institute for Sustainable Development
IO	International Organization
IPCC	Intergovernmental Panel on Climate Change
IR	International Relations
IRENA	International Renewable Energy Agency
JODI	Joint Organisations Data Initiative
NATO	North Atlantic Treaty Organization
NAZCA	Non-state Actor Zone for Climate Action
NDC	nationally determined contribution
OECD	Organisation for Economic Co-operation and Development
OLADE	The Latin American Energy Organization

OPEC	Organization of the Petroleum Exporting Countries
UN	United Nations
UNEP	United Nations Environment Programme
UNFCCC	United Nations Framework Convention on Climate Change
UNSD	United Nations Statistics Division
US	United States
WEO	World Energy Outlook
WIM	Warsaw International Mechanism
WTO	World Trade Organization

About the Author

Laura von Allwörden is a consultant for energy sourcing. Before and when writing this book, she was a postdoctoral researcher and lecturer at the chair of International Relations at Kiel University, Germany. Prior to that she was a doctoral researcher and PhD candidate in the ERC NestIOr research project 'Who gets to live forever? Toward an Institutional Theory on the Decline and Death of International Organisations' at Maastricht University, The Netherlands. In May 2023 she defended her doctoral thesis in Maastricht, way before the funding deadline. In 2022 Laura was a guest researcher at the chair for Political Science, especially concerning international organizations, at the University of Potsdam. Since 2023 Laura has been a fellow in the excellency project DenkRaum 'Energy in Changing Times and a Changing World' at CAU, where she also receives funding. Further, she is an associate in the expert network of the Horizon project ENSURED, hosted at Maastricht University. Also, she is a member of the SECC – Societal, Environmental, and Cultural Change – network at CAU.

In her research, Laura has specialized in international organization, norms, and related practices in the global climate regime. Her focus is particularly on concepts of contestation, legitimation, and crisis in global governance. In her research, she employs qualitative methods of interpretive, and discursive and practice analysis. Here, she conducts open- and semi-structured interviewing as well as ethnographic methods like participant observation. Her work has been published in Bristol University Press, Oxford University Press, *International Relations, Cambridge Review of International Affairs*, and *Zeitschrift für Internationale Beziehungen*.

Acknowledgements

First and foremost, I would like to thank the editors of Bristol University Press, Stephen Wenham and Zoe Forbes, for supporting this book. I would also like to thank Sophia Unger from Newgen in this regard. I want to thank my great PhD supervisors from Maastricht University, Hylke Dijkstra and Esther Versluis, for all your support and advice. I am very lucky to have had you on my side during the process. I want to thank Elke Krahmann and Kilian Spandler, as Professor ad interim at the CAU chair of IR, for their generous support and funding. I am grateful to have received funding from the European Research Council (ERC) under the European Union's Horizon 2020 research and innovation programme (grant agreement No. 802568), in the project NestIOr hosted at Maastricht University, as well as from Deutsche Forschungsgemeinschaft DenkRaum Fellowship 'Energie im Wandel der Zeit und der Welt' hosted at Christian-Albrechts-Universität zu Kiel. I would like to give special thanks my colleague Nadine Wagener-Böck in this regard. Moreover, I would like to thank Merle Damm, Luise Hirsch and Franka Starke for their amazing research assistance and their excellent work. I want to thank all my interviewees at the UNFCCC, IEA, IRENA, and beyond for giving me their time and sharing their insights into the complex world of climate governance. Thank you also for your kindness and making my first fieldwork interview such a positive and confidence-boosting experience. In this regard, I also want to thank Vegard Tørstad for helping me out with my second round of fieldwork rand sharing some golden insights with me. I want to thank the assessment committee of my dissertation that this book is based on. To Sophie Vanhoonacker, Anna Herranz Surralles, Thomas Sommerer and Carmen Wunderlich, for awarding me and my thesis with the doctoral degree and giving such a great assessment. Thank you for your engagement, time, and excellent feedback. I also would like to thank all participants at the several workshops and conferences for their time, feedback, and the discussions of my papers that also helped me in better understanding and writing my research. I want to thank Maria Josepha Debre for her overall support. I would like to thank my colleague and friend Elena Dück for her support within and beyond the academic day to day business. Last, I want to thank my friends and family for their support, and to extend my very special gratitude to Marius for his support.

1

Introduction: Contested International Organizations in Climate and Energy

The reality of climate change manifests itself as a global existential crisis, in which loss and destruction are 'measured in lives' (Mottley, 2021). At the yearly global climate summit (COP), the United Nations Framework Convention on Climate Change (UNFCCC) brings world leaders of 197 countries together, to solve this crisis that affects all of us. At COP26 in Glasgow in 2021, Mia Amor Mottley, the Prime Minister of Barbados, challenged world leaders in her remarkable speech by emphasizing the existential, life-threatening reality of climate change:

> what must we say to our people living on the frontline in the Caribbean, Africa and the Pacific when both ambition and some of the needed faces are absent? What excuse should we give for their failure? ... Our people are watching and taking note. ... Will we act in the interest of our people who are depending on us or will we allow the path of greed and selfishness to sow the seeds of our common destruction? (Mottley, 2021)

Climate change is a global issue, and its effects will continue to rise around the globe. Thus, climate change demands collective action to at least control the extent of, or at best avoid, 'our common destruction' (Mottley, 2021). Mottley is not alone in this claim (see, for example, Benson and Craig, 2014). As the Intergovernmental Panel on Climate Change (IPCC), which is the United Nations body for assessing the science related to climate change, states: 'Human-induced climate change is causing dangerous and widespread disruption in nature and affecting the lives of billions of people around the world' (IPCC, 2022). For example, other organizations such as the United Nations Environment Programme (UNEP) now officially call climate change a climate crisis, that is, an 'emergency', and human-made as 'a direct consequence of our carbon-heavy land-use and agriculture, transport, buildings and industrial processes and our polluting energy sources' (UNEP, 2019).

Vital to solving this crisis is the (final) implementation of the Paris Agreement. This agreement, which was ratified in 2015, is meant to deliver the collective action that is needed to fight climate change. The Paris Agreement requires states to achieve their goals of limiting 'global warming to well below 2, preferably to 1.5 degrees Celsius', and aims to 'reach global peaking of greenhouse gas emissions as soon as possible to achieve a climate neutral world by mid-century' (UNFCCC, nd [a]). When ratified, the Paris Agreement was seen as ultimate success and turnaround in the climate crisis; however, to date not all world leaders share the perception of climate change as a pressing existential threat to humanity. Not only did the US, a major leader when it comes to world politics and international relations, withdraw once from the Paris Agreement in 2017 under President Donald Trump, but twice when he was re-elected in 2025. Climate change has thus not only become a threat itself, but the multilateral endeavour to fight it is threatened from within the political engine room.

Yet not everyone shares this hostile perception. In the past decade a large number of civil societies around the globe have recognized climate change as a priority 'as the science is clearer and consensus grows impossible to ignore' (Nunez, 2019). In particular, since the founding of the Fridays for Future movement (Fridays For Future, nd), in which especially Generation Z (BBC, 2022) across societies protest for climate action during school hours,[1] the demand for politics to get serious about environmental issues and act on climate change has drastically increased. Consequently, global climate action[2] is not just a catchphrase, but rather it has become the norm for global cooperation towards this existential crisis. The norm for climate change action (CCA)[3] speaks to the stronger and more ambitious mobilization and implementation of policies and action by all global actors that are required to achieve the goals of the Paris Agreement (UNFCCC, nd [b]). These must come from governments, cities, regions, and businesses alike as climate change action is a collective endeavour. Thus, the spotlight is not only on national actors but also on respective energy and environmental international organizations (IOs) in the global climate regime.

International organizations, contestations and climate change

In general, IOs are part of the evolving, complex system of global governance, in which states need to constantly re-evaluate 'how they conduct themselves in the storm' (Guzzini, 2013, p 229; cf. Tussie, 2018, p 205). They need to navigate their tasks, mandate, members, network and themselves through this complexity (Barnett and Finnemore, 2004; Rittberger et al, 2019). So, what if the respective organization fails to follow up on the task of navigating international cooperation on climate change or energy transition? Or is perceived to fail in delivering in the mandate to individual or more member states? In the recent past, there have been contestations by powerful states to several IOs, including in different fields, whether it be the World Trade Organization (WTO), the World Bank or the North Atlantic Treaty Organization (NATO) (see, for example, Schuette, 2021; Dijkstra et al, 2022; Zaccaria, 2022). These contestations put these organizations under pressure and simultaneously brought questions about contestation and legitimation to the forefront in academic research (Bäckstrand and Söderbaum, 2018, p 101; see also Barnett and Finnemore, 2004; Barnett and Coleman, 2005; Bernauer and Gampfer, 2013; Zaum, 2013; Tallberg et al, 2018, p 8; Tallberg and Zürn, 2019; Zürn, 2020).

Contestation, which is understood as a social practice through which disapproval is expressed (Wiener, 2014, p 1), ranges from, for example, major powers within the IOs, such as the US, to externals within civil society and scientific experts. Also, scholars find that the global governance system with its hierarchies of inequality itself contains a legitimation problem that produces contestation 'endogenously' (Zürn, 2018, p 6). Contestation entails 'objection to specific issues that matter to people', or even rejection or refusal of the implementation of norms and practices (Wiener, 2014, p 1). For IOs, contestation can have several consequences, all of which have delegitimating potential that can lead to an existential crisis of legitimacy. IOs '[experience] a crisis of legitimacy ... when the level of social recognition that its identity, interests, practices, norms, or procedures are rightful declines to the point where it must either adapt ... or face disempowerment' (Reus-Smit, 2007, p 157). These consequences can range from missing financial contributions that can cause a performance loss and gridlock (see, for example, Hale et al, 2013). The same gridlock potential occurs if member states, although they are not withdrawing, turn their back on the IO by establishing a counter institution that caters better to their demands (Urpelainen and Van de Graaf, 2015). Further, member withdrawal can lead to a domino effect of other members cancelling their membership (Walter, 2021). These consequences can work as de-legitimation and can lead to a loss and crisis of legitimacy.

The navigation of international cooperation on climate change- or energy transition policies is a difficult endeavour. This complexity creates a fragile realm for IOs and puts them in a permanent exertion for legitimacy, which is the belief and recognition of appropriate authority that has the right to act and to govern (Tallberg and Zürn, 2019, pp 582, 585). Therefore, they are in consequent reoccurring need for legitimation, which is the '[practice] of justification ... intended to shape legitimacy beliefs' (Tallberg et al, 2018, p 4). In the past, also within the global climate regime, numerous instances of contestation were followed by de-legitimation (see, for example, Bäckstrand et al, 2017; Hickmann et al, 2019; Well et al, 2020). For example, the failure of US ratification of the Kyoto Protocol in 2001, which was the predecessor to the Paris Agreement (see, for example, Pickering et al, 2018), and the breakdown of COP15 in Copenhagen in 2009 (see, for example, Bäckstrand et al, 2017) were both major instances of contestation, which brought de-legitimation to the global climate regime.

However, what can be empirically observed is that despite several, different instances of contestation originating from different levels of the power hierarchy, some IOs neither experience consequences of de-legitimation nor do they mount to a legitimacy crisis. How can this be explained? Why does contestation of IOs, even though it may come from powerful actors that can have a deep, negative impact on the respective IO's legitimacy, lead to legitimation? We would expect that the more powerful the contester is, the more likely we would see a negative, de-legitimating impact of this contestation. For example, Zaccaria shows how the Trump contestation of the WTO Appellate Body led to a de-legitimation, as the Trump administration successfully rendered it as the 'dysfunctional one of the most powerful courts in the international system' (Zaccaria, 2022, p 322; see also Dijkstra et al, 2022).

As mentioned earlier, the decision by former US president Donald Trump to withdraw from the Paris Agreement in 2017 was such a contestation by a major power to the global climate regime (see, for example, Kemp, 2017; Pickering et al, 2018). Trump claimed that the agreement was unfair to the US and climate change was 'mythical', 'non-existent' and 'an expensive hoax' (Cheung, 2020). Practitioners and scholars alike expected that this contestation would have a severe damaging effect to not only the Paris Agreement but also on the UNFCCC itself (see, for example, Kemp, 2017). De-legitimation and a crisis of legitimacy were potential consequences of this withdrawal. However, what can be empirically observed is the opposite. Contrary to the expectation of de-legitimation, legitimation followed this contestation. Several member states of the UNFCCC opposed Trump's position and engaged in different kinds of legitimation practices. Also, several sub-state and non-state actors on the US level legitimated and supported the agreement as well as opposing Trump's decision to withdraw.

In this respect, this book asks the question: *How and why are IOs in the global climate regime able to self-legitimate despite contestation?* While I do not assume a priori that contestation of IOs being followed by legitimation is always the case and the new normal, this connection between is puzzling, especially when the contestation comes from a powerful actor or from a big majority of the respective community in the regime. Henceforth, I analyse and explain *how and why IOs in the global climate regime can self-legitimate despite contestation*. I argue that contestation can in fact trigger legitimation, which can be understood through conceptualizing contestation and legitimation as an *interlinked process* rather than isolated phenomena as prior International Relations (IR) research has suggested. These processes of contestation and legitimation of IOs are guided by norms as 'guiding frame' as they 'represent the legitimating core of global governance' and 'are considered as standards of behaviour in international relations' (Wiener, 2014, p 21). However, it is not the aim of this book to analyse the guiding norm and norm contestation itself.

As I argue, norms as guiding frames in contestation–legitimation processes, in which a norm is adopted, structure behaviour, determine the legitimacy belief of the community and condition the process. Norms as standards of behaviour do guide this action. Social actors do not start with a blank page when they aim to legitimate and enact what is right, what they believe is right. Also, while norm scholars see norm contestation as an underlying constant, in this context of contestation–legitimation processes of IOs, *contestation of IOs* is viewed as a momentary exception and pointed challenge, when it is carried out openly, hearable and/or visible.

To gain a deeper understanding about the connection between contestation and legitimation, more specific attention to issue areas, such as the global climate regime, and related empirical cases, is necessary. With the research of this book and to explain why contestation was followed by legitimation, I analyse four processes in total of two large IOs, the UNFCCC and the International Energy Agency (IEA). Both experienced severe instances of contestation. The UNFCCC and the IEA are influential cases within the global climate regime as they were confronted with multiple instances of contestation along the lines of two key issues within the global climate regime: the North–South divide and the institutional format for climate governance.

To substantiate this theoretical argument as well as to showcase the newly introduced norm for CCA in the UNFCCC and IEA contestation–legitimation processes, the book builds on a nested research design and a vast qualitative, empirical study. Based on original data of 43 interviews in total and triangulated document analysis of first and secondary literature as well as participant observation at the COP26 at the UNFCCC in 2021, I show that legitimation of IOs can follow contestation when practices reflect what the community regards as appropriate norm. This deconstruction comes alive in tracing the contestation and legitimation practices in four processes. The approach of practice tracing allows interpretive analysis to deconstruct these processes, occurring practices and their meaning, which unveils to the guiding norm. As 'normativity is enacted in practice, because its validity and reach are constituted in social contexts' (Gadinger and Niemann, 2025), in turn, practices are the translation of normative meaning. Through this, I can detect the guiding frame of the processes.

Studies of the global climate regime

Due to the gravity of climate change as an existential threat, IOs in the global climate regime are exposed to a high potential for struggle and thus, contestation. For these IOs, the rising awareness and urgency for climate change action, as well as the variety of actors and stakeholders that are involved in the related policy-making processes, create a persistent struggle (O'Neill, 2009; Pattberg and Biermann, 2012). Further, in the past, member states have not always supported IOs' purposes for various reasons and have sometimes been met with scepticism or even denial among politicians and national leaders (see, for example, Dijkstra et al, 2022). The global climate regime presents a highly evolving and crucial area of global cooperation in this regard (see, for example, Chasek, 2000; Depledge, 2006; Biermann et al, 2009c; O'Neill, 2009; Biermann and Pattberg, 2012; Pattberg and Biermann, 2012; Chasek et al, 2014).

Scholars of environmental politics and climate policy analysis have investigated how the global climate regime is shaped and structured as well as how action to tackle climate change has been implemented – or not (Jordan et al, 2018; Biermann and Kim, 2020; Aykut and Maertens, 2021; van Driel et al, 2022; Partzsch, 2023). Here, not only the relation of climate action and the UN sustainable development goals, that give orientation to aim for more equity and protection of vulnerable societies around the world, has been examined (van Driel et al, 2022; Partzsch et al, 2023).

Also, research has shown that the issue of climate change has become more and more framing for other issue areas. Aykut and Maertens (2021) refer to this as *climatization* of global politics. For example, Biermann and Kim (2020) show that 'international institutions do not operate in a void. All institutions operate instead within complex webs of larger governance settings' (p 1; see also Biermann et al, 2009a, 2009b; Kanie et al, 2010; Zelli, 2011; Hackmann, 2012; Zelli and van Asselt, 2013; Biermann, 2014; Abbott and Bernstein, 2015; Holzscheiter et al, 2016; Scobie, 2019). By pointing out these various connections to other issue areas, research has shown that politics on climate change is not a state-centric endeavour but, a global problem that affects everyone, or 'poly-centric' (Jordan et al, 2018), and it spreads across non-state actor communities, sectors and institutions (Biermann and Kim, 2020). This will be especially seen in Chapters 3 and 4 of this book when examining the contestation–legitimation processes within the UNFCCC.

Further research on environmental politics has gone a long way pointing out the harsh reality of inequity and power politics among 'developed' and 'developing' countries, resulting in 'dysfunctional North-South politics' (Yamin and Depledge, 2004, p 443; see also Orekere, 2018; van Asselt and Zelli, 2018; Lefstad and Paavola, 2023). The so-called North–South divide is one of the main focal points when it comes to fighting against climate change and fighting over just, collective practices for climate action. It encompasses conflicts and struggles among the various involved actors due to their different geopolitical interests and needs (Depledge, 2006; O'Neill,

2009; Biermann et al, 2009c, 2012; Pattberg and Biermann, 2012; Chasek et al, 2014). This will not only be discussed in Chapters 3 and 4 regarding the contestation–legitimation processes within the UNFCCC, but also in Chapters 5 and 6 on the contestation–legitimation processes within the IEA, that needed to move beyond its OECD centrism and expand to associating Global South players.

As mentioned, the global climate regime is not only connected to other issue areas, for example, security (von Uexkull and Buhaug, 2021; Bremberg et al, 2022; Dalby, 2024; McDonald, 2024), but it also interconnects issues of environmental politics, sustainability and energy within itself. Research on the global climate regime has connected, as done here, questions on energy to the environment. For example, the issue of decarbonization has been a vital pillar for a successful energy transition and successfully fighting climate change (Bernstein and Hoffmann, 2018). 'Decarbonisation thus implies attacking climate change at its fundamental core – global reliance on fossil energy – and it is a daunting task, as carbon lock-in arises from overlapping technical, political, social and economic dynamics that generate continuing and taken-for-granted use of fossil energy' (Bernstein and Hoffmann, 2018, p 248). As shown in this book, these issues relate back to the norm for CCA. This will especially be seen in Chapter 6, with the modernization of the to move away from fossil fuels only to include renewables as well as leadership advocating for climate change action.

The norm for climate change action

In contrast to many other norms in global governance that have emerged from the ideas and traditions of science and knowledge in the Western hemisphere, norms in the global climate regime evolved out of the conflict and compromises of the Global North and Global South, and thus its related divide. Norms in the global climate regime are, for example, the norm of sustainable development, climate justice, common but differentiated responsibilities (CBDR) – and the norm for CCA. Climate norms not only affect the local level but also the global sphere and multilateral cooperation through their embodiment in law, institutions or discourse directed at solving the global problem, that is climate change (Höhne et al, 2024).

The norm for CCA grew as standard of appropriate behaviour for collective action in the nexus of energy and environment in the global climate regime, which started in 1992 with the Rio Convention. Even more so, with the Paris Agreement the norm emerged and actors decided to have a multilateral understanding of how to implement these commitments. CCA can be defined as the norm that guides the action of developed and developing countries that collaborate and come together to mitigate, adapt and respond to climate impacts resulting from anthropogenic greenhouse gas emissions

(UNFCCC, nd [b]; UNFCCC, nd [c]; UNFCCC, nd [d]). Chapter 2 takes a deeper look at the norm of CCA, in which it is explained further.

As will be shown, by deconstructing the processes of contestation and legitimation, the parts of this process can tell us that the norm for CCA guides the community in the four processes in this book. Norms shape practices, policies and set the frame of expected and accepted behaviour. This way, they produce legitimacy beliefs that are articulated in de-legitimation and legitimation practices and have strong influence on how global actors conduct international relations and multilateral cooperation.

The case studies: the UNFCCC and the IEA

To understand how IOs in the global climate regime self-legitimate despite contestation and, why contestation can be followed by legitimation in the global climate regime, rather than de-legitimation as an expected negative consequence due to contestation's refusing, objecting nature, I analyse four processes in total within two cases, thus two processes each. For these case studies, I selected two large IOs within the global climate regime, the UNFCCC and the IEA. Large IOs can be defined as: (1) having at least three member states; (2) holding a plenary session at least every 10 years; and (3) having a secretariat and correspondence address (Pevehouse et al, 2004).

A case study can be defined 'as an intensive study of a single unit for the purpose of understanding a larger class of (similar) units' (Gerring, 2004, p 342; see also Gerring, 2006). A unit can be 'a spatially bounded phenomenon, e.g. a nation state, revolution, political party, election, or person observed at a single point in time or over some delimited period of time' (Gerring, 2004, p 342). Processes within IOs can also be classified as such units. The units I am interested in are those processes that start with a contestation against the IO specifically and are followed by legitimation. Cases that have an influential role in the global climate regime have to be chosen, in order to be able to understand the 'larger class' regime itself and the units (processes in the global climate regime) within it (see, for example, Gerring, 2004, 2006; Seawright and Gerring, 2008; Gerring and Cojocaru, 2016).

As influential cases, the UNFCCC and IEA have a profound impact not only on the regime empirically, but also answering questions on why contestation to IOs in this regime can be followed by legitimation contrary to the first-hand logic of negative consequence due to contestation's objecting nature. Further, in statistics, influential cases are those 'that play an influential role—understood as cases that, if removed from the sample, would have the largest impact on the total model' (Gerring and Cojocaru, 2016, p 403). With all IOs from the global climate regime, if the UNFCCC and the IEA cases were missing, this would impact the outcome on explaining why contestation was followed by legitimation as a significant number of processes (units) would be subtracted. Further, the UNFCCC and IEA are influential cases within the global climate regime as they have been confronted with multiple instances of contestation along the lines of two key issues within the global climate regime: the North–South divide and the institutional format for climate governance.

As a large IO, the UNFCCC has 198 parties of which 197 are member states and approximately 450 (UN, nd [a]) staff members. The UNFCCC's main task is to provide technical expertise and assist in the 'analysis and review of climate change information reported by parties and in the implementation of the Kyoto mechanisms', as well as maintaining 'the registry for Nationally Determined Contributions (NDC) established under the Paris Agreement, a key aspect of implementation of the Paris Agreement' (UN, nd [a]). Beside holding the big summit of the Conference of the Parties (COP) each year, there are several side events that involve the UNFCCC, states and non-state actors (UN, nd [a]). For the UNFCCC, the first process is the walkout of the G77 countries at the COP19 conference in Warsaw in 2013, which can be allocated to the North–South divide. The second process is the US contestation of the Paris Agreement by former president Trump in 2017. This was directed against the institutional format within the UNFCCC, namely the Paris Agreement.

The IEA has 31 member states and 11 associated countries. There are approximately 500 (IEA, nd [b]) staff members. Beside holding the high-level 'Ministerial Meeting' (IEA, nd [c]) every two years, the IEA organizes working groups, which consist of member state government officials, several times a year. Further, the IEA holds a different range of programmes and 'co-operates with a broad range of international organizations and forums working in the field of energy', hosts 'a number of multilateral organizations at its headquarters in Paris, including the Clean Energy Ministerial (CEM) Secretariat and the Energy Efficiency Hub', and facilitates 'the BioFuture Platform' (IEA, nd [d]). For the IEA, two contestations manifested in the creation of the International Renewable Energy Agency (IRENA) in 2009 by three member states: Denmark, Germany and Spain (Van de Graaf and Lesage, 2009, p 303). The first process for the IEA is the contestation of the IEA's OECD-only membership, which manifests along these global lines, since countries of the Global South were largely excluded, and the IEA did not represent international energy politics as its name implies. The second process is the contestation of the IEA's oil-only approach. This process focuses on an institutional format in the climate regime (see Table 1.1).

Findings and contribution

By analysing the two influential IOs that experienced severe contestation, I conceptualize contestation and legitimation in an interlinked process and

Table 1.1: Key issues in the global climate regime North–South divide and institutional format and cases

Case	North–South divide	Institutional format
UNFCCC	G77 walkout	Trump contestation of Paris Agreement
IEA	OECD-only membership	Oil-only approach

address such puzzling cases of contestation being followed by legitimation. The UNFCCC and the IEA have been contested multiple times in the past as they are at the heart of international cooperation on global climate change action. As I argue, the norm for CCA frames the processes of contestation and legitimation in the global climate regime. As norms 'represent the legitimating core of global governance' (Wiener, 2014, p 4), and 'are considered as standards of behaviour in international relations' (Wiener, 2014, p 21), they frame these processes and condition the contestation as well as legitimation. As mentioned earlier, it is thus important to stress that this book's theoretical framework is about the *contestation of IOs* and their legitimation thereafter and how this is enabled by the adopted norm dynamics that work in global governance.

To be able to explain how IOs self-legitimate amid contestation and why contestation can lead to legitimation rather than having a negative, weakening effect in the investigated processes in this research, I will turn to what is empirically observable, namely the practices (Bourdieu, 1998; Schatzki et al, 2001; Adler and Pouliot, 2011a, b; Bueger, 2014; Bueger and Gadinger, 2018; Lechner and Frost, 2018). Epistemologically, practices are one of the most observable data we can find as '[p]ractices ... are the foundations, or the smallest units, of social life' (Mattern, 2011, p 70). Previous research has just started to map practices of legitimation, such as praise or protest (see, for example, Halliday et al, 2010; Gronau and Schmidtke, 2016; Bäckstrand and Söderbaum, 2018; Bernstein, 2011, 2018; Gregoratti and Uhlin, 2018; Tallberg et al, 2018; Tallberg and Zürn, 2019). Yet, only a little explanation has been given to these practices and their normative implications and guidance (Scholte, 2018, p 97).

This book is situated at the intersection of IR and environmental politics, offering an international perspective on international organizations and norms in the global climate regime. It fits in with several research publications on the topic (Wiener, 2014; Tallberg et al, 2018; Zürn, 2018; Dingwerth et al, 2019), but takes research in a new direction. My book advances the conversation of contestation and legitimation in IR as these theoretical concepts have been covered in-depth but separately. Contestation has been studied vastly by scholars of norm contestation, while legitimacy and legitimation has been discussed broadly by scholars of international institutions. This book seeks to bridge this divide by asking about the role of norms as guiding frames when it comes to the contestation and legitimation of IOs. Hence, it conceptualizes the connection of contestation and legitimation in *an interlinked process* and deconstructs the process to its guiding norm. After reading this book, readers will have gained new knowledge on contestation and legitimation of IOs in the global climate regime. The aim of this book is to understand what informs the processes of contestation and legitimation, and what norm guides actors to act the way that they do within the global climate regime.

Another part of my contribution is the comparison of two different IOs, which address different mandates, one in the environmental area and the other in energy. I identify them as part of the wider global climate regime, which speaks to scholars of environmental politics and IR alike. The processes of the two case studies can be allocated to two of the main issues in global climate regime, namely the North–South divide and the institutional formats in climate governance. With this research on the contestation–legitimation processes of the influential cases within the global climate regime, the UNFCCC and the IEA, I can make a novel empirical contribution. By combining the two case studies of the large IOs in the field, the UNFCCC and the IEA, this book can take a broader view and at the same time a deeper connection between the two issue areas, environment and energy, in the global climate regime. Thus, this book provides new empirical insights into global climate governance and the cooperation on environmental- and energy-related issues.

I was able to collect puzzling findings on the four processes of contestation and legitimation. For the case of the UNFCCC, the first process is the walkout of the G77 countries at the Warsaw COP19 in 2013. Although this contestation instance has not received attention in the past, I argue that this instance deserves to be analysed. It is a prime example of the North–South divide. Also, the mechanism on 'loss and damage', which was debated at COP19, is key in politically addressing the damaging and existential threat of climate change that is for now affecting the globe unequally. The walkout of the G77 led to an abrupt break in COP19. Although this division occurring in the Warsaw COP19 could be bridged and the parties came to an agreement after the break of the walkout, this divide is a continuous challenge to the UNFCCC and the global climate regime. This also means that due to this struggle, the UNFCCC is constantly in a position where its legitimacy will be questioned.

In this process, I find that this contestation was followed by legitimation. Further, I find in my research that these kinds of contestation and following legitimation practices are traced back to COP15 in Copenhagen in 2009. Here, the conference ended in a total breakdown, as parties could not come to any agreement at all. The disagreement was especially along the lines of this North–South divide (Busby, 2013). The previous experience in Copenhagen and thereafter established practices led to the rekindling of the conference and thus re-legitimized COP19 and its negotiations despite the contesting walkout. The norm for CCA frames the overall process and thus conditioned the legitimation after contestation. Establishing a collective mechanism to prevent loss and damage due to climate change is a vital part of the norm.

The second process is the US contestation with the announcement of withdrawing from the Paris Agreement by former president Trump in 2017. With this contestation, it was anticipated that a domino effect of further contestation would follow along with withdrawal by other member states, especially those with similar protectionist and climate action hostile positions. Concern over the US withdrawal damaging the 'goodwill at international negotiations' (McGrath, 2018) not only at the UNFCCC but worldwide grew further. However, as I find, contrary to these apprehensions and de-legitimation, legitimation followed this contestation. Several members of the UNFCCC, for example, France, Germany, the EU and China, opposed Trump's position and engaged in different kinds of legitimation practices, supporting and emphasizing the importance of the Paris Agreement, the UNFCCC and climate change action. Also, several sub-state and non-state actors on the US level openly supported the agreement and contested Trump's decision to withdraw, thereby engaging in several different legitimation practices.

I find that this process of legitimation, too, is guided by the frame of the norm for CCA. The legitimation practices of the UNFCCC itself can be traced back to past experience with US contestation, on the one hand, and its own orchestration efforts at building a strong supportive network beyond its member states, on the other (see, for example, Abbott and Snidal, 2009; Abbott, 2014; Abbott et al, 2015; Hickmann et al, 2019). The failure of US ratification of the Kyoto Protocol in 2001 provides the background to the 2017 contestation. As one of my UNFCCC interviewees put it, 'we have seen this movie before' (per UNFCCC#1 in list of interviews in Appendix A). Also, the election of Trump in 2016 presented the opportunity to prepare for this kind of contestation to happen. Thus, the UNFCCC already has a strong backup that drove the legitimation.

For the IEA, I identify two processes of contestation and legitimation that manifested in the creation of the IRENA by three IEA members as a direct competitor to counter the IEA in 2009. The members, Denmark, Germany and Spain, did not regard the IEA as an appropriate organization for reform in terms of membership inclusivity and expertise for renewable energy beyond oil (Van de Graaf and Lesage, 2009; Van de Graaf, 2012, 2013; Faude and Fuss, 2020). In the first process, the non-inclusivity of membership of the IEA's exclusive 'club' membership of OECD countries only is contested. This non-universal frame meant a neglect of including rising powers, such as India and China, which have heavily increased their energy consumption over time (Van de Graaf, 2012, 2013). This speaks to the unequal burden of the effects of climate change and related emissions and energy consumption by states.

The second process contests the exclusion of the IEA's renewable energy, which stood in tension to the reality of climate change and the demand to transition to more sustainable energy sources. Its focus on oil did not reflect the changing realities of its member states and the demands of a changing world in the light of finite fossil energy resources. Yet, I find that, despite the dawning legitimacy crisis, the IEA engaged in self-legitimation practices and was able to come back as the most 'suitable' organization to organize the energy policy field (IEA#7). This legitimation, too, is guided by the frame of the norm for CCA. The understanding of the norm by the community implied the need to change towards a more sustainable and inclusive political procedure. In response to both contestations, the IEA started modernizing, especially from 2015 onwards, by incorporating the association membership of non-OECD countries as well as transitioning its expertise to all energy sources, beyond just fossil energy (Heubaum and Biermann, 2015). These processes show that contestation, despite being followed by a dawning legitimacy crisis, can lead to self-legitimation.

These findings of the two case studies and the four processes show that, first, contrary to the expectation of negative consequences of contestation as a destructive rupture, contestation can in fact lead to legitimation. As I argue, the norm CCA is the guiding frame in contestation–legitimation processes in the global climate regime. Therefore, I can show why contestation can be followed by legitimation in the global climate regime and answer this book's research question. When deconstructing the practices to the two core aspects of the norm, and by viewing contestation and legitimation in a connected process and their related backgrounds, I can detect the different stages of norm adoption of the parts of the respective communities.

The adoption informs the contestation practice towards the IOs as well as legitimation engagement after the contestation. In contestation–legitimation processes, norm adoption can tell us why contestation of a specific, empirical target is met with legitimation engagement and not de-legitimation. The aim of this book is to answer exactly this question, as I show which norm guides action and structures behaviour. It is not the aim to analyse the guiding norm and norm contestation itself. As I argue, norms as guiding frames in contestation-legitimation processes structure behaviour, determine the legitimacy belief of the community and condition the process.

Both the UNFCCC- and the IEA-related communities share the understanding that to successfully act on climate change, action needs to be taken collectively since it is a global issue that affects everyone. The legitimation of the processes discussed here differs regarding whether the norm for CCA had already been adopted and by whom. For example, the IEA needed to adopt the norm to legitimate itself, which demanded institutional transformation, while after the US contestation of the Paris Agreement, the UNFCCC kept in the background. The most explicit legitimation engagement came from the rest of the community that reinforced their legitimacy belief in CCA as the norm by opposing Trump's contestation.

Part of my contribution is the comparison of two different IOs, which address different mandates, one on the environmental area and energy, and the other on identifying them as part of the wider global climate regime under the umbrella of the norm for CCA. The processes of the two case studies can be allocated to two of the main issues in the global climate regime, namely the North–South divide and the institutional formats in climate governance. With this research on the contestation–legitimation processes of the influential cases within the global climate regime, the UNFCCC and the IEA, I am not only able to make a novel empirical contribution but move beyond the isolated understandings in the IR literature of the theoretical concepts of contestation and legitimation. Further, by taking the perspective and identifying the relation between contestation and legitimation as an interlinked process, I can deconstruct and discover what informs these processes: the norm for CCA. Through this I add a novel finding to our understanding of the global climate regime, its guiding norms and practising IOs. The two cases show a common understanding, a standard of appropriate behaviour within the community of the global climate regime, which frames these contestation–legitimation processes.

By pursuing this argument, I add to contestation and legitimation research. As I view contestation and legitimation in an interlinked process rather than as separate, conceptual phenomena, I can show the explicit connection between contestation and legitimation. For this purpose, I connect the knowledge of contestation and legitimation research alike. I will engage with the previous research of both scholar fields that have established a large body of literature on legitimacy and legitimation of IOs (see, for example, Buchanan and Keohane, 2006; Reus-Smit, 2007; Johnson, 2011; Symons, 2011; Ecker-Ehrhardt, 2012; Bernauer and Gampfer, 2013; Zaum, 2013; Lenz and Viola, 2017; Bes et al, 2019; Tallberg et al, 2018, p 8; Tallberg and Zürn, 2019). This will be coupled with contestation by norm scholars (Wiener, 2014; Lantis and Wunderlich, 2018; Deitelhoff and Zimmermann, 2019; Sandholtz, 2019; Schmidt and Sikkink, 2019; Welsh, 2019; Deitelhoff, 2020). Turning to the concept of contestation by norms research is useful for investigating the contestation of IOs as here we can find a deeper conceptualization of contestation in relation to legitimacy, through the legitimacy gap (Wiener, 2014). This fusion is necessary to successfully explain and profoundly understand *why* the investigated empirical cases of my research result in legitimation rather than de-legitimation despite severe instances of contestation.

Outline of the book

This book is structured as follows. After setting the scene of the reality of global climate change and the related global governance regime, as well as outlining my detailed contribution of this research and its findings in this introduction of Chapter 1, I move into a detailed discussion of the theoretical framing and concepts in Chapter 2. Here, I engage with the previous research on contestation and legitimation, and outline my analytical framework based on their findings. Here, I identify the different stages of contestation–legitimation processes and related concepts, which are contestation, and through this the indicated legitimacy gap and legitimation potential, legitimacy, and norms and their adoption. Further, I outline the practices of de-legitimation and legitimation that can be identified in contestation–legitimation processes as well as the analytical vehicle of practices and the methodological approach of practice tracing that enable a deconstruction of the four processes.

With Chapter 3, I move into the analysis of the empirical cases of this research. Chapter 3 covers the analysis of the UNFCCC case and the two contestation–legitimation processes with the G77 walkout at COP19 in 2013. In Chapter 4, I analyse the US withdrawal from the Paris Agreement. The structure of the processes' sub-chapters first covers the background, then the contestation, followed by the legitimation and concludes with a summary. The practices of contestation and legitimation will be deconstructed to the two core aspects of the norm for CCA and will also show the adoption stage of the norm.

In Chapters 5 and 6, I analyse the second case, the IEA, and the two contestation–legitimation processes of the OECD-only membership and the oil-only approach. The first process in Chapter 5 is the IEA's non-inclusivity of membership, its exclusive 'club' membership of OECD countries only. I will elaborate on the contestation–legitimation processes by introducing the contestation. The legitimation practices that the IEA engaged in after the contestation will be analysed afterwards. The same structure applies for the second process in Chapter 6, which starts with the contestation of the IEA's oil-only approach, which speaks to the non-inclusion of renewable energy. I conclude each process by summarizing my findings regarding my argument of the norm for CCA as a guiding frame that explains why contestation can be followed by legitimation in the global climate regime.

In Chapter 7, I compare these two cases and the four related contestation–legitimation processes. The focus in comparing the UNFCCC's and the IEA's contestation–legitimation processes will be twofold. On the one hand,

I will order the cases by two bigger main issues in global climate governance that were contested. Thus, the G77 walkout of the UNFCCC case and the IEA OECD-only membership can be allocated to the North–South divide in global climate governance. The other two processes, the US contestation of the Paris Agreement by former president Trump and the contestation of the IEA's oil-only approach, are about the contestation and legitimation of an institutional format in the climate regime.

When comparing the processes in this structure, it will be possible to clarify further which aspect of the norm becomes visible in the contestation and legitimation. On the other hand, to further carve out the norm and to show why contestation can be followed by legitimation in the global climate regime and answer this book's research question, I will compare the processes regarding the norm adoption of the community in each process. To show that the norm for CCA is the guiding frame of the four processes I will start by comparing the processes that can be allocated to the North–South divide. Afterwards, I will move on to comparing the processes in which the institutional format was contested and legitimated. I will summarize the comparative chapter by reflecting on the norm for CCA and the implications of contestation–legitimation processes in the cases analysed here.

The conclusion of Chapter 8 summarizes this research's findings, reflects its limitations and discusses possible avenues for future research.

2

Understanding Norms as Guiding Frames in Contestation–Legitimation Processes

Within the global climate regime, numerous instances of contestation were followed by de-legitimation and legitimacy crises in the past. But also, contrarily, contestation has been followed by legitimation (see, for example, Bäckstrand et al, 2017; Hickmann et al, 2019; Well et al, 2020; von Allwörden, 2025). Therefore, this book asks the guiding question: *How and why are IOs in the global climate regime able to self-legitimate despite contestation?* The purpose here is to unpack the puzzling processes as well as to understand the connection between contestation and legitimation of IOs.

Henceforth, in this chapter I will delve into the relevant concepts of the different stages of contestation–legitimation processes. These concepts are contestation, its indicated legitimacy gap and legitimation potential, legitimacy, as well norms (here as guiding frames) and their adoption. Further, I outline the analytical vehicle of practices and the methodological approach of practice tracing, which enables a deconstruction of the four processes. Here, I also incorporate which practices of de-legitimation and legitimation can be identified in contestation–legitimation processes. As mentioned earlier, it is important to stress that this book's theoretical framework and study is about the contestation of IOs and their legitimation thereafter and how this is enabled by the adopted norm dynamics that work in global governance. It is about the role that norms play as guiding frames in distinct processes, for the survival and development of IOs to counter contestation and self-legitimate.

In International Relations research (IR) international organizations, their role in global governance and how they (can) act within it have been discussed from various angles. Further, IR scholars have investigated how IOs are contested and how and if they can react to contestation. For example, realist voices would expect that contestation by a hegemonic power will trump the contested target and de-legitimation will follow (see, for example, Carr, 1946; Morgenthau, 1948). In this logic, they would not be able to explain why contestation can be followed by legitimation. Also, as they regard legitimacy as means to an end by states to act in their interest and to their advantage (see, for example, Krasner, 1999), they would not be able to say what guides this course of action in contestation–legitimation processes. Further, while liberal institutionalists acknowledge legitimacy as a function to foster collective action between states (see, for example, Buchanan and Keohane, 2006), in which IOs have an 'important political function of collective legitimization' (Claude, 1966, p 12 in Tallberg et al, 2018, pp 11–12), they are more focused on strategic, explicit adaption aspects of legitimation. Accordingly, they might not ask about the aspects that drive legitimation after contestation and are more interested in how legitimation can avoid the consequences of contestation (see, for example, Hirschmann, 2021; Heinkelmann-Wild and Jankauskas, 2022).

These approaches cannot fully tell us about what guides practice – adaptive or legitimizing, strategic or not. They also do not ask about what communities believe in and what role norms play for IOs. So, similarly they miss out on what guides their course of action in contestation–legitimation processes. Action can be both explicitly and implicitly guided by the belief of what is rightful and legitimate. Norms as standards of behaviour do guide this action. Social actors do not start with a blank page when they aim to legitimate and enact what is right, what they *believe* is right. The aim of this book is to understand what informs the processes of contestation and legitimation, and what guides actors to decide and act within the global climate regime. Thus, I am siding with a more functionalist-constructivist notion that rather emphasizes the relational, intersubjective component of legitimacy, how it is shaped and challenged among states, and focus on their 'shared understandings' (see, for example, Clark, 2005; Clark and Reus-Smit, 2007; Brunnée and Toope, 2019).

While the IR literature has partially addressed questions about the direct relationship between contestation and legitimation, there is a large scholarship that addresses legitimation and contestation separately. The research on legitimation and norm contestation in IR today is essentially divided into two vibrant camps. The first works on legitimacy, de-legitimation and legitimation in global governance (see, for example, Buchanan and Keohane, 2006; Reus-Smit, 2007; Johnson, 2011; Symons, 2011; Ecker-Ehrhardt, 2012; Bernauer and Gampfer, 2013; Lenz and Viola, 2017; Tallberg et al, 2018, p 8; Bes et al, 2019; Tallberg and Zürn, 2019). The other works on norms, their contestation and related concepts, such as norm robustness, diffusion, erosion (Lantis and Wunderlich, 2018; Deitelhoff and Zimmermann, 2019; Sandholtz, 2019; Schmidt and Sikkink, 2019; Welsh,

2019; Deitelhoff, 2020; Wiener, 2014, 2018; Zimmermann et al, 2023; Orchard and Wiener, 2024).

Surprisingly, the two have not been connected yet. As the conversations of both camps show ontological differences, the normative component of legitimation practices has only been researched to a marginal extent. Legitimation scholars have scarcely asked what this legitimation is really informed by, so on a normative, cultural level, and which role norms play in this regard (see, for example, Buchanan and Keohane, 2006). Also, they have understood legitimation thus far mostly in connection with legitimacy and legitimacy crisis. Despite contestation being used as conceptual term by legitimation-research scholars, little conceptual depth has been given to contestation and the role of norms (Zürn, 2018). Yet, processes of de-legitimation that can lead to a legitimacy crisis have an initiating point, which is most often contestation. Further, as shown in this book, contestation can relate to other entities than norms. The fusion of the conceptualization of contestation by norms research deepens the analysis of IO contestation as it relates contestation to legitimacy, through the legitimacy gap (Wiener, 2014).

I will fuse the theoretical insights of both camps. The connection is beneficial for this book's analytical framework to successfully explain and profoundly understand *how* and *why* the investigated empirical cases of this book resulted in legitimation rather than de-legitimation and destruction, despite severe instances of contestation. As I argue, the legitimation (or de-legitimation) after contestation is conditioned by a guiding frame of this interlinked process, which is the appropriate standard of behaviour, which is the norm that guides the community and how this community understands the contestation in the light of the norm. When norms emerge in practical translation, the norm is adopted. These practices will reflect this norm adoption towards the community. In turn, the community will measure behaviour against the norm to judge legitimacy. The practices of contestation and legitimation reveal the adopted norm as guiding frame of the process. Thus, in this book, the theoretical framework is built on the premise that the norm can guide the contestation and the following legitimation depending on the adoption of the norm within the community.

The stages of contestation–legitimation processes in brief

In contestation–legitimation processes, *contestation* signals a legitimacy gap in the contested target (here IOs). At the same time, a legitimation potential is revealed by this legitimacy gap. The norm within the given community guides how this contestation and indicated gap are perceived and responded to. If the community believes that abiding by the norm that is perceived as an appropriate standard of behaviour is necessary, connected legitimacy beliefs will be articulated within the contestation and legitimation practices. Here, explicit or implicit reference to the norm in practice, which needs to be deconstructed in the analysis, enables the adopted norm to be found. This unveils the norm as the guiding frame, which will finally answer why contestation leads to legitimation. The guiding frame is the frame that informs and reasons the individual processes, the initiation contestation and the legitimation responses. This means it determines the local and contextual understandings actors are situated in and conditions in which circumstances contestation and legitimation are not only justified and understood but how they are enacted. In other words, it refers to the normative self-understanding of the governance regime in which actors find themselves in, which frames and conditions their thinking and acting. The frame sets and conditions the appropriate standard of behaviour, the norm, which works as a guiding frame to structure this behaviour within the regime.

Generally, processes include a starting point or trigger, some events or a story within the process and an outcome. Processes take place in a certain setting, an environment that frames and conditions the trigger, and it is possible for the following events to happen in response to this starting trigger and consequently to end in the outcome. In contestation–legitimation processes, contestation marks the start that leads to either de-legitimation or legitimation. The common understanding, the appropriate standard of behaviour, the norm, frames the process and conditions how the contestation is perceived and responded to through (potential) legitimation. Figure 2.1 illustrates this interplay of the theoretical concepts in contestation–legitimation processes.

The *contestation* starts the process that can either result in de-legitimation or legitimation. Contestation is the practice of disapproval, objection, rejection or refusal of implementation (Wiener, 2014, p 1). It is essentially a struggle over what is perceived as legitimate, thus over the IO's legitimacy. Contestation has the power of determining, changing or underlining the meaning of norms, practices, procedures and hence their institutions (Wiener, 2014, p 10). This, as mentioned before, can have a positive, strengthening, legitimizing effect 'as it is the condition for a shared understanding over meanings ... can generate ... legitimacy' (Deitelhoff, 2020, p 717).

In response to the contestation and as contestation triggers a review of legitimacy, this review will be based on the 'setting' responding actors find themselves in, which is the common understanding, the appropriate standard of behaviour: the *norm*. The norm frames the process. To have this conditioning, framing effect the norm must be adopted. The norm moves on the stages of adoption regarding how the norm has emerged and is adopted by which part of the community in the respective process. Since the community in the institution of responding actors believe that abiding

Figure 2.1: Conceptual connection contestation–legitimation processes

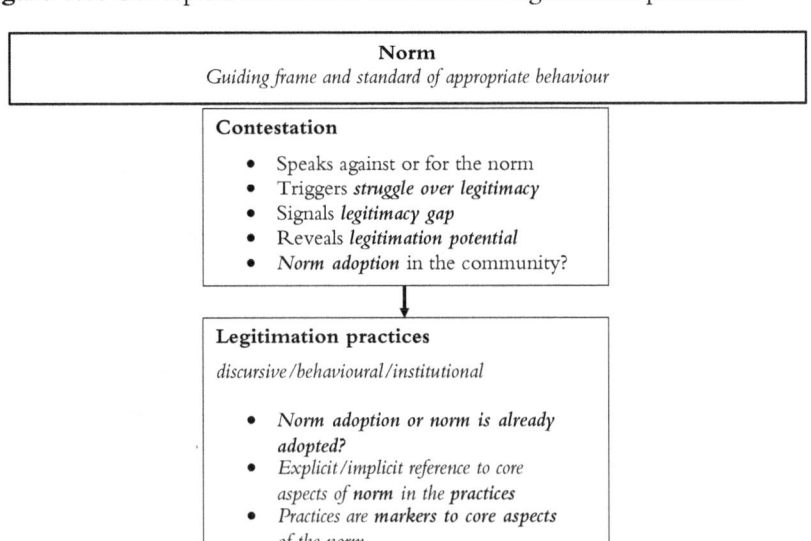

the common standard of behaviour is necessary and legitimate, adoption of the guiding frame (norm) within the governance regime is needed to fill the legitimacy gap and fulfil the legitimation potential. This way, the response traces back to the norm, which can be uncovered in the contestation and legitimation practices within the process. These practices can be *discursive contestation* (for example, speech, shaming), *behavioural contestation* (for example, written statements, walkout, protest) or *institutional contestation* (for example, creating a new institution, membership withdrawal) (see, for example, Wiener, 2014; Bäckstrand and Söderbaum, 2018; Tallberg and Zürn, 2019).

The response to contestation in form of *legitimation practices* is informed by the guiding frame, the norm. This reflects the responding, legitimating actors' understanding of the situation. This also reflects how they finally act. But it also reasons possible adaptation to overcome the contestation and in turn, legitimate what is being contested. Legitimation becomes visible through the observable practices. As norms are 'meaning in use' (Wiener, 2008, p 57), practices are the translation of this normative meaning. Such practices legitimation can be *discursive*, *behavioural* or *institutional* (see, for example, Halliday et al, 2010; Bernstein, 2011, 2018; Gronau and Schmidtke, 2016; Bäckstrand and Söderbaum, 2018; Gregoratti and Uhlin, 2018; Tallberg et al, 2018). For example, *discursive* practices of (de-)legitimation can be speeches, coming from IOs, their members, other internals and externals alike, expressing either their discontent or praise (Bäckstrand and Söderbaum, 2018, pp 109–10). The practices carry this meaning by speaking to the core aspects of the norm. As norms are often not 'out in the open' but 'adopted', they come through in practical translation and in reference to the community's legitimacy belief, which will be explained in due course in this chapter. By deconstructing the processes and looking into the contestation and legitimation practices, and what they are referring to, I can trace the practice back to the guiding norm that frames the process. Through this, I can assess the stage of adoption of the norm within parts of the community at that given moment in time, when the process unfolded.

Starting the process: contestation

To understand contestation–legitimation processes, I will discuss the research on norm contestation (see for example Finnemore and Sikkink, 1998; Wiener and Puetter, 2009; Wiener, 2014, 2018; Lantis and Wunderlich, 2018; Deitelhoff and Zimmermann, 2019; Sandholtz, 2019; Schmidt and Sikkink, 2019; Welsh, 2019; Deitelhoff, 2020; Zimmermann et al, 2023; Orchard and Wiener, 2024), in order to provide the conceptual clarity on contestation itself and show its connection to norms, legitimacy and legitimation through the legitimacy gap (Wiener, 2014) in the following. When analysing processes that result in (de-)legitimation and started with contestation, not including contestation as a concept in this analysis closes the door to fully understanding why de-legitimation or legitimation occurs. As empirics show, contestation of IOs can be, and is usually, the initiation of de-legitimation processes, and part of a legitimacy crisis as a potential consequence. Yet, contestation itself does not necessarily and exclusively lead to de-legitimation. Instances of contestation can in fact be followed by legitimation, as will be seen in this research. Contestation has a rather 'ambivalent nature' (Deitelhoff, 2020, p 716).

Contestation is the act of signalling discontent, while de-legitimation is a processual consequence of this act. Contestation points towards a legitimacy gap in the contested target (Wiener, 2014). This at the same time opens the potential for de-legitimation or legitimation, depending on whether the contestation claim is valid and met. If the contestation is perceived as valid by the community but the contestation is not met, the contested target will be delegitimized. Moreover, although acknowledging that contestation can have different consequences, the aforementioned (de-)legitimation scholars are not zooming out to the contestation itself. Thus, the necessary step has been missing that can explain why legitimation happens despite contestation in particular processes.

While to the contrary, norm-contestation scholars have engaged in a critical conversation, they have indeed mentioned the strengthening, legitimizing effect of contestation (Wiener, 2014; Deitelhoff and Zimmermann, 2019; Deitelhoff, 2020, p 717). However, they have not conceptualized contestation and legitimation as an interlinked process or emphasized the role of norms *for IOs* explicitly, although norms build 'the legitimating core of global governance' (Wiener, 2014, p 4). So, here too, the conversation has remained conceptually one-sided and does not span further into the analysis of the specific connection between contestation and legitimation. Although acknowledging contestation's positive, strengthening, legitimizing effect 'as a shared understanding over meanings of norms … can generate norm legitimacy' (Deitelhoff, 2020, p 717), few have gone beyond the space of norms themselves and actively engaged with social entities such as IOs (see for instance Zürn, 2018).

While norm-contestation scholars have focused on critically engaging on contestation as practice itself and its impacts on norms, they have not yet approached processes in which contestation and legitimation are connected. Therefore, we are still missing out on the explanatory understanding of *why* contestation of IOs, as a 'mode of critique' (Wiener, 2014) can lead to legitimation rather than de-legitimation. As defined in norms research, contestation is the 'social practice of merely objecting to norms (principles, rules, or values) by rejecting them or refusing to implement them' (Wiener, 2014, p 1). However, by focusing on 'merely' norms (Wiener, 2014, p 1), the wider scope of the actual contested target, and thus other targets that are contestable, misses the larger dimension of contestation itself, especially in connection to legitimation. What needs to be considered to theoretically conceptualize contestation and its connection to legitimation is the target of contestation – which can, in fact, be a policy, a structure, a performance or IOs. While norm scholars see norm contestation as an underlying constant, in this context of contestation–legitimation processes of IOs, *contestation of IOs* is viewed as a momentary exception and pointed challenge; when it is carried out open, hearable and/or visible.

While few have gone beyond the space of norms themselves and actively engaged with social entities such as IOs, Zürn for example conceptualizes contestation in the realm of international institutions in global governance as two reactive kinds, namely 'contestation by societal actors mainly in the form of politicization and contestation by state actors mainly in the form of counter-institutionalization' (Zürn, 2018, pp 95–96). Here, Zürn links authority, legitimacy and contestation, as his two kinds of contestation both show 'the legitimation problems of the global governance system' that with its hierarchies of inequality produces contestation itself 'endogenously' (Zürn, 2018, p 6). He claims that these inequalities lead to four mechanisms of contestation of which the outcome is de-legitimation, via increased politicization or counter-institutionalization (Zürn, 2018, pp 63, 99). These are either a deepening or a decline of the institution of either state or societal contestation. In response to de-legitimation, authority holders will attempt to engage in re-legitimation (Zürn, 2018, p 99).

While acknowledging this complex interplay of authority, legitimacy and contestation, as well as recognizing that 'contestation may lead to a deepening of global governance in other cases, when institutional adjustment is symbolic at best, they spur institutional fragmentation and decline' (Zürn, 2018, p 99), I note two problems. First, although including the necessity for legitimation, it seems that Zürn almost always views contestation and de-legitimation as inevitably linked. However, as I show in this book, there are cases where contestation flags a potential problem or criticism but there is no show of de-legitimation happening. Yet, as can be seen for example in both processes of the United Nations Framework Convention on Climate Change (UNFCCC), the process directly emerged from contestation to legitimation, as actors engaged in legitimation practices. Second, Zürn does not discuss the normative component that affects either contestation or legitimation. Although norms are in themselves contestable, they are flexible and stable at the same time (Wiener, 2014). This way, they guide behaviour and what is perceived as appropriate to do and this is also in response to contestation or when contesting an institution, agreement or practice.

Subsequently, as mentioned earlier, legitimation scholars of international institutions have not yet opened the conversation on contestation connected to legitimation as an interlinked process. Despite contestation being used as to start of conversations about de- and legitimation, little conceptual depth has been given to contestation in regard to investigated de-legitimation or legitimation instances (see, for example, Halliday et al, 2010; Bernstein, 2011, 2018; Gronau and Schmidtke, 2016; Gregoratti and Uhlin, 2018; Tallberg et al, 2018; Tallberg and Zürn, 2019). Further, they do not ask what role norms play for IOs in instances of de- and legitimation. Also, they do not analyse in depth, in which normative setting, communities and here, legitimating actors find themselves and how they understand and perceive contestation, the contester or the contested target. They do not ask what informs the process. Thus, they also miss out on *why* legitimation happens after contestation and not de-legitimation.

In order to understand this nature of contestation and show its relation to legitimation, I will first draw on previous explanations by norm researchers that have been able to uncover and explain the *productive potential of contestation* (Wiener, 2014; Lantis and Wunderlich, 2018; Deitelhoff and Zimmermann, 2019; Sandholtz, 2019; Schmidt and Sikkink, 2019; Welsh, 2019; Deitelhoff, 2020). The fusion of research on legitimation and contestation of norms research is not only plausible but it is necessary as the creation of legitimacy, and its legitimacy beliefs, is 'less the fact of having consented, but rather having consented to a certain normative reasoning, linking shared values and principles to practice type norms' (Steffek, 2003, p 264; see also, for example, Scholte, 2018; Scholte and Tallberg, 2018). In regard to this book, I aim to go a step further theoretically and show why contestation can lead to legitimation, due to the adoption of norms and their role as guiding frames of the contestation–legitimation processes of IOs.

In general, contestation is 'the range of social practices that discursively express disapproval'[1] (Wiener, 2014, p 1). It can be of a discursive, substantial or procedural nature, expressed directly or indirectly. As 'social activity', contestation is a 'social practice [that] entails objection to specific issues that matter to people' and has different modes of being expressed, mostly verbally (Wiener, 2017, p 1). These include 'justification, deliberation, arbitration or contention, and the latter especially does not necessarily involve language' (Wiener, 2017, p 1). In Wiener's conceptualization, contestation is the 'social practice' of objection, rejection, or refusal of implementation, 'and as a mode of critique through critical engagement in a discourse' about '*merely* norms (principles, rules, or values)' (Wiener, 2014, p 1; emphasis added).

This reading of contestation as applicable only to norms, however, misses the wider processual dimension of contestation itself, especially in connection to legitimation. While Wiener criticizes earlier norms research for their perspective on norm internalization as (presumably) final and attesting norms a prescriptive character (Wiener, 2008; Wiener, 2014), Deitelhoff and Zimmermann, despite sharing Wiener's critique of norms being static, understand norms from a rather empirical dynamic. This means that they do see norms as guiding in practice as long as they are not contested themselves (Deitelhoff and Zimmermann, 2020; see also Loges, 2021, p 54). This way, they circle back to some essentialist understanding of norms as stable and guiding principles of the appropriate standard of behaviour with a causal effect (Loges, 2021, p 54).

In this book, it is neither assumed nor shared that norm internalization is final. However, in accordance with the criticism of internalization, this book will speak of norm adoption to conceptualize norms as guiding frame in contestation–legitimation processes. As Wiener (2008; 2014) and Deitelhoff and Zimmermann (2020) argue, norms are contestable and will find re-interpretation as change in global governance is constant and inevitable. Norm internalization thus never finalizes, as the re-interpretation and the life cycle of the norm goes on. This way, speaking of norm adoption in IO climate communities is more fruitful.

Moving back to understanding contestation–legitimation processes, norm adoption can tell us why contestation of a specific, empirical target is met with legitimation engagement and not de-legitimation. The aim of this book is to answer exactly this question and show which norm guides action and structures behaviour. It is not the aim to analyse the guiding norm and its contestation itself. Further, what needs to be considered to theoretically conceptualize contestation and its connection to legitimation is the target of contestation, a policy, a structure, a performance or even actors or institutions that have not adopted the norm yet. But the IOs are contested for precisely this missing norm adoption, which the relevant community demands. Thus, there is no contradiction in moving contestation research beyond the scope of contested norms.

The understanding that the contested target 'will always lose some salience just in virtue of being publicly challenged' (Deitelhoff, 2020, p 717) refers to the commonly perceived negative, weakening effect of contestation. However, this is not always the case. As contestation triggers a critical engagement about the contested target and the underlying guiding norm, this points to the target's legitimacy and potential 'legitimacy gaps' (Wiener, 2014, p 3). These in turn leave room for de-legitimation or legitimation. Wiener connects contestation and 'legitimacy gaps' in her research on norm contestation with the following:

> The principle of contestedness reflects the global agreement that, in principle, the norms, rules and principles of governance are contested and that they therefore require regular contestation in order to work. For the legitimacy gap between fundamental norms and standardised procedures to be filled, therefore, access to regular contestation (as opposed to ad hoc contestation) needs to be facilitated, in principle, for all involved stakeholders. ... Given that norms entail a dual quality (i.e. they are both structuring and constructed) they must be contestable so as to both indicate potential legitimacy gaps and to overcome them. (Wiener, 2014, pp 3–4)

In other words, contestation is necessary to fill this 'gap' by addressing the legitimacy deficit between the contested target and related practical implementations. This shows that contestation *is* about legitimacy and in consequence always has the potential for de-legitimation or legitimation. Contestation functions as a review of the alignment between the normative position and herein carried legitimacy beliefs of the community contra the target, its procedures and performances. Contestation is an act of signalling discontent, while de-legitimation can be a processual consequence of this act. However, as this research shows and as can be empirically observed, the result can be either de-legitimation or legitimation, depending on whether the contestation claim is valid and met. When contestation occurs and legitimation potential is laid open by pointing to a legitimacy gap, the norm within the given community guides how this contestation and indicated gap are perceived and responded to. If the contestation is perceived as valid by the community and is met, legitimation may occur. But if the contestation is valid and not met, the contested target will be delegitimized.

In further development on this relation of norms and their contestation, Deitelhoff and Zimmermann, understand contestation as either strengthening or weakening, depending on the context and given circumstances (Deitelhoff and Zimmermann, 2020, p 1; see also Niemann and Schillinger, 2017). They show that different types of contestations and the given context can tell us more about the different forms and consequences of contestation (Deitelhoff and Zimmermann, 2020, p 1; see also Niemann and Schillinger, 2017). Here, they differ between the contestation contesting the application of the norm on the one hand and the overall appropriateness or righteousness of the claims a norm makes, so contesting its general existence on the other (Deitelhoff and Zimmermann, 2020, p 1).

Henceforth, contestation has the power of changing or underlining the meaning of norms, practices and hence their institutions (Wiener, 2014, p 10). Thus, it can have a positive, strengthening, *legitimizing* effect. As acted out by social actors, in the same way as social practice, contestation is 'constitutive for social change, for it always involves a critical redress of the rules of the game' (Wiener, 2014, p 2). This is also the case for legitimacy. As Lantis and Wunderlich find, 'deliberation over norm meanings may be necessary to produce legitimacy insofar as contestatory discourses open the way for processes of understanding, of joint meaning creation, which will lend sociocultural legitimacy and power to norms' (2018, p 575).

Thus, contestation has the significant potential of changing the dynamics within communities, and also between IOs, their members and civil society (for example, Seabrooke, 2007, p 264; Ecker-Ehrhardt, 2018, p 526). Reoccurring instances of contestation reflect this change of global governance and its structures, and this is also the case for IOs. This fragility poses a struggle for legitimacy that creates the constant potential for delegitimation and need for legitimation, which I will elaborate on in the following section.

The struggle of contestation–legitimation processes: legitimacy

Previous research on legitimacy has encompassed legitimacy's different dynamics, relevant entities and effects (see, for example, Buchanan and Keohane, 2006; Reus-Smit, 2007; Johnson, 2011; Symons, 2011; Ecker-Ehrhardt, 2012; Bernauer and Gampfer, 2013; Zaum, 2013; Lenz and Viola, 2017; Tallberg et al, 2018, p 8; Bes et al, 2019; Tallberg and Zürn, 2019). As Zürn notes, legitimacy matters in global governance as 'any system of rule and any authority that is considered legitimate is *ceteris paribus* much more efficient and effective than one without legitimacy' (2020, p 200).

For IOs, legitimacy affects their relevance and recognition as appropriate agents to coordinate policies and to solve problems. Further, legitimacy will determine the IO's degree of agency and its ability to develop new rules and norms. The respective degree of legitimacy translates into support by governments, non-state actors, elites and citizens. Since IOs depend on the compliance of their members rather than coercive rule, high legitimacy can support an IO's cause and ability to act (Tallberg and Zürn, 2019, p 582). When having legitimacy, it implies that the respective community follows 'the [governors'] rules, commands or decisions as they acknowledge them as binding' (Steffek, 2003, p 255). Between the governing actor and the community exists the consensus understanding of shared norms that inform the way the governor will practise its authority (Bernstein, 2011, p 21; Habermas, 1996, p 119; Steffek, 2003, p 264). Henceforth, the respective community is the responsible audience to delegitimate or legitimate the respective governing actor, especially in the context of IOs, including both state and non-state actors. So, 'to gain lasting support from societal actors, IOs are in desperate need of normative recognition as legitimate, given that IOs notoriously lack alternative sources of social power' (Ecker-Ehrhardt, 2018, p 527).

This community can consist of both state and non-state actors, so all kinds of political actors, governments and civil society from the public and private sector (Gronau and Schmidtke, 2016, p 543; Tallberg et al, 2018, p 5). Legitimacy is socially embedded (see, for example, Keohane, 2006; Bernstein, 2011; Beetham, 2013; Tallberg et al, 2018). As a central, linking component between the governing and the governed, legitimacy is relational (Jackson, 2002, pp 448–49; MacKay, 2019, p 718). It 'is primarily the result of the relationship between actors, processes, and institutions, as perceived by the audiences, be it states, non-state actors, or individuals' (Tussie, 2018, p 201). Thus, it is not constant and static, but fluid and prone to change and decline. The social embeddedness of legitimacy implies 'the possibility for actors to affect legitimacy beliefs through practices of legitimation and delegitimation' and can open up 'spaces for actors to draw on prevailing norms to shape legitimacy perceptions' (Tallberg et al, 2018, p 11, referring to Finnemore and Sikkink, 1998). But its processual fragility also implies the risk of crisis.

Scholars of legitimacy and legitimation have widely discussed different terms and aspects of legitimation audiences (see, for example, Halliday et al, 2010; Tallberg et al, 2018; Tallberg and Zürn, 2019; Bexell et al, 2020). In general, legitimation audiences can be defined as:

> the sets of actors that a global governance institution explicitly acknowledges as an audience it intends to address in its efforts to legitimize itself. Such a conceptualization accentuates that the communities that grant legitimacy are far from pre-set and stable, but are constructed by and through their interaction with the global governance institution that seeks to present itself as legitimate. (Bexell et al, 2020, p 10)

IO audiences have been distinguished as internal audiences, member states and their publics, and external audiences, non-member states and their citizens (Zaum, 2013). The internal-external distinction resembles the differentiation between constituencies and observers (Tallberg and Zürn, 2019). While the former implies the institutionalized political link to a governing authority of the audiences, the latter misses such a link. However, this implies a fixed set-up of different audiences a priori. IO communities include member states, IO staff and civil society (Gronau and Schmidtke, 2016).

Taking the audiences of legitimation into account is necessary to be able to unpack contestation–legitimation processes, to identify the community, as they 'may vary widely in composition, power, and relevance across institutions and geographies, with significant implications not only for who matters, but also for what gets legitimated, and with what consequences' (Tallberg et al, 2018, p 18). With regard to IOs, audiences become more and more diverse due to the 'broader trend towards increased politicization of global governance, leading to more public discussion, political mobilization, and contestation' (Zürn, 2014, cf. in Bexell and Jönsson, 2018, p 121). This 'more variable set-up of audiences' also increases the potential for normative contestation of IO legitimacy (Bernstein, 2011, cf. in Bexell and Jönsson, 2018, pp 121–22).

Instead of referring to audiences, in this book, I refer to community. In the following, I will reflect on the concept of community in contestation–legitimation processes. According to its definition,[2] an audience is mostly passive and does not associate with the agency that the 'audience' possess in contestation–legitimation processes. Instead of referring simply to audiences, in this research, I include audiences of legitimation within the broader term of the community as I analyse not only the legitimation but the whole process, in which contestation is followed by legitimation. Thus, community consists of all relevant actors in the process: the contesters, the audience of legitimation and the contested, and the legitimating actors. Also, after contestation, the community refers to the norm adoption in the process and which legitimacy gap, as well as legitimation potential, needs to be filled.

However, it is worth reflecting on what role audiences play in the second part of the process, the legitimation, as this speaks to the necessary norm adoption after contestation. This adoption must be reflected through the legitimation towards the 'audience', the rest of the community, as '[w]e only know what is appropriate by reference to the judgments of a community or society. We recognize ... norm conforming behavior because it produces praise' (Finnemore and Sikkink, 1998, p 892). Due to the relational character of legitimacy, it involves a relationship between an organization and its audiences (Suchman, 1995, p 594; see also Bexell and Jönsson, 2018, p 122). In the next section, I will introduce said norm adoption in accordance with the analytical framework of contestation–legitimation processes in which norms work as guiding frames.

Norms as guiding frames of contestation–legitimation processes

In the following, I will explain how norms are understood conceptually, their impact on political practice as well as how they work as guiding frames in contestation–legitimation processes of IOs. Norms 'represent the legitimating core of global governance' and 'are considered as standards of behaviour in international relations' (Wiener, 2014, p 21). They shape practices and policies (Wiener and Puetter, 2009, p 2). Further, norms 'set key contours of expected and accepted behavior in world politics', and in this way, they shape legitimacy beliefs that are articulated in de-legitimation and legitimation practices (Scholte, 2018, p 87). Henceforth, to 'state that norms matter is no longer controversial' (Björkdahl, 2002, p 9).

In the first wave of norms research, Finnemore and Sikkink conceptualize norm development with the 'life cycle' of norms, how they influence state and non-state behaviour, and which 'norms will matter under what conditions' (1998, p 894). When the 'critical mass' of actors within a community adopts the norms, the norm moves beyond the tipping point, emerges in importance and necessity, and thus manifests as an appropriate standard of behaviour in practice (Finnemore and Sikkink, 1998, p 901). Identifying the three stages of the life cycle, norm emergence, tipping point as an in-between step, and cascade and internalization (Finnemore and Sikkink, 1998, p 896), the authors made way for conceptualizing norms and providing the conceptual tools to identify which norms 'make it in the end'.

As 'norms do not appear out of thin air' (Finnemore and Sikkink, 1998, p 896), stage one of the life cycle is related to the agent that promotes the norm in the role of the so-called 'norm entrepreneur', in order for the norm to emerge. By bringing attention and relevance to the respective issue that will be framed as the norm, norm emergence proceeds. When norm entrepreneurs have convinced the critical mass within the relevant community, norm emergence reaches the so-called 'tipping point' from which the norm 'cascades' (Finnemore and Sikkink, 1998, pp 901–2). The 'cascade' stage leads to a different dynamic that translates this normative change into norm internalization, which will find practical implementation, for example, in the form of new institutional formats, agreements or corporation. This practical translation marks the third stage of the 'life cycle' as norm internalization. Practices that speak to the aspects of the norm and the appropriate standard the norm constitutes will reflect this norm internalization towards the community. In turn, the community will measure (future) behaviour against the norm to judge legitimacy. As Finnemore and Sikkink state:

> We only know what is appropriate by reference to the judgments of a community or society. We recognize norm-breaking behavior because it generates disapproval or stigma and norm conforming behavior either because it produces praise or, in the case of a highly internalized norm, because it is so taken for granted that it provokes no reaction whatsoever. (1998, p 892)

This shows that norms are the key link to what is perceived as legitimate, and the recognition of which guides the respective community. When contestation occurs, it depends on the community to judge the adopted norm and the indicated legitimacy gap and the necessary legitimation potential. For example, if the community perceives the signalled legitimacy gap as valid, it needs to be filled. So, as norm still must be adopted further, re-engagement with the contestation in the form of legitimation is necessary. To legitimate and to not run into a severe legitimacy crisis, the legitimation practices need to reflect the norm and its core aspects to show norm adoption.

Norms themselves, just like actors and institutions, of course, can be contested and legitimated as well. As norms are based on the shared understanding of appropriateness and are part of the changing, complex realm of global governance, they are not static but shaped and changed over time through instances of contestation that contribute to their development (Krook and True, 2012; Brunnée and Toope, 2019; Deitelhoff and Zimmermann, 2019). So, simultaneously, norms are only as legitimate 'as perceived by their addressees' (Finnemore and Sikkink, 1998, p 892). As Deitelhoff and Zimmermann summarize, contestation of norms can have two effects:

> Existing research offers two competing hypotheses: One branch of norm research often conceptualizes contestation as a sign of norm weakening. By contrast, another branch assigns contestation a normative power of its own, which strengthens norms. It does not specify the limits of such normative power, however. … contestation per se is a poor predictor of norm robustness. (Deitelhoff and Zimmermann, 2020, p 1)

Thus, to be robust, norms are also in need of legitimation in order to be adopted, and in turn guide behaviour and social interaction. Adopting a norm in the sense of the life cycle does not stand in contradiction to changing the understanding of what is appropriate. In other words, although internalization of a norm is necessary to guide practice, norm interpretation continues. Thus, contestation can lead to a new interpretation and adjustment of the norm, which might also lead to norm discarding and replacement.

In light of the changing nature of global governance, in further developing the theoretical understanding of norms in the second wave with research on for example the 'boomerang-effect' (Risse and Sikkink, 2016, p 131), the third wave of norms research has encompassed the 'dual quality of norms' (Wiener, 2008, pp 9, 50). In this interpretation, norms are always both stable and flexible, as they are embodied in social practices. Wiener denotes this character of norms as 'meaning in use' (Wiener, 2008, p 57), which refers to the everyday practice of a norm's interpretation and application in the interaction between actors (Schillinger and Niemann, 2021, p 146). In Wiener's words: '[w]hile norm validity is in principle contested, *norm recognition does structure behaviour*. In turn, as a social practice, behaviour has an effect on the type and meaning of a norm' (Wiener, 2008, p 50; emphasis added). What is important to stress here is the clear recognition that 'norms lie in practice' (Wiener, 2018, p 27). At the same time, acknowledging the 'dual quality' of norms themselves does not stand in contradiction to the characteristic of norms as guiding frames of social practice within a process at a particular time within a given community. When norms are adopted, they guide until social interaction produces a profound change that results in new interpretations or even new norms.

For state actors, there is a complex tension between the demands of the state's domestic contexts and the parallel task of aligning with norms of the international community, when adopting a norm. Scholars have theorized this tension by referring to 'norm diffusion as driven by moves towards a shared world culture, boomerang effects facilitated by transnational advocacy networks, ... spiral models of domestic change and resistance' (Krook and True, 2012, p 104). So, if the norms match the existing cultural context, they are potentially adopted more easily while others will remain disregarded (Krook and True, 2012, p 111). When adopted, 'norms are more robust when they enjoy diverse support' (Simmons and Jo, 2019, p 20). Diverse and widespread support includes 'a range of state actors from different normative traditions, cultural perspectives, and material interests; both official state actors and international organizations; a range of nonstate actors; and a range of institutions at international, regional, and domestic levels' (Simmons and Jo, 2019, p 20).

In accordance with this research's theoretical framework, it is necessary to clarify that this book's aim is not to cover the 'story' of the norm itself that frames the process and shows why the processes result in legitimation despite contestation. It is not about researching the 'birth' of the norm, but its adoption as a guiding frame. Through this, I can explain why contestation was followed by legitimation. To do so, I will deconstruct the processes and analyse its contestation and legitimation and their related practices. Hence, while acknowledging that norms themselves can change, I am interested in their informative, conditioning characteristic as guiding frames of what, and which behaviour, is perceived as appropriate and legitimate. These practices reveal the adopted norm. In the following, I will explain the connection of norms and legitimacy beliefs in legitimation practices.

Legitimacy beliefs

In the following, I will reflect on the conceptualization of legitimacy beliefs in de-legitimation and legitimation and their relations to norms. The creation of legitimacy, and its legitimacy beliefs, is 'less the fact of having consented, but rather having consented to a certain normative reasoning, linking shared values and principles to practice type norms' (Steffek, 2003, p 264; see also, for example, Scholte, 2018; Scholte and Tallberg, 2018). The beliefs shaping legitimacy are informed by the shared norms that 'set key contours of expected and accepted behavior in world politics' (Scholte, 2018, p 87). While norms provide the overall structure and the guiding frame to processes, legitimacy beliefs are much more obvious in the (de-)legitimation itself. Legitimacy beliefs are embedded, and shaped, in daily practice in international institutions. They are articulated in the practices of de-legitimation and legitimation. Thus, they are part of the legitimation practice and the channel through which the *belief* in the appropriate standard of behaviour, the norm, is articulated. Legitimacy beliefs 'are held by individuals and refer to regulatory institutions; however, this interplay of subjects and their governing bodies unfolds amidst a social architecture' (Scholte, 2018, pp 75–76). These beliefs thus reproduce the prevailing sense of legitimacy (Scholte, 2018, p 79).

Legitimacy beliefs are formed around what is known, consciously as well as unconsciously. As the 'cultural values' differ around the globe, so do legitimacy beliefs (Scholte and Tallberg, 2018, p 69). Also, the political system informs the criteria that shape legitimacy beliefs. Societies in democracies may rather 'form legitimacy beliefs vis-à-vis [IOs] on the basis of democratic procedure than audiences in countries with autocratic rule' (Scholte and Tallberg, 2018, p 68). The perception of IOs can also differ in regard to their issue area, whether they are directed toward a specific task (for example, UNFCCC) or general or more purposes (for example, European Union) (see, for example, Rittberger et al, 2012; Lenz et al, 2015), and also whether their task is directed towards executive, legislative or judicial performance (Scholte and Tallberg, 2018, p 67).

Legitimacy beliefs are articulated in the de-legitimation and legitimation practices and they point us to the guiding frame of the process. They can lay open the 'shared rules, rituals, and beliefs that shape the members of the organization's decision-making processes by specifying the basic assumptions, or the correct way to perceive, think, and feel' (Nelson and Weaver, 2016, p 923; see also Dingwerth et al, 2020, p 717). Considering that the societal and political upbringing of IO representatives highly informs and determines the design, performance and procedures of the IO, it in turn leads to a continued reproduction and adoption of these beliefs. The shared principles, the norms, 'set key contours of expected and accepted behavior in world politics' (Scholte, 2018, p 87; see also Keck and Sikkink, 1998; Bernstein, 2001; Barnett and Finnemore, 2004; Lechner and Boli, 2005; Clark, 2007). As norms are embedded in the social structures, they guide how legitimation is carried out, how beliefs are formed, and where legitimacy is drawn from (Clark, 2007, p 182; Scholte, 2018, p 87).

Due to the diverse demands of states' domestic contexts, the parallel task to align with norms of the international community can have different, complex outcomes for implementation. As contexts do not stand still but change constantly, normative understandings and the demand for implementation of new norms and practices change over time (Finnemore and Sikkink, 1998; Wiener, 2014; Lantis and Wunderlich, 2018; Deitelhoff and Zimmermann, 2019; Sandholtz, 2019; Schmidt and Sikkink, 2019; Welsh, 2019; Deitelhoff, 2020). This also entails implications for legitimacy beliefs, changing perceptions and thus the potential for contestation, de-legitimation and legitimation. Targeted audiences in de-legitimation or legitimation shape their legitimacy beliefs through the occurring practices, and in doing so shape the practices of (de-)legitimation themselves in turn (see also Bernstein, 2018, p 195). As de-legitimation and legitimation practices are 'charged with power' (Bexell et al, 2020, p 7; see also Tussie, 2018), these also reflect the power structures in which community and producers find themselves. In the next section, I will portray practices of de- and legitimation before explaining how practices work as vehicles to deconstruct processes of contestation and legitimation, to unveil the norm as the guiding frame and answer why legitimation followed contestation.

Practices of de-legitimation and legitimation

Legitimation is an 'activity which can be observed ... it is something people do' (Barker, 2001, p 24, in Bäckstrand and Söderbaum, 2018, p 103). As practices have 'no existence other than in their unfolding or process' (Jackson and Nexon, 1999 in Adler and Pouliot, 2011b, p 6; see also Jackson and Nexon, 1999), legitimation is observable in practice. Yet, too little research has focused on the actual deconstruction of legitimation and de-legitimation practices to unveil their normative meaning and what they are guided by (Bäckstrand and Söderbaum, 2018, p 101; see also Zaum, 2013). Broadly speaking, while de-legitimation is depreciating, consequential, disapproving, legitimation is the practice 'of justification ... intended to shape legitimacy beliefs' (Tallberg et al, 2018, p 4; see also Tallberg and Zürn, 2019). Further, it is the practice that shapes, enables and manifests legitimacy.

These practices of justification aim to translate and establish 'what is acceptable behavior and [make] certain behavioral choices inappropriate' (Dingwerth et al, 2019, p 33). Practices of de-legitimation and legitimation are socially embedded, they simultaneously inform and are the result of the structures, which are the relationship between actors, processes, and institutions and their audiences (Bernstein, 2018, p 198; Tussie, 2018, p 201; MacKay, 2019, p 718; Jackson, 2002, pp 448–49). Here, '[legitimacy] claims and practices destined to enhance or reinforce the legitimacy of an institution are rarely uncontested; institutions face oppositions and are confronted with attempts geared towards their delegitimation' (Rittberger and Schroeder, 2016, p 586). In the case of IOs, these cannot only come from non-state actors but also from member states and even staff (Zaum, 2013; Bäckstrand and Söderbaum, 2018, p 102; Gregoratti and Uhlin, 2018). Legitimation practices are successful when they speak to 'established normative frames' within the community (Dingwerth et al, 2019, p 39). Thus, actors can judge what kind of practice will transport the belief of legitimacy and in consequence channel de-legitimation or legitimation.

De-legitimation and legitimation practices are 'charged with power' (Bexell et al, 2020, p 7; see also Tussie, 2018), as they aim to undermine or justify existing power and authority relations (Clark, 2005, p 254; Bernstein, 2011, 2018; Bexell et al, 2020). As de-legitimation and legitimation are socially embedded and relational, they shape each other (Bäckstrand and Söderbaum, 2018, p 102). Further, as de-legitimation can be the result of contestation, so can legitimation. The contestation claims may be mirrored by legitimacy claims and vice versa (see, for example, Clark, 2005; Reus-Smit, 2007; Hurrelmann and Schneider, 2014; Bäckstrand and Söderbaum, 2018). These claims, that are either to justify or to undermine, are carried by the legitimacy beliefs conforming to the social embeddedness of de-legitimation or legitimation (Scholte and Tallberg, 2018, p 65).

So, which de-legitimation and legitimation practices can be found in global governance? Practices of de-legitimation and legitimation are used by IOs, their audiences and contesters alike (Steffek, 2003, p 251). Thus, IOs, their members and other internals and externals are most often 'simultaneously both producers and audiences of legitimation' (Bäckstrand and Söderbaum, 2018, p 106). In this regard, scholars have distinguished the different existing practices: for example, Gronau and Schmidtke (2016)[3] conceptualize among governmental practices, thus geared towards governments as audience; bureaucratic, directed towards their own bureaucratic staff; and societal practices, thus societal audiences. These are separated into top-down and bottom-up legitimation regarding the relationship between producers and audiences. These, however, cannot always be as neatly separated, as legitimation is complex, and the undertaken practices can be directed towards multiple audiences (see, for example, Bäckstrand and Söderbaum, 2018; Bexell and Jönsson, 2018). Such practices can be *discursive, behavioural* or *institutional* (see, for example, Halliday et al, 2010; Bernstein, 2011, 2018; Gronau and Schmidtke, 2016; Bäckstrand and Söderbaum, 2018; Gregoratti and Uhlin, 2018; Tallberg et al, 2018).

Discursive legitimation may involve praise and support of the IO and/or their norms, procedures, performance and so on (Steffek, 2003; Reus-Smit, 2007; Halliday et al, 2010). Generally, these are attempts to establish legitimacy 'through public self-justification of their actions and/or through the construction in rhetoric and other messages of positive impressions of their rule' (Bäckstrand and Söderbaum, 2018, p 106). Here, the producers associate themselves with the 'perceived sources of legitimacy', which can relate to democratic credentials, technocratic standards, and fairness of procedures (Bäckstrand and Söderbaum, 2018; Scholte and Tallberg, 2018).

Discursive self-legitimation attempts by IOs, in contrast to their usually neutral semantic in discursive communication, are often 'value-laden ... to (re)define and present the institution as a force for a normative good' (Gronau and Schmidtke, 2016, p 542). Antagonistically, de-legitimation can consist of verbal or written criticism of, or discontent with, the IO and its procedures (Bäckstrand and Söderbaum, 2018, pp 102–3). Discursive practices can come in different forms, such as texts and speech acts, mission statements, constitutional documents, speeches, policy papers, press releases, public relations communications, social media, straplines, protest slogans, spontaneous talk in negotiations and so forth (cf. Bäckstrand and Söderbaum, 2018, p 108; see also Steffek, 2003; Schneider et al, 2007).

Behavioural practice of de-legitimation and legitimation, such as protests, speeches and statements, coming from IOs, their members, other internals and externals alike, can include a discursive component (Bäckstrand and Söderbaum, 2018, pp 109–10). They often come combined, as 'discursive often spills over into behavioral delegitimation' (Bäckstrand and Söderbaum, 2018, p 113; see also Derman, 2014; Orr, 2016). The emphasis of behavioural de-legitimation and legitimation, however, is on action. They can consist of performance reviews, visual representations, opinion polls, external validation, street protests and campaigns (cf. Bäckstrand and Söderbaum, 2018, p 112). Non-state actors' de-legitimation practices in particular are behavioural, and can involve peaceful petitions, demonstrations and strikes but also disruptive blockades and occupations or even the use of property and physical violence (Gregoratti and Uhlin, 2018). But also state actors or representatives of member states and even of IOs themselves engage in behavioural practices that can be cyber-protests, critical action research, monitoring of IO activities (Bäckstrand and Söderbaum, 2018, p 113) or walkouts from meetings or conferences.

Institutional de-legitimation and legitimation practices most often evolve around self-legitimation by IOs towards their members, but also by 'opening up' to civil society actors (cf. Bäckstrand and Söderbaum, 2018, p 106; see also Scholte, 2011; Zaum, 2013; Tallberg et al, 2018). Institutional self-legitimation attempts to foster the audience's perceptions of its own legitimacy, internally or externally (Steffek, 2003; Gronau, 2016; Gronau and Schmidtke, 2016; Bexell et al, 2020). These 'may be conducted by a multitude of units, sections and individuals working at the institution's interface with outside actors' (Bexell et al, 2020, p 21). Institutional legitimation, however, can also be combined with the other two forms of de-legitimation practices. It 'prioritizes form over function, signaling to important and powerful audiences to encourage their continued material and political support' (Zaum, 2016, p 1). They can consist of constitutional reforms, administrative reorganizations, transparency initiatives, civil society engagement programmes and policy adjustments in response to criticism (cf. Bäckstrand and Söderbaum, 2018, p 110). There is also institutional isomorphism or mimicry, thus remodelling one's own organization in regard to another, mostly competitor organization (Bäckstrand and Söderbaum, 2018, p 110; see also Heubaum and Biermann, 2015; Lenz and Burilkov, 2017; Faude and Fuss, 2020).

One common practice of and within the processes of IOs is the practice of consent. Although scholars count this practice as institutional (Zaum, 2013; Bäckstrand and Söderbaum, 2018), I regard it as a combined formation of all three kinds of legitimation practices. It can be institutionally embedded as a processual requirement, such as in the UNFCCC processes. The act, however, can come in both discursive and behavioural form. It can be spoken or written, but also expressed by joining an IO, the acceptance of rules acquired by this membership, shown in practices such as voting in support of the IO's policies and programmes (Zaum, 2013; Bäckstrand and Söderbaum, 2018). The lack or absence of consent can, nevertheless, be a severe practice of de-legitimation. The most expressive and powerful intensification of this kind of practice is final withdrawal (see, for example, Kemp, 2017; Jotzo et al, 2018; Pickering et al, 2018). In the next section, I will explain how practices work as vehicles to deconstruct processes of contestation and legitimation, to unveil the norm as the guiding frame and answer why legitimation followed contestation.

Practice tracing in contestation–legitimation processes

As outlined previously, contestation is the practice of criticism and refusal. Thus, we would expect rather negative consequences after contestation, such as de-legitimation, which can even lead to a legitimacy crisis and pose an existential threat to IOs. However, as I will show in this book, the opposite can be the result, as here contestation was ultimately followed by legitimation. Therefore, I ask: *How and why are IOs in the global climate regime able to self-legitimate despite contestation?* Considering this question, I focus on two large IOs. I study these two cases with two contestation-legitimation processes each. The purpose is to unpack the puzzling processes as well as to understand the connection between contestation and legitimation.

As I argue, contestation and legitimation are conditioned by the guiding frame of the norm for climate change action (CCA), which frames the process. In order to be able to understand the connection between contestation and legitimation in the processes, I trace the occurring practices of the contestation and its legitimation in an interlinked process, and I engage in an altered form of process tracing (see, for example, Bennett, 2010; Collier, 2011; Beach and Pedersen, 2013; Beach, 2016). My approach of 'practice tracing' (Pouliot, 2009) allows interpretive analysis to deconstruct the processes, related practices and their 'meaning in use', and the guiding norm.

I combine an interpretive form of process tracing, which 'is also an effective and "doable" research strategy' (Pouliot, 2009, p 258; see also Pouliot, 2007; Bueger, 2014; Cornut, 2015). Combining the originally more positivist method of process tracing and an interpretivist epistemology allows me to generate an in-depth understanding and to unfold a more interlinked picture of the process and the question of why contestation can result in legitimation. Embracing interpretivism and 'working intentionally to grasp the other's meaning' (Vandamme, 2021, p 377) 'shifts the researcher's expert role from technical-rational subject-matter expertise to process expertise' (Yanow, 2003, p 11, cf. Vandamme, 2021, p 377).

Due to its interpretive nature, practice tracing makes it possible to uncover and understand how and why contestation can have a positive, legitimizing effect 'as it is the condition for a shared understanding over meanings ... can generate ... legitimacy' (Deitelhoff, 2020, p 717), rather than result in delegitimation, total disruption and a crisis of legitimacy. As this book aims to understand the 'why' in the observed processes, it is required to look behind at what is formally observable. Through interpretive analysis, I will be able to fully understand and explain, but more importantly, reason this book's findings regarding the legitimizing nature of contestation by deconstructing the meaning of the practices in the processes.

By choosing a practice tracing approach, I will turn to what is empirically observable, namely the practices (Bourdieu, 1998; Schatzki et al, 2001; Adler and Pouliot, 2011a, b; Bueger, 2014; Bueger and Gadinger, 2018; Lechner and Frost, 2018). These are identifiable in people's everyday doing and saying, henceforth the interview material and conducted participant observation of this study not only give insight but are essential methods to gather these practices in the material. Epistemologically, practices are one of the most observable data we can find as '[p]ractices ... are the foundations, or the smallest units, of social life' (Mattern, 2011, p 70). Previous research has just started to map practices of legitimation, such as praise or protest (see, for example, Halliday et al, 2010; Gronau and Schmidtke, 2016; Bäckstrand and Söderbaum, 2018; Bernstein, 2011, 2018; Gregoratti and Uhlin, 2018; Tallberg et al, 2018; Tallberg and Zürn, 2019). Yet, only a little meaning has been given to these practices and their normative implications and guidance (Scholte, 2018, p 97).

Practice tracing builds on the 'practice turn' that has proceeded since the early 2000s in social theory (Schatzki et al, 2001). Definitions of practice vary within the literature (Bourdieu, 1998; Schatzki et al, 2001; Adler and Pouliot, 2011a, b; Bueger, 2014; Bueger and Gadinger, 2018; Lechner and Frost, 2018). Broadly defined they are the 'nexus of doings and sayings' in everyday life (Schatzki, 1996). While Bourdieu connects practice to 'habitus' (Bourdieu, 1990), Lechner and Frost, for example, define practice in connection to rules as 'a distinctive domain of rule-following activity, defined by concrete constitutive rules and espoused as common understanding by a group of participants' (2018, p 115), which stresses the collective understanding by a group of actors, by pointing to the understanding of norms in IR as 'common understanding of appropriate behaviour' (Lechner and Frost, 2018). In this book, I rely on definitions by Adler and Pouliot (2011b). Here practices are: 'competent performances. More precisely, practices are socially meaningful patterns of action, which, in being performed more or less competently, simultaneously embody, act out, and possibly reify background knowledge and discourse in and on the material world' (Adler and Pouliot, 2011b, p 4).

Further, they describe practices as '... not merely descriptive "arrows" that connect structure to agency and back, but rather the dynamic material and ideational processes that enable structures to be stable or to evolve, and agents reproduce or transform structures' (Adler and Pouliot, 2011a, p 6). As 'world politics can be understood by practices' (Adler and Pouliot, 2011a, p 5), practices give entry to 'conceive of the social as bundles of ideas and matter that are linguistically, materially, and intersubjectively mediated in form of practice' (Adler and Pouliot, 2011a, p 13). Henceforth, they are both material and meaningful, in other words analysing practices closes the divide 'between ideas and matter' (Adler and Pouliot, 2011a, p 14). This way, it is possible to deconstruct the doings and sayings of contestation–legitimation processes to its core meaning, namely the norm that guides this action. As practices are 'constructed collectively by a community' (Stein, 2011, p 89) while 'performed by an individual, it acquires meaning only through collectively shared understandings of competency, of what is well done or poorly done. ... practices join together people or organizations that share an interest in doing and that share standards of competence that have been internalized over time' (Stein, 2011, p 89).

As practices are the translation of normative meaning and are themselves 'imbued with normativity' (Gadinger and Niemann, 2025), I can detect the guiding frame of the processes. By deconstructing the processes and looking into the contestation and legitimation practices, and what they are referring to, I can trace the practice back to the guiding norm that frames the process. Through this, I can assess the stage of adoption of the norm within parts of the community at that given moment, when the process unfolded. An interpretive guidance helps me unveil this frame by incorporating the social context of the process and the ongoing practices (Geertz, 1973; Schwandt, 1999; Yanow, 2000, 2003; Guzzini, 2013; Pouliot, 2014; Norman, 2015, 2016; Yanow and Schwartz-Shea, 2015). This allows me to capture the practices of contestation and legitimation, interpret the meaning of the discursive and behavioural action and thus the process in which they are performed, and finally, put these into causal context with one another.

When tracing practices that are being acted out in the empirical world, we can see the reality they are causing. These can be observed, heard and read in the collected materials, especially interviews and participant observation. Practices have 'casual power in the sense that they make other things happen' (Pouliot, 2009, p 241). As practices unfold in a specific context, it is necessary to find the meaning behind them. Through practices, I can use the visible, hearable reference about the norm in the related events, documents, speeches and interviews as a reference point to grasp that meaning, in line with the aim of interpretivist research. Here, 'the line of inquiry finds its source in phenomenological presuppositions, according to which analytical focus is put on experience and narratives with a primacy on context specificity' (Vandamme, 2021, p 377).

Further, for finding the nuances that help uncover why contestation does not play out as a destructive rupture but rather as legitimation, it is necessary to get behind the guiding frame of the process, thus the common understanding, the standard of appropriateness the involved actors find themselves in. Interpretation in practice tracing requires '[incorporating] an in-depth understanding of intersubjective social worlds' as it 'is intrinsically entwined with attempts to specify the causal element of particular processes' (Norman, 2016, p 35; see also Beach, 2016). It enables us to capture the meaning of the contestation and legitimation practices, interpret the meaning of the discursive, institutional and behavioural practices and thus the process in which they are performed, and finally, abstract them into a causality and explain contestation–legitimation processes.

Practices can point as markers to ways of understanding and belief and thus point to norms. Contestation and legitimation practices 'link both to the dispositions of actors in terms of their perceptions of legitimacy (which can inform their motivations to support or withdraw support from an institution) and also define the types of strategies and reasons or arguments at their disposal' (Bernstein, 2018, pp 195–96).

Due to the reflexive quality of norms, the contestation can either be aligned with the norm, embodied in the contestation claim indicating the legitimacy gap, or the contestation cannot be in line with the norm of the community. When norms are not themselves the explicit target of contestation, they either lie in the contestation claim itself, which then influences possible legitimation in light of the norm. The signalled legitimacy gap in the contested target also describes legitimation potential. This can be fulfilled through adoption of the norm and engaging in legitimation practices that reflect the norm towards the community. Or the norm is embodied in the contested target itself and reinforced through the community that believes in the standard of appropriate behaviour given by the norm and opposes the contestation. Norm adoption, however, does not equal missing recurrence of conflict or disagreement within IOs and among their communities. Norms guide behaviour and thus frame contestation–legitimation process and condition these.

As practices are the translation of normative meaning, I can detect the guiding frame of the processes. Further I decode the norm for CCA in its two core aspects, namely the *collective endeavour* and *policy implementation* aspect. By focusing on the two core aspects, I can analyse the contestation and legitimation practices in their contextual depth. By deconstructing the processes and analysing the contestation and legitimation practices, and what they are referring to, I can trace the practice back to the guiding norm that frames the process. Through this, I can assess the stage of adoption of the norm within parts of the community at that given moment, when the process unfolded.

In contrast to many other norms in global governance that have emerged from the ideas and traditions of science and knowledge in the Western hemisphere, norms in the global climate regime evolved out of the conflict and compromises of the Global North and Global South, and thus its related divide. Norms in the global climate regime are, for example, the norm of sustainable development, climate justice, common but differentiated responsibilities (CBDR) – and the norm for CCA.

The norm for CCA grew as standard of appropriate behaviour for collective action in the nexus of energy and environment in the global climate regime. Even more so, with the Paris Agreement the norm emerged, and actors decided to have a multilateral understanding of how to implement these commitments. CCA can be defined as the norm that guides the action of developed and developing countries that collaborate and come together to mitigate, adapt and respond to climate impacts resulting from anthropogenic greenhouse gas emissions (UNFCCC, nd [b]; UNFCCC, nd [c]; UNFCCC, nd [d]).

The development of the norm for CCA dates to 1992, when the Rio Convention addressed the issue of acting collectively on climate change. The norm for CCA is not the activity to fight climate change itself, but it frames the urgency and desirable need to commonly act on climate change. The norm for CCA evolved as political stakeholders recognized increasingly that climate action is necessary in order to tackle the threat of climate change. The norm thus emerges through the very practices of policy-making and political processes in the global climate regime. The norm for CCA emphasizes collective action, not only encompassing states but all global actors. This must come from governments, cities, regions, businesses and investors. The commitments of all actors are recognized in the decision text of the Paris Agreement. The norm for CCA is now explicitly institutionalized through the Paris Agreement, both in the document itself, as well as in the pledges and practices that come with the multilateral agreement. These set the goal to pursue efforts to limit the temperature increase even further to 1.5°C and to foster the ability of countries to deal with the impacts of climate change.

Through its definition the two core aspects of CCA can be extracted: the collective endeavour aspect and the policy implementation aspect for CCA. The collective endeavour aspect that emphasized that acting on climate change can only work if 'everyone', 'all actors' 'collaborate' 'together' and 'commit' to the (appropriate) institutional format to tackle climate change. Thus, policies need to be implemented that guide action to 'mitigate and adapt to climate impacts' and for 'effectively implementing' the Paris Agreement, which is the second core aspect of the norm for CCA. Further, for example, Article 7.6 of the Paris Agreement stresses 'the importance of support for and international cooperation on adaptation efforts and the importance of taking into account the needs of developing country Parties, especially those that are particularly vulnerable to the adverse effects of climate change' (UN, 2015). The speech by Patricia Espinosa, former UNFCCC executive secretary, is an example to illustrate this further:

> If the 1990s was the decade of optimism, the 2020s must be the decade of action. It means we must act now. It means nations must complete and implement the Paris Agreement. ... It means recognizing that governments can't do it on their own. We need all people and all segments of society on board. ... we'll never get there if we're divided. We'll only succeed by working together. (Espinosa, 2020)

CCA is widely associated with the Paris Agreement, which is the major institutional format for global cooperation on climate change. This means that definitions and attributes of CCA can be derived from the underpinnings of the agreement and from associated actions in the global climate regime, especially facilitated through the UNFCCC. However, since the analysed processes in this research cover a time span from 2009 to 2017, the historical component of CCA is relevant to acknowledge. As mentioned, the development of the norm started with the first attempts at global cooperation on climate change in the 1990s. Back in 1992, Principle 7 of the Rio Convention acknowledged that '[s]tates shall cooperate in a spirit of *global partnership to conserve, protect and restore the health and integrity of the Earth's ecosystem*. The 'Rio Convention' was constituted at the 'Earth Summit', which

> was held in Rio de Janeiro, Brazil, from 3 to 14 June 1992. This global conference, held on the occasion of the 20th anniversary of the first Human Environment Conference in Stockholm, Sweden, in 1972, brought together political leaders, diplomats, scientists, representatives of the media and non-governmental organizations (NGOs) from 179 countries for a massive effort to focus on the impact of human socio-economic activities on the environment. (UN, 1992)

In view of the different contributions to global environmental degradation, states have common but differentiated responsibilities' (UN, 1992, p 2). Also, in light of the Kyoto Protocol, climate action was suggested through different policies and measures, for example through enhancing energy efficiency, protecting and enhancing greenhouse gas sinks, promoting renewable energy, carbon sequestration and other environmentally friendly technologies, removing subsidies and other market imperfections for environmentally damaging activities and encouraging reforms in relevant sectors to promote emission reductions and others (cf. UNFCCC, 2002, p 25).

As will be shown, by deconstructing the processes of contestation and legitimation, the parts of this process can tell us that the norm for CCA guides the community in the four contestation cases in this book. Norms can guide processes as they 'represent the legitimating core of global governance' and 'are considered as standards of behaviour in international relations' (Wiener, 2014, p 21). They shape practices, policies and set the frame of expected and accepted behaviour. This way, they produce legitimacy beliefs that are articulated in de-legitimation and legitimation practices and have strong influence on how global actors conduct international relations and multilateral cooperation. Table 2.1 illustrates these markers within practices of contestation and legitimation, and to which aspect of the norm for CCA these can be allocated and from which I can infer the normative meaning that enables the deconstruction of the process to the norm as the guiding frame.

For legitimation practices, this can mean that (a) actors support the contested target in their legitimation practice and praise it. It can also mean

Table 2.1: Markers in practices to deconstruct guiding frame, here: norm for CCA

Norm for CCA aspect	Marker in practice	Practice
Collective endeavour	• everyone (else) • all countries • all/other members • all actors • universal • collective • cooperate • association • include/inclusive/inclusion • together	• *discursive contestation* (e.g. written statements, speech, shaming, criticism) • *behavioural contestation* (e.g. protest, walkout, refusal) • *institutional contestation* (e.g. creating new institution, membership withdrawal) • *discursive legitimation* (e.g. written statements, speech, praise) • *behavioural legitimation* (e.g. consensus, building alliances/cooperation) • *institutional legitimation* (e.g. modernization, ratification, consensus)
Policy implementation	• policies (needed) • mechanism • adapt • mitigate • transform • transition • renewables • energy transition • act on climate change • climate action • successfully implement(ation)	• *discursive contestation* (e.g. written statements, speech, shaming) • *behavioural contestation* (e.g. refusal, protest) • *institutional contestation* (e.g. creating new institution, membership withdrawal) • *discursive legitimation* (e.g. speech, praise) • *behavioural legitimation* (e.g. written statements, consensus, transform) • *institutional legitimation* (e.g. modernization, ratification, consensus)

that (b) on a behavioural level, legitimating actors negotiate to legitimate after contestation, write statements, form coalitions or initiate transformation and inclusion in some way that speaks to the norm, (c) institutionally, the actors have access to a wider network, or rebuild the contested target, and thus (d) adapt in a way that is more in line with the conditioning norm and related expectations. Here, contextual understanding and an incorporation of the context of the process are necessary, to find the markers in the form of implicit or explicit reference to the norm in the practices. The deconstruction of the legitimation practices to their markers enables the detection of the frame and the adoption stage of the norm.

In the analysis of the four contestation–legitimation processes, I will first introduce the background to the cases and the respective processes that will help in understanding the emergence of the process itself, on the one hand, but also of the norm adoption, on the other. In other words, the background will give information on the status quo on how the process started with the contestation and how legitimation could occur. The start of the process, the contestation, will be analysed afterwards. Here, I will examine the practices regarding the markers that enable the deconstruction of the practices to the aspects of the norm for CCA. This will also unveil the adoption stage of the norm, and how contestation indicates a legitimacy gap and legitimation potential. Then, I will move over to the response to the contestation: the legitimation practices. Here, I will show what was done after the contestation and in what way the core aspects of the norm were addressed to respond to the legitimacy gap and fulfil the legitimation potential. By connecting the contestation and legitimation in an interlinked process that is framed under the guiding frame, the norm, I can show what connects the contestation and the legitimation. I can explain how the concepts and their subcategories are connected in *practice* in empirical cases. And in this way, I can answer why contestation was followed by legitimation.

To conclude: the contestation–legitimation process framework

To summarize my previous outline, this book's theoretical framework is based on the contestation–legitimation processes and norms as the guiding frame of these processes. As norms 'represent the legitimating core of global governance' (Wiener, 2014, p 4) and 'are considered as standards of behaviour in international relations' (Wiener, 2014, p 21), they shape practices. Thus, the norm as the guiding frame directs practices of contestation and legitimation, which reflect the adoption of the norm.

Contestation is 'the range of social practices that discursively express disapproval' (Wiener, 2014, p 1). This research does *not* concentrate on norm contestation but, as stated in the introduction, on the contestation of other targets that are constituting parts of the analysed IOs. When analysing de-legitimation or legitimation, not including contestation as a concept in this analysis closes the door on fully understanding why de-legitimation or legitimation occurs. As contestation triggers a critical engagement about the contested objects and the underlying guiding norm, this points to the object's legitimacy and potential 'legitimacy gaps' (Wiener, 2014, p 3). These in turn leave room for de-legitimation or legitimation. With contestation, disapproval and questioning of legitimacy occur. The legitimacy gap opens a struggle for legitimacy that can go both ways – de-legitimation or legitimation can follow.

At the same time, this opens a legitimation potential. In turn, the standard of appropriateness within the community, thus the norm, guides how this contestation and indicated gap are perceived and responded to. If the community believes that abiding by the norm that is perceived as an appropriate standard of behaviour is necessary, connected legitimacy beliefs will be articulated within the contestation and legitimation practices. Here, explicit or implicit reference to the norm in practice, which needs to be deconstructed in the analysis, enables the adopted norm to be found, and thus the guiding frame and finally the answer to the question of why contestation leads to legitimation. In the following four chapters, I will analyse the cases of the UNFCCC and the International Energy Agency and deconstruct their contestation–legitimation processes.

3

Emergence of the Norm for Climate Change Action: The UNFCCC and Contestation of Global South

For states to protect their societies against the severe consequences of climate change, they are required to adapt and transition. Especially, countries in the Global South have been affected more heavily by climate change (see, for example, Benson and Craig, 2014). At the same time, since wealth is not distributed equally around the globe, some countries do not have the means to adapt sufficiently and to act on climate change. Thus, climate change demands collective action. Wealthier countries are asked to support the less wealthy countries on a compulsory basis and agree on policies to achieve the environmental goals to successfully act on climate change. However, at the Conference of the Parties (COPs) of the United Nations Framework Convention on Climate Change (UNFCCC), Global North countries are often reluctant to commit to agreements that speak to this inequity and distribute wealth in this collective endeavour of climate action. In turn, Global South countries respond by contesting this non-solidaric behaviour.

This was also the issue at COP19 in Warsaw in 2013 with the G77 walkout, which is the first contestation–legitimation process that will be analysed. The G77 walkout consisted of three walkouts in total and was also followed by a walkout of civil society. This contestation is at the heart of the North–South divide conflict. As the term 'walkout' indicates, all representatives from G77 countries literally walked out of the negotiation room in Warsaw, leaving Global North negotiators behind in astonishment. At the opening of the conference, Yeb Saño, Climate Change Commissioner of the Philippines, criticized the slow motion of the loss and damage mechanism, 'making an emotional appeal to delegates to "stop the madness" and "act decisively on climate change"' (Busby, 2013). The mechanism of loss and damage was the key issue of the debate and conflict at COP19, which aimed to address the damaging and existential threat of climate change. The mechanism shall ensure:

> the implementation of approaches to address loss and damage associated with climate change impacts, in a comprehensive, integrated and coherent manner ... . The mechanism is established under the United Nations Framework Convention on Climate Change to assist developing countries that are particularly vulnerable to the adverse effects of climate ... . Through these functions, the mechanism implements Article 8 of the Paris Agreement. (UN, nd [b])

The negotiation of the loss and damage mechanism had been a fixed negotiation item since 2010 and at the same time had been a struggle. Over the years, the divide between the Global North and G77, including other parties from the Global South, hardened and mistrust from the G77 towards Western parties manifested (Hermwille et al, 2017). The urgency to consent on this mechanism due to the severe consequences, especially for the Global South, that Yeb Saño stressed in his contribution at the opening of COP19 was echoed later during the conference by Tiarite George Kwong, the Minister of Environment, Lands and Agriculture Development of the small island state of the Republic of Kiribati:

> Security challenges posed by climate change continue to undermine our efforts, the *global family* of nations, to achieve sustainable development. [Our] efforts as a global community to work towards peace and security. *For some of us, it is a plea for basic survival.* As such, I also wished to support and align my statement with those made by Fiji on behalf of the G77 and China, Nepal on behalf of least developed countries and Nauru on behalf of the Alliance of Small Island Developing States. ...
>
> The *establishment of an international mechanism on loss and damage is crucial and must be in place now here in this meeting as we have decided in Doha.* For countries like Kiribati, *loss and damage can no longer be avoided through mitigation nor can it be avoided through adaptation.* In this regard, loss and damage must be treated with the urgency it demands. ...
>
> Time is running out for us. Climate change ... has become a survival issue. (Kwong, 2013; emphasis added)

In 2013, the norm for CCA, and its aspects of collective endeavour and need for policy implementation, were already at the core of the issue of loss and damage. When the negotiation on this mechanism did not go further, as Western parties did not want to agree to upcoming proposals, the G77 countries decided to bring the conference to an abrupt break with a walkout. The escalation of this walkout that contested the behaviour of Western parties indicated a legitimacy gap in the negotiation process on the loss and damage mechanism over the years, as one interviewee emphasized (UNFCCC#7).

In the following I will show why this contestation was followed by (re-)legitimation instead of a full breakdown of climate change negotiations. Further, as I find, this kind of contestation and following legitimation practices trace back to COP15 in Copenhagen in 2009. The previous experience in Copenhagen and thereafter established practices that led to the rekindling of the conference and thus re-legitimized the COP and its negotiations despite the contesting walkout. The norm for climate change action (CCA) frames the overall process and thus conditioned the legitimation after contestation. Establishing a collective mechanism to prevent loss and damage due to climate change is a vital part of the norm. I will first elaborate on the contestation itself and discuss how the background for the contestation evolved over a longer course of time than 'only' in the 'heat of the moment' of the negotiations in 2013. The G77 contestation in Warsaw came with a built-up frustration as the plan for negotiating the mechanism for loss and damage started in fact earlier, namely in 2010 at COP16 in Cancun, and was pushed year after year leading up to 2013.

At COP19 in Warsaw, the walkout of the G77 countries was supported by civil society, which staged a walkout on the last day of the conference as well. After discussing this contestation and how it relates to the norm for CCA, I will analyse the following legitimation practices that contributed to the rekindling of the conference process and the final successful negotiation of the loss and damage mechanism. In particular, the UNFCCC secretariat played an important role in the re-legitimation. Their engagement in legitimation practices comes from experience after the 'disaster' of the breakdown of COP15 in Copenhagen. Due to this 'deep trauma' from Copenhagen, the UNFCCC secretariat developed their legitimation practices portfolio to bring the negotiation processes back on track.

The background of the G77 walkout: the norm for CCA and loss and damage

The G77 is the main coalition of 'developing'[1] countries and representatives of the Global South in the UN with 135 member states. Joanna Depledge summarizes the history and purpose of this coalition as follows:

> The G77 was formed in 1964 during negotiations on a 'New International Economic Order' explicitly to counter the might of the developed world. This history, combined with persistent inequalities and the development and equity dimensions of climate change, are carried through to a deep North–South divide that permeates every aspect of the climate change negotiations. The G77 has always

perceived climate change as a development issue, invoking equity as the fundamental principle for addressing it. The G77 also emphasizes the need for financial assistance and technology transfer, informed by a belief in multilateral cooperation. ... North-south relations in the climate change regime are indeed characterized by generalized mutual mistrust. (Depledge, 2005, p 30)

Thus, China and the G77 often ally in the negotiations and the UNFCCC to represent non-Western interests. The North–South divide is at the core of the various conflicts among UNFCCC members and stakeholders that challenge the UNFCCC negotiations. This divide has proven itself to be highly complex and difficult, which is most often at the centre of discussion and ruptures at the UNFCCC COPs. Within the UNFCCC processes, developed countries should take prior responsibility in combating climate change, a provision that has been a 'core conflict ever since the UNFCCC process started' (Hermwille et al, 2017, p 158). The contestations of parties from the Global South are significantly driven by the principle of 'common but differentiated responsibility' (O'Neill, 2009, p 88), reflecting the involved asymmetries of wealthy and less wealthy countries. These asymmetries, and the diverse number of actors that need to be considered in environmental policies, add to the problem of broad and complex issues of climate change and collective action.

In 2013, the frustration around the loss and damage debate was particularly high and widened the gap of the North–South divide. This led to the contestation and the walkout and to a crucial break in the negotiations at COP19. The debate on loss and damage, as mentioned earlier, was not new in 2013 but started around 2010 at COP16 in Cancun. The legitimation practices that the UNFCCC had in their portfolio were increasingly strengthened and developed after the breakdown of COP15 in Copenhagen in 2009, which also plays a part in this process. The following table shows the different stages of the loss and damage debate building up to the walkout in 2013.

At COP15, the conference ended in total breakdown, as parties could not come to any agreement. The 1997 Kyoto Protocol gave legally binding emission-reduction targets for developed countries only, which all parties should have been committed to by the expiration date of 2012 (Walker and Biedenkopf, 2020). In 2007, preparations were made for a global agreement to be adopted in 2009 (Walker and Biedenkopf, 2020). The failure to agree and the related conflict were especially along the lines of this North–South divide (see, for example, Walker and Biedenkopf, 2020). It was an 'unmitigated disaster' (UNFCCC#1). The breakdown at COP15 not only led to the end of the negotiation process but furthermore to questioning the ability of the UNFCCC to handle multilateral processes overall (UNFCCC#1). This led the UNFCCC into the momentum of a legitimacy crisis (Hickmann et al, 2019, p 12).

The contestation of the COP15 walkout and breakdown caused a delegitimation for the UNFCCC (see Table 3.1) The public accusation of 'failure' of the UNFCCC, in fact, resulted in the resignation of the executive secretary at the time (UNFCCC#1). The secretariat itself fell into 'a nervous breakdown', overwhelmed by the struggle and the mistakes that had been made at the conference (UNFCCC#1). It led to the revision of internal processes but also to the strengthening of external engagement with the expertise of non-state actors (UNFCCC#1), in order to make improvements for the next COPs and to become open 'to new ideas to bolster the existing global response to climate change' (Hickmann et al, 2019, p 12).

This 'deep trauma' informed the negotiation practices of the UNFCCC and the awareness of the necessity to act immediately when breakdowns occur (UNFCCC#4). Yet despite this, Copenhagen turned out to function as a 'catalyst' leading to more suggestions for a bottom-up approach and the initiation of a more active non-state actor engagement to achieve collective agreement that cannot be agreed upon by consensus in the international system (UNFCCC#11). In this way, despite its breakdown, COP15 in Copenhagen provided a starting point for alternative ways for the UNFCCC to navigate the COP processes beyond the level of national governments.

At COP16 in Cancun, the group of 'least developed' countries demanded the implementation of a loss and damage mechanism, and the term was put into the Cancun adaptation agreement for the first time (UNFCCC#7). Also, the following year at COP17 in Durban, 'the complexity of loss and damage became evident', leading to consulting a series of experts to discuss

Table 3.1: Timeline of G77 walkout and loss and damage debate

Year	Event/Stage	Content
2009	COP15 in Copenhagen	• unsuccessful and failure of negotiation process • UNFCCC's legitimacy crisis
2010	COP16 in Cancun	• term 'loss and damage' first appeared in the Cancun adaptation agreement
2011	COP17 in Durban	• complexity of loss and damage became evident; higher demand for mechanism
2012	COP18 in Doha	• decision on negotiations about establishing actual loss and damage mechanism at COP19
2013	COP19 in Warsaw: Walkout	• loss and damage a difficult topic to reach consensus • strong division leading to walkout; contestation

and clarify 'the needs associated with assessing and addressing loss and damage in developing countries at the national, regional and international levels' (Roberts and Huq, 2015, p 151). At COP18 in Doha, a 'wide range of actions that could help to limit the pre-2020 ambition gap' were discussed, in addition to the goal-setting of incorporating stronger non-state actors particularly regarding developing countries and the loss and damage mechanism (Bäckstrand et al, 2017, p 565). In Doha, the loss and damage mechanism became an agenda item, which was followed by intense negotiations that 'went into overtime' (UNFCCC#7).

The negotiations about the mechanism for loss and damage were pushed into the following year at COP19 in Warsaw. This was very much opposed by the developed countries (UNFCCC#7), but the developing countries were for once 'extremely united and they pushed it and made that a condition to ... discuss it next year' (UNFCCC#7). Thus, 'parties agreed that "comprehensive, inclusive and strategic" approaches are needed to address loss and damage' and also clarified the role of the convention (Roberts and Huq, 2015, p 151). However, due to the opposition from developed countries, it was anticipated that negotiations at COP19 would be continuously difficult, despite the commitment of 'coming together' (UNFCCC#8). Here, not only did the North–South divide become particularly visible in the debate around this mechanism, but also the perceived necessity to act on global climate change. This shows that the process was framed and conditioned by CCA, as loss and damage is one of the many components for the implementation of the norm in practice.

The G77 walkout: contestation for loss and damage and CCA

The process analysed here started with the contestation of the G77 group and their walkout, which caused an abrupt break at COP19. The walkout can be counted as behavioural contestation practice. The core issue of the contestation was the loss and damage mechanism. This mechanism represents aspects of the norm CCA as collective endeavour and demanding a policy for reflecting the reality of climate change. Consenting to this mechanism also included a collective-norm adoption. The hardlining of Western countries indicated that norm adoption was not processed, especially regarding the collective aspect of CCA that was already promoted by parts of the community, the UNFCCC itself and countries of the Global South. The G77 contestation was based on the aspects of the norm for CCA. Figure 3.1 shows the different stages of the process that will be deconstructed and analysed in the following section.

As most of my interviewees confirm, in negotiations there is always a moment of disruption or conflict where the process becomes 'intense' and

Figure 3.1: UNFCCC: Process of G77 walkout

Guiding frame
'Norm for climate change action'
Standard of appropriate behaviour

North–South divide

Contestation

G77 walkout COP19, Warsaw 2013

Contestation: Challenge
- G77 contesting negotiation on loss and damage mechanism
- Struggle over legitimacy of negotiation item: loss and damage mechanism
- Indicating **legitimacy gap** in negotiation: failure of negotiating since 2010; north 'hardlining', south mistrust
- **Legitimation potential:** a just, differentiated agreement to collectively act on climate change and reach consensus for adoption of the Norm for CCA

↓

Legitimation practices

Actor: UNFCCC

Practices:
- *Moderating, conflict-solving communication (discursive legitimation)*
- *Informal practices of fostering trust (behavioural legitimation)*
- *Convince negotiators, especially Global North (behavioural legitimation)*
- *Mediate, bring Global South back in (behavioural legitimation)*
- *Active role of presiding officers (behavioural legitimation)*
- *Involving non-state actors (behavioural and institutional legitimation)*

CCA norm and practices:
- *Norm adoption or norm is already adopted:*
  Norm not yet adopted fully
- *Explicit/implicit reference to core aspects of norm in the practice: bring forward to the negotiation, reach consensus and push CCA*
- *Practices are markers of core aspects of the norm: all countries, together, policies (needed), mechanism, mitigate, adapt*

'doors get slammed' with participants walking out (UNFCCC#4). It happens 'all the time to some extent' (UNFCCC#6). This might also be a reason why some of the representatives from the Global North perceived the walkout at COP19 as a 'non-event' (UNFCCC#1; UNFCCC#6; UNFCCC#14). Yet, since the UNFCCC negotiations are based on consensus by all parties, such a contestation cannot be left without response (UNFCCC#3). It is thus a necessity to mobilize and re-legitimize the negotiation process, as the discontent, contestation partakers need to return for final agreement (UNFCCC#4).

Walking out signals contestation as it comes with a strong symbolic value and with practical implications in the form of breaking up the process, even if it is just for a moment (UNFCCC#2; UNFCCC#3; UNFCCC#5; UNFCCC#12; UNFCCC#13; UNFCCC#14). Further, it signals a legitimation potential, as here the legitimacy gap of negotiation on the mechanism was indicated. This legitimacy gap points towards the demand of the norm for CCA as collective endeavour that the community needs to collectively act against climate change. Thus, the contestation of the G77 parties in 2013 was in line with this aspect of the norm. In the COP processes, contestation cannot be left without response; due to the consensus clause, decisions cannot be made without all parties involved being present. When this kind of contestation occurs, informal practices, such as talks and negotiating 'behind closed doors', are often enough (UNFCCC#7). This was part of bridging the contestation and re-legitimating the process after the G77 walkout in Warsaw. However, at this COP, these kinds of informal practices were not satisfactory for the G77 countries.

As already mentioned, at the heart of the contestation was the negotiation of the mechanism for loss and damage. Although, this mechanism addressing loss and damage was finally established at COP19 as the 'Warsaw International Mechanism' (WIM). At that time of the negotiations, the process was still in the so-called 'technical negotiating phase', which 'needed to move to a political level to reach its success' (UNFCCC#6). The negotiation processes follow formal and informal rules. Decisions within these processes are informed by the key actors, government officials, diplomats and ministers, who ultimately are also responsible for the final agreement. These negotiators are authorized to do so via a mandate from their individual national government. Decisions are thus most often informed by the national discourse of national delegates and negotiators (Hermwille, 2018, p 452). 'The national discourse and dominant narratives therein delimit the scope of the "politically feasible"' as politicians need to justify their decisions at their national level (Hermwille, 2018, p 453).

However, some space for bargaining for the individual negotiator does often exist. This way comprises can be made to get to final decisions. As for COP19, both delegates from the Global South and North kept pushing for their national agenda and interests. This ultimately led to the walkout by the G77 to make their mark. Here, many developed countries 'objected to the creation of a new mechanism because of its political implications', as the debate was about equity elements (Busby, 2013). This meant 'that loss and damage will imply blame or liability', and 'suggests culpability for climate-related loss' (Busby, 2013).

To push the negotiations, the G77 staged the walkout publicly to the media. The G77 chose to give a press conference explaining their walkout and framing loss and damage as a non-negotiable issue. Further, the G77 engaged in discursive legitimation by choosing to portray their concerns in a rather accusatory way not only with the press but also on social media to get attention, build support, and engage with civil society (UNFCCC#6). In this way, on the one hand, the urgency of the situation was demonstrated, as well as their determination and unity in not going 'home without something', on the other (UNFCCC#7). Their protest was 'quite vocal', 'pointing at Australia' (UNFCCC#6) and exposing the lack of trust that was delivered by the UNFCCC system (UNFCCC#8). For example, Claudia Salerno, the lead climate negotiator for Venezuela, said in an interview with the NGO 'Democracy Now!':

> When you see developed countries being so bold as to tell you that they are not even considering reducing their emissions, but they are not even considering paying for the costs that those inactions have in the life of others, that is really rude and hard to handle it politically, that we are heading to a point in which countries are not ready to take responsibility for their acts. (Democracy Now!, 2013)

Giving these very strong messages was not only regarded as a necessity for the current negotiations but also perceived as important considering future COPs, especially regarding the final negotiation on the Paris Agreement in 2015 (UNFCCC#8). For 2013, due to the walkout and the accompanied exposure, the G77 countries were able to pressure the developed countries to move and to accept the creation of the loss and damage mechanism (UNFCCC#6). When negotiating the mechanisms for loss and damage, countries of the Global South felt pushed by developed countries (UNFCCC#2). Australia, which had just had a change in government a few months prior, suddenly took 'a much harder line', creating a lot of 'mistrust' (UNFCCC#6). Further, as shared by spokeswoman for the Climate Action Network, Australian negotiators were perceived as not taking the negotiations seriously, allegedly being too casually dressed and 'gorging' snacks throughout the negotiations (Vidal, 2013). These hard lines divided the parties even further and created 'a moment when tensions were high and there was a lack of trust in the room' (UNFCCC#6).

Before the agreement was decided, in contrast to previous years when negotiating the mechanisms for loss and damage, the G77 put forward 'a very strong proposal' (UNFCCC#7). This was quite unusual, as previously the G77 were unlikely to put forward propositions of their own, rather always refusing what was drafted from the other parties or not being able to find a consensus among their own group (UNFCCC#7). In turn, this strong proposal even brought more leverage to the negotiations, which made these 'very, very tough … late into the night for several nights' (UNFCCC#7). Due to this leverage, the North–South clash and the non-solidaric behaviour of Western parties indicated a legitimacy gap in the negotiation process on the loss and damage mechanism, which led to the abrupt walkout of the G77 in the middle of the night (UNFCCC#6).

Negotiators made clear that 'without having a mechanism this discussion is not going to move forward' (UNFCCC#8). The point was reached when 'you can't go further' (UNFCCC#6). Partakers from the Global South claim that the UNFCCC negotiators, in fact, were 'shaken' for the time being, before taking the relevant steps to pick up the negotiations (UNFCCC#8). As this contestation resembled the breakdown of the conference in 2009 in Copenhagen, another total breakdown resulting in de-legitimation was possible, and potentially a legitimacy crisis that could involve further consequences for the UNFCCC processes. However, the breakdown of COP15 in Copenhagen 2009 informed the legitimation practices that were put in place to respond to the G77 contestation in Warsaw, which will be discussed later in this chapter.

Contestation doubled: the walkout of civil society

The G77 walkout did not remain the only contestation of this kind. In fact, civil society followed the G77 example by engaging in behavioural contestation and staging a walkout on the last day of the COP. In this way, they emphasized their support and solidarity for the G77's concerns and interests (UNFCCC#1; UNFCCC#5; UNFCCC#6; UNFCCC#7; UNFCCC#14). Here, the need to act on and push for climate change action was underlined in their contestation as civil society 'exposed' the lack of climate justice, claiming that 'justice [implies that] countries that are responsible for the crisis have to do most and that was not happening' (UNFCCC#8). Without the persistence of the G77 group, in combination with the agency of civil society, the implementation and the continued incorporation of loss and damage in the Paris Agreement in 2015 would not have been achieved (UNFCCC#7). The walkout certainly played a crucial role in this endeavour. Further, the support by non-state actors as part of the community speaks to the aspects of the norm for CCA as collective endeavour and the need for policy implementation. The collective aspect of the norm is stressed by this coalescing move of civil society.

The walkout was thus a critical addition to the previous event of the G77 walkout pointing towards legitimacy. Although members of civil society are not part of the official negotiation process, they in fact shape the process as advisers to state delegates (UNFCCC#8). Their special role and expertise are giving 'input on a real-time basis', providing 'all that is missing' (UNFCCC#8). This is especially the case for 'developing' countries and those who do not have the capacity to send large delegate groups, in contrast to, for example, the US. As one of my interview participants from civil society stated, 'practically there is no distinction between a civil society person and a negotiator because they really work hand in hand ... and if you're not in the room it does make a difference' (UNFCCC#8). In fact, as previous research has also already shown, non-state actors, and so partakers of civil society, take over the role of lobbyists or 'NGO diplomats' (Betsill and Corell, 2008, p 3).

Since COP15 in Copenhagen in 2009, civil society has been increasingly incorporated by the UNFCCC. In 2009, despite the breakdown of the conference, the UNFCCC was able to reach a turning point towards more inclusive cooperation and multipolarity by replacing the legally binding Kyoto Protocol with a 'decentralized climate policy architecture' and including more non-state actors (Bäckstrand et al, 2017, p 563). Through this engagement it was possible for civil society to voice their support for the G77 countries. Of course, their follow-up walkout on the last day of the conference did not bring a break to the negotiation. However, it is a signpost of non-state actor engagement at the COP that should not be left overlooked, as the walkout received attention in the public media, exposing the lack of climate change action and justice within the UNFCCC negotiation processes.

Bringing parties back on track for CCA: legitimation by the UNFCCC

Why did the G77 contestation result in legitimation rather than a breakdown of the COP and a de-legitimation of the UNFCCC processes? In the following section, I will analyse the response to the contestation by the UNFCCC as the most prominent legitimating actor. The re-legitimation of COP19 was not only necessary to bring the process back on track but moreover is in line with the UNFCCC's perception of CCA as an appropriate standard and norm, which frames the process. Furthermore, the UNFCCC has been key to pushing the norm for CCA in the global climate regime. The UNFCCC is intrinsically motivated by this effort towards CCA, which explains their legitimation response after the G77 contestation. The UNFCCC, therefore, has a special interest in moving parties forward towards a consensus in favour of global climate change action, which is also in accordance with the aspects of the norm of collective endeavour and the need for policy implementation.

After the G77 contestation, we can see mostly behavioural and discursive legitimation practices by the UNFCCC. These include practices of moderation and conflict-solving communication (discursive legitimation). Also, there were informal practices of fostering trust (behavioural legitimation) and mediating to bring the Global South back in (behavioural legitimation). Also, negotiators, especially from the Global North, needed to be convinced to recognize the G77 proposal (behavioural legitimation) to negotiate to reach consensus. This way, also the norm adoption can be reflected.

To prevent a repetition of Copenhagen, the UNFCCC negotiators needed to engage in legitimation practice to bring all parties back to the table and to reach consensus (UNFCCC#3; UNFCCC#4). Also, the UNFCCC is intrinsically motivated to promote CCA, which explains their legitimation response after the G77 contestation to move parties forward to consensus in favour of global climate change action. For example, in 2009 in Copenhagen, the UNFCCC's Executive Secretary Yvo de Boer made clear in his opening statement that a push for policies that would foster collective action on climate change was necessary: 'Copenhagen will only be successful if it delivers significant and immediate action that begins the day the conference ends. ... Developing countries desperately need tangible, immediate action on these crucial issues. ... The time has come to *reach out to each other*' (de Boer, 2009; emphasis added).

To pick up the negotiations and to not let COP19 result in a breakdown as experienced in COP15, there are 'methods in place and modalities to bring everybody back to the table and seek consensus again' (UNFCCC#3). The UNFCCC re-engaged with the contesters, but also the contested counterpart. Thus, parties were mediated towards reaching consensus on the loss and damage mechanism. This mechanism was perceived as a just, collective policy to act on climate change, which speaks to the aspect of CCA as collective endeavour. Therefore, the decision on this mechanism and the necessity to re-legitimize the negotiation process to reach consensus was a necessary mean that not only reflected the legitimacy belief in CCA but also the adoption of the norm by all parts of the community. Legitimacy beliefs can be made visible through examining the legitimation practices and they indicate the guiding frame, the norm, that works as the guiding frame of the process.

As previously mentioned, the legitimation practices that the UNFCCC had in their portfolio were increasingly strengthened after the breakdown of COP15. In response to the G77 contestation, the UNFCCC mostly engaged in several informal but also formal practices that involved discursive and behavioural legitimation. Here, the UNFCCC's discursive, communicatory practices were key to re-legitimize the negotiation process. Discursive legitimation involves support for the contested object and related procedure (Steffek, 2003; Reus-Smit, 2007; Halliday et al, 2010). Generally, this is the attempt to legitimate through the 'self-justification of ... actions and/ or through the construction in rhetoric and other messages of positive impressions' (Bäckstrand and Söderbaum, 2018, p 106).

On a behavioural level, the re-engagement with the contesters and convincing them in informal talks at an interpersonal level will help to clarify concerns, such as the reaching out of the presiding officers to the heads of delegation or group chairs (UNFCCC#3). The UNFCCC as a facilitator of the COPs delivers the conditions for this (UNFCCC#14). The UNFCCC offers, besides formal negotiation, informal ways for parties to regain trust and negotiate. The so-called 'informal consultations are convened by the presiding officer (COP President or SBSTA/SBI Chair)' (Depledge, 2005, p 115). Here,

> [t]he presiding officer typically invites a delegate (sometimes two) to consult on a particular topic and report back to plenary, but advertised meetings are not held. The expectation, instead, is that the consulting Chair will discuss the issue at hand in private with representatives of the main negotiating coalitions and interested delegations in order to forge a consensus. (Depledge, 2005, p 115)

At the COPs, the presiding officers are regarded to have a 'very strong relationship of trust with the group chair' making it 'personally just to get to the heart of the concern and try to understand what options might help to resolve that concern, ideally in an as informal way as possible to save face' (UNFCCC#3). The interpersonal relationships help to clarify 'the real issue' (UNFCCC#3). Here, 'trust is key', and it is the role of the UNFCCC to help to rebuild it if lost (UNFCCC#5). In these cases, it is important to 'immediately try to solve the problem' (UNFCCC#5). This urgency rests upon the risk of losing trust and confidence, which only become harder to rebuild the more time passes (UNFCCC#6).

These practices that will rebuild trust are a strong vehicle for legitimation and for bringing the COPs back on track. These can be behavioural and discursive. 'Trust in the chairs of global negotiations is a decisive factor facilitating successful outcomes. When negotiators trust the chair, they allow her to go beyond her formal procedural role by acting as a mediator, fostering the reaching of agreement' (Walker and Biedenkopf, 2020, p 440). Trust can be defined as acceptance of 'vulnerability based upon positive expectations of the intentions or behavior of another' (Rousseau et al, 1998, p 395). Trust helps negotiation chairs bridge the process to help 'parties to navigate the complex landscape of multilateral negotiations' (see, for example, Jepsen et al, 2021). This, in turn, contributes to legitimation after contestation. If more official engagement is needed, the ministers or even the COP presidents also must be involved to unblock the process (UNFCCC#5; UNFCCC#6). Conversations can be 'very opaque, very one on one' or 'a big open conversation so that everybody gets back on the same page' (UNFCCC#3). This way no party is excluded and 'every voice is heard even from smaller countries', which essentially is 'the idea of multilateralism' (UNFCCC#5).

Further, on an institutional legitimation level, COP19 was a breaking point for the North–South divide and the agency of members from the Global South. Institutional legitimation practices often evolve around self-legitimation by international organizations (IOs) by 'opening up' to civil society actors (cf. Bäckstrand and Söderbaum, 2018, p 106; see also Scholte, 2011; Zaum, 2013; Tallberg et al, 2018). This also included a further outreach to non-state actor engagement, which can be observed in COP20 the following year, when the incorporation of non-state actors was stretched beyond the technical level. At COP20 in Lima, President Manuel Pulgar-Vidal opened the conference with his speech about the contribution of civil society, business representatives and subnational governments and launched the 'Non-state Actor Zone for Climate Action' (NAZCA), which is now manifested in the Paris Agreement. Thus, COP19 and the walkout of the challenger G77 countries not only created a break in the negotiation process in 2013 but also gave a push to the UNFCCC negotiations to an even more inclusive practising and enhanced the promotion of the norm for CCA. In turn, this also expanded the community of the norm for CCA.

Conclusion: Successful legitimation after contestation in the name of CCA

The G77 walkout may not have caused a total breakdown of COP19 and the negotiation process, potentially followed by a legitimacy crisis of the UNFCCC as was almost the case at COP15 in Copenhagen. Nonetheless, it was a challenging moment of contestation that the UNFCCC needed to overcome. Here, the UNFCCC had to perform the balancing act of building trust among the parties, providing solutions that met the diverse interests and at the same time fulfilling its purpose of promoting CCA.

Creating the visibility for the interests of parties from the Global South and persisting with the inclusion and consensus on the loss and damage mechanism predominantly determined the subsequent negotiations and the designing of the Paris Agreement (UNFCCC#12). At the same time, the North–South divide remains a continuous possibility for contestation within the UNFCCC process (UNFCCC#12). As a guiding frame, the norm for CCA, however, gives the framing to upcoming processes and possible contestations that are largely in the interest of nations that are, for now, most affected by climate change. In this way, CCA conditions how contestation will be met and why contestation will be followed by legitimation, rather than de-legitimation, as CCA is the community's standard of appropriate behaviour in the global climate regime.

Contestations that are not in line with the norm for CCA, such as by protectionist members that contest the fairness and effectiveness of the UNFCCC and its policies, create tension and the need to prevent de-legitimation and to uphold legitimacy. In the next section, one such process will be analysed, namely the contestation of the Paris Agreement by US President Trump in 2017. Here, although the US remains a major power in global governance, Trump's contestation and announcement to withdraw from the Paris Agreement was followed by legitimation. Here, both state and non-state actors opposed Trump and responded with legitimation rather than following his example. I argue that this is due to the adoption of the norm for CCA by most of the community as well as their legitimacy belief on policies that ensure collective action on climate change.

4

The UNFCCC, US Contestation and Guidance by the Norm for Climate Change Action

When President Trump announced to withdraw the US from the Paris Agreement on 1 June, 2017, in the White House Rose Garden (White House, 2017), the worries of climate change action proponents became reality (Kemp, 2017). In line with his protectionism and moves away from other international forums and multilateralism, this announcement posed a major challenge to continued cooperation on climate change. It was anticipated that the contestation by this major power would have a negative, delegitimising consequence for the Paris Agreement and, ultimately, the United Nations Framework Convention on Climate Change (UNFCCC). Further, this contestation had the potential of resulting in a crisis of the UNFCCC's legitimacy, since the agreement relies on 'universal participation for legitimacy' (Kemp, 2017, p 86). As the US used to be perceived as the lead nation in international relations (UNFCCC#4; Kemp, 2017), the anticipation was this contestation could lead to a domino effect of further member withdrawal, particularly of those states with similar tendencies towards climate change (UNFCCC#4). The US contestation was perceived as potentially damaging the 'goodwill at international negotiations' not only at the UNFCCC but worldwide (McGrath, 2018). It was declared as one of the 'darkest' moments in US diplomacy and 'a huge blow to global efforts' (BBC, 2019).

In the following, I will analyse this process of contestation which – against all odds – was followed by legitimation. First, I will engage with the past experiences of the UNFCCC with US contestation in the case of the non-ratification of the Kyoto Protocol in 2001. In addition to this, the Trump election in 2016 is another background experience that influences the process. Furthermore, I will show how the UNFCCC itself contributed to the emergence of legitimation by both state and non-state actors. Furthermore,

I will show how the UNFCCC contributed to building the norm for climate change action (CCA), which frames this contestation–legitimation process. The UNFCCC has engaged beyond nation-state members, especially since 2015, and orchestrated a wide forum of non-state actor engagement. This orchestration of facilitating exchange with civil society organizations, non-profit entities and the private sector not only pushes the UNFCCC's climate change agenda within, but beyond the negotiation processes, which ultimately fostered CCA's strength to frame the process.

In contrast, Trump's foreign policy decisions, especially on climate change, are driven by a populist ideology that has received discontent and disapproval from both state and non-state actors, resulting in opposition and legitimation responses.[1] In the following, I will explain the background to this contestation as well as the background of the legitimation practices, which both trace back to the guiding frame of CCA. I will then showcase the contestation by Trump, and furthermore, I will analyse the legitimation practices that the UNFCCC, but also state and non-state actors, actively engaged in after the withdrawal announcement.

The US, the UNFCCC and CCA: the Kyoto Protocol experience and the Trump election

To understand why the process analysed here resulted in legitimation after the contestation, it is important to include the background of this process. The UNFCCC did not only face contestation by the US in 2017 but experienced this before with the US non-ratification of the Kyoto Protocol in 2001. The withdrawal announcement in 2017 brought back memories of this history, as the UNFCCC had 'seen this movie before' (UNFCCC#7).

Back in 2001, the US government under George W. Bush withdrew from the Kyoto Protocol. This had been set up with the previous Clinton administration in 1998, but still needed to be ratified by the US senate (Pickering et al, 2018, p 820). 'US president George W. Bush formally rejected the protocol, which he considered "fatally flawed"' (cf. Zelli, 2018, p 177; alterations added). At the time, this caused 'real worry about what could happen to the treaty regime that was being put in place to deal with climate change' (UNFCCC#1). These concerns especially manifested when Australia under Prime Minister John Howard refrained from ratifying as well (Pickering et al, 2018, p 823). Although the protocol still came into force in 2005, the years of US non-participation were found to have weakened the protocol's effectiveness and legitimacy (Pickering et al, 2018, p 820). The following table shows the important stages in the particular contestation–legitimation process of this case (see Table 4.1).

When dealing with the withdrawal announcement in 2017, the UNFCCC was somewhat prepared as they had had a similar experience in 2001 with

Table 4.1: Timeline of US contestation of the Paris Agreement

Year	Event/Stage	Content
2001	Kyoto Protocol non-ratification	• US senate under George W. Bush does not ratify the agreement
2015	Paris Agreement	• Paris Agreement ratified
2016	Trump election and COP22	• Donald Trump elected at the same time as COP22 in Marrakech
2017	US announcement to withdraw from Paris Agreement	• announcement discussed as a threatening moment of US non-cooperation towards climate change and the UNFCCC
2016–18	Legitimation by state and non-state actors	• legitimation by state actors through active opposition to Trump and recommitment to support the Paris Agreement • sub- and non-state actor initiatives, for example, 'Climate Mayor' (2016/17), 'Americas pledge' (2016), 'We're still in' (2017), 'Global climate action summit' (2018) • UNFCCC non-state actor engagement prior to contestation benefited the responses

the US non-ratification of the Kyoto Protocol (UNFCCC#2). Yet even though both instances are US contestations, they differ in their circumstances despite ideological similarities. The US was a ratified member of the Paris Agreement, which was not the case for the Kyoto Protocol. The design of the Paris Agreement as an agreement instead of a treaty was a crucial step initiated by the previous Obama administration to get it ratified by the US Senate and House of Representatives (UNFCCC#4). It made possible to 'withstand a judicial challenge' as it was designed 'as a pledge and review agreement with varied legality order' (Kemp, 2017, p 87). Further, this enabled the US president to 'join it via executive action only', which additionally made it easier to bypass a full senate vote (Pickering et al, 2018, p 822). In this case, it helped Obama to partake in the Paris Agreement despite the objections of the Republicans. But this also meant that a withdrawal and at the same time a rejoining, the latter taking 30 days after notification, would be easier (Jotzo et al, 2018, p 813; Pickering et al, 2018, p 822).

The withdrawal from the Kyoto Protocol before its full ratification brought 'into question whether the protocol would ever come into force' (UNFCCC#1), which ultimately prolonged the process. This was different at the time of the announcement of withdrawal from the Paris Agreement, because the agreement had already been ratified by 148 countries and the European Union including the US (UNFCCC#1). This way, the Paris Agreement started off with strong legitimacy. The UNFCCC's history and previous experience of US withdrawal, which was influenced based on an 'ideological decision' by Trump's opposition to multilateralism (UNFCCC#1), frames the conditions in which the UNFCCC could act after the announcement in 2017.

Informed by the perspectives of the UNFCCC officials and Conference of the Parties (COP) negotiators interviewed for this research, it becomes clear that the announcement to withdraw from the Paris Agreement was not the first 'shock'. The first stage of the process and the actual 'bombshell' (UNFCCC#1) or 'shell shock' (UNFCCC#12) was the election of Trump in November 2016. It left UNFCCC staff and negotiators in shock and in stand-by mode in the wait for possible consequences of the election (UNFCCC#9). Here, according to Trump's 2016 election campaign, the 'first inkling was that something would go wrong' (UNFCCC#1) as his positions were 'actively hostile' towards climate action (UNFCCC#6; see also Betsill, 2017; Bomberg, 2017).

The election took place during COP22 in Marrakech (UNFCCC#6), which cast a 'dark shadow over the event' (UNFCCC#1), and left a lot of people 'very, very disappointed' (UNFCCC#7; UNFCCC#13; UNFCCC#14). In particular, the staff members of the American delegation who worked under the Obama administration at the time 'were very much supportive of action on climate change and they were very, very heartbroken' (UNFCCC#7). After the election of Donald Trump, the understanding was that the new administration was 'not going to be extremely actively positive on acting on climate change' (UNFCCC#6). Indeed, UNFCCC staff uniformly agreed that the US withdrawal had already been expected (UNFCCC#1; UNFCCC#5). It was expected as 'the natural repercussion of the election' (UNFCCC#1; UNFCCC#8; UNFCCC#11).

Another difference of this instance to the Kyoto Protocol was the high non-state actor engagement of the UNFCCC. Since the Kyoto Protocol, and especially after the ratification of the Paris Agreement was signed, the UNFCCC has strengthened this engagement (Bäckstrand et al, 2017; Pickering et al, 2018, p 822). Thus, compared to the situation of the Kyoto Protocol, the UNFCCC could rely on broader support for the Paris Agreement from a wider range of actors (Pickering et al, 2018, p 822). Before, the Kyoto Protocol was set up as largely state-centric and non-state actors were only included in the 'Clean Development Mechanism' in the role of implementing entities or financial intermediaries (Pickering et al, 2018, p 823). In contrast, the Paris Agreement now gave non-state actors the opportunity to join the UNFCCC processes and give their support, as they could not formally join the Paris Agreement themselves (Pickering et al, 2018, p 823).

By doing so, the UNFCCC contributed to promoting and manifesting the norm for CCA, which frames this process as a standard of appropriate behaviour. Even beyond the discussed processes of this research, the

UNFCCC continuously enforces deeper engagement with non-state and sub-national actors. This way, the UNFCCC reaches beyond its state members, as it had built 'an open forum' of integrated non-state actors in the policy dialogue (Hickmann and Elsässer, 2020, p 6). By orchestrating this 'open forum', the UNFCCC has successfully established itself as 'a manager and information hub, emerging as a co leading institution, and taking on the role of a spearheading actor' of non-state actor engagement (Hickmann and Elsässer, 2020, p 14). Figure 4.1 shows the different stages of the process that will be deconstructed and analysed in the following section.

Figure 4.1: UNFCCC: Process of US contestation of the Paris Agreement

---

Guiding frame
'Norm for climate change action'
Standard of appropriate behaviour

Institutional format
Contestation

Withdrawal A. Paris Agreement US, 2017

Contestation: Challenge
- Major power contesting the UNFCCC's institutional format (Paris Agreement)
- Struggle over legitimacy: US major power impactful contestation
- Indicating **legitimacy gap**: Paris Agreement 'unfair' to the US
- **Legitimation potential**: option to underline norm by reinforcing belief in the importance of Paris Agreement and acting collectively on climate change

↓

Legitimation practices
Background: Kyoto 2001, US election 2016, UNFCCC developed strong network with sub- and non-state actors

Practices: UNFCCC
- *Non-state actor engagement (behavioural and institutional legitimation)*
- *Moderating, neutral communication (discursive legitimation)*
- *Filing exit in accordance with the Paris Agreement (institutional legitimation)*

Practices: State actors and non-state actors
- *Statements of praise and taking leadership role for CCA (discursive legitimation)*
- *Opposing statements contra contestation (discursive legitimation)*
- *Networks and events after contestation, e.g. 'We're still in' (behavioural legitimation)*
- *Financial compensation (behavioural legitimation)*

CCA norm and practices:
- *Norm adoption or norm is already adopted:*
  Norm is adopted
- *Explicit/implicit reference to core aspects of norm in the practices: reinforcing importance of Paris Agreement*
- *Practices are markers of core aspects of the norm: collective, climate action, successfully implemented*

The contestation: the US withdrawal from the Paris Agreement

In this section I will examine the contestation by President Trump and how it was guided by the norm for CCA. With his contestation, Trump spoke out against the aspects of the norm that are embodied in the Paris Agreement. This contestation involves the discursive (announcement), behavioural (speech) as well as institutional (filing withdrawal) levels of contestation practices. As I argue, the legitimacy gap that was indicated by his contestation also includes a legitimation potential. This, in turn, in line with the norm, led to legitimation by several parts of the community. Trump signalled his contestation by announcing the US withdrawal from the Paris Agreement with the following words:

> I am fighting every day for the great people of this country. Therefore, in order to fulfil my solemn duty to protect America and its citizens, the United States will withdraw from the Paris Climate Accord. ...
>
> The Paris Agreement handicaps the United States' economy in order to win praise from the very foreign capitals and global activists that have long sought to gain wealth at our country's expense. They don't put America first. I do. And I always will. ...
>
> As president, I have one obligation and that obligation is to the American people. The Paris Accord would undermine our economy, hamstring our workers, weaken our sovereignty, impose unacceptable legal risk and put us at a permanent disadvantage to the other countries of the world. (NPR, 2017)

Throughout the academic and public discourse, the US announcement and the withdrawal from the Paris Agreement were perceived as a threatening moment towards climate action and the UNFCCC (Zhang et al, 2017; Pickering et al, 2018; Urpelainen and Van de Graaf, 2018). Many believed that without the US, 'the Paris deal was dead' (Bomberg, 2017, p 961). As can be seen from Trump's speech to announce the US withdrawal from the Paris Agreement, it was particularly framed by ideological, domestic interests and protectionism. Trump claimed that the agreement was only giving other countries 'a financial advantage over the United States' (The White House, nd) and was unfair to the US and its taxpayers (Betsill, 2017, p 189). This makes the withdrawal a predominantly ideological decision as 'climate change is an ideological issue' to Trump (Jotzo et al, 2018, p 813), which is along the lines of protectionism, financial interests and the imperialist legacy of the North–South divide (Interviewee#12). From Trump's protectionist perspective, the policy implementation and collective aspect of CCA are a legitimacy gap in the Paris Agreement and the UNFCCC-facilitated regime.

From this perspective, the constitution of the agreement puts the US at a disadvantage with unjust, unequal treatment compared to the other parties, and hence it is perceived as illegitimate.

One of the greatest concerns after the US contestation was potential further member withdrawal (UNFCCC#6). Member withdrawal from the Paris Agreement would have meant that states do not regard this agreement as the appropriate solution to climate change. Thus, not only the legitimacy of the Paris Agreement but the legitimacy of the organization itself would be questioned, as the Paris Agreement is the essential part of the UNFCCC's mandate. This kind of legitimacy loss would make the UNFCCC even more vulnerable to further contestation of its 'substantive status quo' (Cottrell, 2016, p 45). With the withdrawal of an important country such as the US, which used to be a leading negotiator in the UNFCCC (UNFCCC#4) and remains one of the most influential powers in global governance, the potential of further member withdrawal increased. Regarding similar positions towards finance and the implementation of climate change action (UNFCCC#6), Brazil is mentioned very often in this context, as President Bolsonaro of Brazil took similar positions on several issues to Trump.

Yet, in the years after 2017, the opposite could be seen. No other withdrawals were announced, and Brazil, for example, also remains in the Paris Agreement (UNFCCC#6). However, the missing input of the US regarding the negotiations and implementation of the Paris Agreement, as well as its budget cuts to the Paris Agreement, contribute to an anticipated loss of strength. In fact, the US used to deliver the highest contribution to the so-called 'Green Climate Fund' that was set up by the UNFCCC in 2010 and played a crucial part in the Paris Agreement (Green Climate Fund, nd). This contribution amounted to US$3 billion that needed to be compensated (Kemp, 2017; Jotzo et al, 2018). This meant that funding for climate action in developing countries was at stake (Jotzo et al, 2018, p 815; Urpelainen and Van de Graaf, 2018), which gave another negative push to the North–South divide. The already relatively weak key issues in the Paris Agreement of adaptation, loss and damage, and finance were further weakened after the US contribution was cut (Jotzo et al, 2018, p 815). The Global Climate Fund (GCF) secretariat itself, and with it the UNFCCC, was in a 'moment of uncertainty' that created a demand and at the same time an opportunity for learning and developing new practices, as alternative policies for funding, and for less dependency on nation-state funding, needed to be considered (UNFCCC#9).

The change in the US administration and its withdrawal from the Paris Agreement was seen as a 'setback to global cooperation on the biggest global problem that the whole planet is facing together and that cannot be denied' (UNFCCC#7). It created uncertainty and was indeed regarded as problematic, as a second term of the Trump administration would have prolonged the anticipation of obstruction. Also, without the 'nationally determined contribution' from the US it was clear that 'the system is … weak …, much weaker than it needs to be' (UNFCCC#6). After the announcement, the US was 'less active in building additional ambition under the system' (UNFCCC#6).

However, no blockage in the negotiations was initiated by the US, which was also due to pressure by other negotiation parties (UNFCCC#9; UNFCCC#13; Jotzo et al, 2018, p 814). Here, despite remaining in the negotiation processes at the UNFCCC Conferences of the Parties (COPs), a critical issue was whether the US was still meeting its obligations under the Paris Agreement (UNFCCC#8). The previous government had been key in pushing for and negotiating rules for the actual implementation of the Paris Agreement. The termination of this input by this 'key player' and 'absence is a problem' (UNFCCC#6), although this 'absence … may in the end only be a temporary absence … . But [the UNFCCC also has] to live with the possibility that the US is out of the Paris Agreement for a longer period', which 'could undermine the collective enterprise' (UNFCCC#6).

Although the US still sent delegations to the COPs in the following years, their involvement particularly concerned 'less political issues' that were not of a financial nature (UNFCCC#12). Yet, the US involvement from 2017 onwards was perceived as coming with less enthusiasm and depending on the individual interests of partakers in the negotiation. Representatives of the Global South, for example, have regarded the behaviour of the US with more discontent, particularly criticizing the US for its 'resistance in areas around finance, … long-term finance issues, such as loss and damage where they've had rather restrictive positions' (UNFCCC#6). This was also recognized as 'obstructionism' towards the UNFCCC and the COPs, which could put 'negative pressure on getting consensus … and therefore, getting consensus has become increasingly difficult' (UNFCCC#7).

The withdrawal from the agreement as a protectionist decision rather focused on issues of geopolitics, finance and economics (Jotzo et al, 2018, p 814). Besides this, although President Trump's focus was not on environmental policies and climate change, the US remained in the UNFCCC altogether, even though an exit from the UNFCCC would have been possible. In fact, this would even have been a less time-intense process as 'according to Article 25.2 of the Convention, the United States could declare their withdrawal at any time', and after the US senate's ratification of the exit it 'would take effect only one year later and would also entail the withdrawal from the Paris Agreement, which is a dependent treaty of the UNFCCC' (Obergassel et al, 2017, p 18). Yet this would have meant having no more possibilities, agency or power in the UNFCCC. Although exiting the UNFCCC would have been a much stronger statement following Trump's election campaign promises, the fact of not having the opportunity to influence and sit at the international negotiation table seemed to be a bigger disadvantage for the US in the long run.

With his contestation, Trump claimed a legitimacy gap in the Paris Agreement and the UNFCCC-facilitated regime. The legitimation potential lay in the reinforcement and the belief in the importance of the Paris Agreement and acting collectively on climate change. From the UNFCCC's side it was acknowledged that this contestation, although expected at the time, was a crucial moment of contestation that needed to be taken seriously. In the next section I will analyse the legitimation practices after the announcement. By further deconstructing the whole process, I can show why this major contestation was followed by legitimation rather than the anticipated de-legitimation. Via this deconstruction I argue that the norm for CCA framed the contestation–legitimation process analysed here.

Legitimation practices by the UNFCCC

After the contestation the UNFCCC engaged in different forms of legitimation practices. These were prior non-state actor engagement (behavioural and institutional legitimation) and neutral communication as well as moderating (discursive legitimation), and the UNFCCC filing the US' exit in accordance with the rules of the Paris Agreement (institutional legitimation). Although the UNFCCC anticipated the US contestation within Trump's legislature, the UNFCCC secretariat reacted with 'regret' (UNFCCC#1; UNFCCC#3; UNFCCC#4). However, there was a sense of 'inevitability' (UNFCCC#1) after the initial shock of the election of Trump in 2016, as mentioned earlier. A 'sort of shock panic reaction, … didn't really happen' (UNFCCC#1). Yet, despite this anticipation and inevitability of the US withdrawal that was felt, this did not change the fact that the US was still perceived as an impactful leader in international politics. The US is still regarded as a trendsetter and one of the key players (UNFCCC#4). The previous government was perceived as a 'big champion' and, together with China and the EU, 'instrumental' in reaching the Paris Agreement and negotiating rules for implementation (UNFCCC#2; UNFCCC#6).

For the UNFCCC, it was a crucial task to not only 'uphold the positive spirit' (UNFCCC#4) that it received throughout the US withdrawal from the Paris Agreement. Ultimately, the whole process of withdrawal is a 'phase to be bridged' (UNFCCC#9). The decision to withdraw was regarded as not being made on 'rational' grounds but as an 'ideological decision' (UNFCCC#1). Accordingly, there was not 'much hope that this could be turned around' (UNFCCC#1). UNFCCC officials admitted that the withdrawal 'was a situation you didn't want to be confronted with', as the Paris Agreement is seen as a 'milestone' (UNFCCC#3) and 'the only global answer to climate change' (UNFCCC#5). Hence, the withdrawal of one of the key players was initially 'discouraging' (UNFCCC#5). Additionally, the US not partaking anymore from 2020 in the Paris Agreement is a problem as it is counted as the second-biggest emitter of greenhouse gases (Urpelainen and Van de Graaf, 2018, p 840).

Despite the regret, the reaction in 2017 was 'calm' and the UNFCCC remained rational and 'factual' (UNFCCC#1; UNFCCC#3; UNFCCC#4). Taking a strong opposition, as member states and sub- and non-state actors did after the US announcement, was not an option for the UNFCCC, since the UNFCCC COPs and negotiations on global climate policies remain a member state-driven process. Not accepting the US's sovereign decision and thus, contesting its autonomy and sovereignty had the potential of dissatisfying other member states with the organization. This would have meant an increased risk of further member withdrawal. Instead, the UNFCCC itself had to remain relatively neutral (UNFCCC#1; UNFCCC#5).

Here, the UNFCCC carefully assessed the US announcement in consultation with the UN Secretary General in New York (UNFCCC#1; UNFCCC#2). This way, a coherent, appropriate response could be filed that reflects the importance of the US in the Paris Agreement but moreover underlined the position of the UNFCCC. However, the importance of the rules of the process of exiting the Paris Agreement should be stressed, as well as communicating that the US will remain in the negotiations until the final withdrawal in 2020 and will still be part of the UNFCCC (UNFCCC#5; UNFCCC#6). Additionally, it was made clear that the renegotiation of the Paris Agreement is generally possible but 'not at the request of one country' (UNFCCC#1). It was also stressed that the US was welcome to 'come back any time if they decide to change their position' (UNFCCC#5; UNFCCC#3).[2]

Moreover, the US withdrawal was anticipated as the kind of challenge 'that you can't really do something about except messaging and moderating' (UNFCCC#1). The UNFCCC's calm response was also influenced by the institutional level, namely the existing exit rules and precluding steps of the Paris Agreement itself. In general, Article 28 of the Paris Agreement regulates the exit process, stating that members can 'at any time after three years from the date on which this Agreement has entered into force ... withdraw from this Agreement by giving written notification to the Depositary', and that it 'shall take effect upon expiry of one year from the date of receipt by the Depositary of the notification of withdrawal' (UNFCCC, 2017). The possibility of a member state exiting the Paris Agreement is regarded as a 'natural' part of international cooperation (UNFCCC#3). The US legally remained in the Paris Agreement until November 2020 and generally remained a member of the UNFCCC after the withdrawal (UNFCCC#6; UNFCCC#7).

Further, on a discursive level, the UNFCCC practised continuous, constructive contact with the US government but also enforced engagement with US non-state actors (UNFCCC#9). After the experience of the US contesting the Kyoto Protocol, the UNFCCC had set up a wider non-state actor network that benefits the legitimation after the contestation. After 2001, the UNFCCC enforced its non-state actor engagement (Bäckstrand et al, 2017; Pickering et al, 2018, p 822). By doing so, the UNFCCC contributed itself to promoting and manifesting norm for CCA over the past few years, which now frames processes in the global climate regime as a standard of appropriate behaviour. The UNFCCC's history of practising non-state actor engagement has not only contributed to successfully establishing itself as 'a manager and information hub, emerging as a co leading institution, and taking on the role of a spearheading actor' of non-state actor engagement (Hickmann and Elsässer, 2020, p 14), but moreover to building a basis on which the contestation of the US in 2017 could be dealt with. Practising non-state actor engagement, and with this, also practising norm promotion, provided a basis for the following legitimation by a wide range of US sub- and non-state actors.

Thus, the collective endeavour aspect of the norm for CCA in particular can be observed with this non-state actor engagement (Betsill, 2017, p 190; UNFCCC#1; UNFCCC#4; UNFCCC#6). Hence, the UNFCCC itself engaged in legitimation through its non-state actor orchestration. So, after the Trump contestation in 2017, the UNFCCC benefited from this network with which the UNFCCC enlarged the relevant community for CCA. Thus, in 2017, this network was particularly influential in legitimation after the contestation. This engagement with more non- and sub-state actors played a significant role in the responses of the respective actors after the announcement. The initiatives that were launched in this particular process were driven by sub-national bodies, cities and regions, as well as non-state actors such as non-governmental organizations, civil society groups and also private companies in the US (Hickmann et al, 2019, pp 2–3), which will be discussed in the next section.

Legitimation practices of member state actors, sub- and non-state actors

Next to the impact of the UNFCCC itself, member state actors and sub- and non-state actors engaged in legitimation after the contestation. In contrast to the expectations of a domino effect of further member withdrawal, a positive, legitimating (re-)commitment to the Paris Agreement can be observed – 'no one else [was] saying "well, since they're going, we'll go too"' (UNFCCC#6). Member states primarily engaged in discursive legitimation by giving statements to praise the Paris Agreement and to take on a leadership role for global cooperation on climate change. They also openly opposed Trump's contestation. Additionally, on a behavioural level, they suggested giving financial compensation. Sub- and non-state actors also openly opposed Trump. Further, they engaged in behavioural legitimation by building networks and organizing events after contestation. As I argue, this is due to CCA being established as a legitimate norm that frames the appropriate standard of behaviour within the process and conditions the engagement in legitimation practices. Especially in the COPs, delegates, negotiators and others involved took more of a position of non-concern if not 'positive defiance' (UNFCCC#4), going from 'it didn't matter, we're going to carry on without the US' (UNFCCC#7), to 'it doesn't make any difference' (UNFCCC#7), officially stating the will to stay committed to the Paris Agreement.

Indeed, many countries actively stated their commitment to the Paris Agreement and intention to continue implementing it. Germany, Italy and France gave out a joint statement, saying 'the momentum generated in Paris in December 2015 is irreversible, and we firmly believe that the Paris Agreement cannot be renegotiated, since it is a vital instrument for our planet' (Walsh, 2017). Likewise, the European Union Commissioner has stated that the EU was 'ready to lead the fight' (Bomberg, 2017, p 962). These discursive legitimation practices pointed to the irreversibility of the Paris Agreement and show that CCA serves as a norm that manifests in the community-belief system of these actors. The discursive commitment and narrative of the belief in the Paris Agreement as legitimation practices indicate this community belief in the norm. Further, this underlines both core aspects of the norm – namely, the belief that to successfully act on climate change, it is necessary to have ratified policies that direct and manifest global climate action as collective endeavour.

These aspects of the norm for CCA span through all legitimation practices of the community after the contestation. Other member states, such as China (UNFCCC#6), Canada, New Zealand and the G77 group, also engaged in discursive legitimation (UNFCCC#4). In particular, the G77 group has a special interest in the implementation of the Paris Agreement, as these countries are particularly vulnerable to the effects of climate change, as could already be clearly seen in the process of the G77 walkout. China's president Xi Jinping claimed to 'take a leadership role' and contribute to climate action, however, 'as long as the diplomatic, economic and domestic environmental opportunities presented by such action remain' (Bomberg, 2017, p 962). Shortly after the announcement, the Chinese president, for the first time in Chinese history, committed to a bilateral agreement with a sub-national actor, declaring that the country would 'boost cooperation on green technology' in corporation with Governor Brown of California (Hermwille, 2018, p 458).

On a behavioural level, since the US withdrawal would impact the UNFCCC's funding, alternatives for funding and for less dependency on nation-state funding needed to be considered (UNFCCC#9). Initially, other nation state members, especially the European states, were put on the spot to compensate the financing responsibility (UNFCCC#9). Contrary to the likelihood of expecting a refusal to accept this responsibility, for example, Germany announced that it was doubling its contribution, leading to other European countries strengthening their commitment to the Paris Agreement, and thus to the UNFCCC (UNFCCC#9). This engagement in legitimation practices by several member states showed clear opposition to Trump's contestation and also emphasized the support of the Paris Agreement.

As I argue, when deconstructing this dynamic, CCA works as a guiding frame of the process and conditions the behaviour after the contestation, and thus the norm for CCA. The vow to take over leadership showed not only support but in turn an understanding of what is legitimate and where these actors locate themselves normatively. Thus, legitimation is particularly driven by the context of the announcement and CCA as the normative status quo of the community. Additionally, the variety and differences between the domestic realities of these actors, articulating their support in a similar way, demonstrate that they assign themselves to the community of CCA contrary to the contestation by Trump that was normatively unaligned with the community.

Despite the reactions of state actors after the announcement, the initiatives by sub- and non-state actors had a 'catalyst function', gave the UNFCCC and CCA a 'strong boost' (UNFCCC#4). The UNFCCC'S previous non-state actor engagement 'in a very active way in a much wider ecosystem' provided grounds for the 'engagement with many actors from the US' (UNFCCC#6). 'Confidence grew' when other actors, particularly from the US, took over to continuously promote acting collectively on climate change nationally as well as internationally (UNFCCC#1; UNFCCC#6). In the US, several initiatives were launched in response to the announcement, which included discursive and behavioural legitimation practices. Even before the reaction in 2016 immediately after the Trump election, mayors from the so-called 'Climate Action Mayors' signed an open letter to President-elect Trump:

> Dear President-elect Trump,
>
> As Mayors, we have taken it upon ourselves to take bold action within our cities to tackle the climate crisis head-on. We write today to ask for your partnership in our work to clean our air, strengthen our economy, and ensure that our children inherit a nation healthier and better prepared for the future than it is today. ... And we ask that you shift to embrace the Paris Climate Agreement and make U.S. cities your partner in doing so. ... The time for bold leadership and action is now. (Climate Mayors, 2016)

After the withdrawal announcement they further stated:

> The President's denial of global warming is getting a cold reception from America's cities. As 305 US Mayors …, we will adopt, honor, and uphold the commitments to the goals enshrined in the Paris Agreement. We will intensify efforts to meet each of our cities' current climate goals … We will continue to lead. We are increasing investments in renewable energy and energy efficiency. (Climate Mayors, 2017)

In the same vein, in 2017, several US corporations, including, for example, Apple, Google, Unilever and others, issued full-page ads (C2ES, nd) in *The New York Times*, the *New York Post* and the *Wall Street Journal* (Betsill, 2017, p 190). Here they urged President Trump 'to keep the United States in the Paris Agreement on climate change' as 'U.S. business is best served by a stable practical framework facilitating an effective and balanced global response. The Paris Agreement provides such a framework' (C2ES, nd). Beyond this, the Paris Agreement and its implementation was continuously supported by some US states contrary to the position of the federal government. These states, including, for example, California, New York and Washington, represent almost two-thirds of the US's economic performance. California and New York account for 10% of the US's total emissions. At the same time, they both committed to the use of renewable energy and to supply 50% of the state's electricity through renewables by 2030 (Bomberg, 2017, p 960).

Another significant example of opposing sub-state actor engagement is the 'Global Climate Action Summit' (Global Climate Action UNFCCC, nd) that was also initiated by Governor Jerry Brown of California in September 2018. The summit gathered local, sub-state actors and several non-state actors, again including big US corporations, to address climate change and the continued support for the Paris Agreement and engaging in climate action (UNFCCC#11). This is another indicator of the community understanding of CCA as collective endeavour. The goal was to take 'ambition to the next level with a wave of fresh and brave climate action announcements that, if implemented, would generate over 65 million new, low-carbon jobs by 2030' (UNEP, 2018). By having US sub-state governments and a major part of the US economy still committed to the Paris Agreement, this commitment sent a strong message, despite risking possible tensions with the federal government by taking an opposition stance (UNFCCC#4; UNFCCC#6).

Further legitimation on a discursive and behavioural level came from the coalition of 'America's pledge' initiated by the 'Bloomberg Foundation' and the governor of California. It aimed to prevent the UNFCCC from long-term financial issues and to further promote climate change action. Here, Bloomberg offered not only to pay parts of the contributions of the US budget, indicating that the UNFCCC could continue its agenda with the Paris Agreement despite the US withdrawal (UNFCCC#1), but also through this coalition keep meeting the targets of the climate change agenda within the Paris Agreement (Hermwille, 2018, p 458). In addition to 'America's pledge', another movement was 'We Are Still In' (Betsill, 2017, p 190; UNFCCC#1; UNFCCC#4; UNFCCC#6). Since June 2017, more than 3,800 leaders from America's city halls, state houses, boardrooms and college campuses, representing more than 155 million Americans and US$9 trillion of the US economy, have signed its declaration. This movement collectively opposed the US government's decision, calling the US withdrawal 'out of step with what is happening in the United States' and declaring that they 'will continue to support climate action to meet the Paris Agreement' (Betsill, 2017, p 190). Further, the movement gathered several kinds of sub-initiatives, which contributed to research and invest in climate change action (We Are Still In, nd).

Building coalitions and initiatives between state, sub- and non-state actors shows that collective action is part of the legitimacy belief of this community. As I argue, the legitimation practices reflect the fact that the legitimating actors of the community recommitted to and praised the importance of the Paris Agreement and its implementation. It was stressed that acting on climate change can only be successful when all global actors act collectively. The praising of the Paris Agreement and open opposition to Trump by member state leaders, sub- and non-state actors, especially in giving out a joint statement, as Germany, France and Italy did, or through the several coalitions between the diverse actors on the US and international level, shows the collective aspect of the norm. The different reactions on the sub and non-state actor level and the combination of discursive and behavioural legitimation practices, like those of the state actors, but also the similarity of responses, underlined their common, collective understanding of what is the legitimate norm, namely CCA as a guiding frame.

Conclusion: Diverse, collective legitimation in the name of CCA after contestation

By analysing the contestation–legitimation process of the US withdrawal from the Paris Agreement, I could show that, in contrast to the previous experience of the US non-ratification of the Kyoto Protocol in 2001, CCA has been established as the legitimate, guiding norm. The process of the US contestation of the Paris Agreement presents the dual quality of norms as a stable and flexible guiding frame. As I argue, it is also possible to carve out the guiding norm of a process, also if the contestation speaks against the community norm. Trump's contestation claimed the Paris Agreement would handicap the US for the benefit of the other parties of the agreement and the wider community, which speaks out against the aspect of CCA as collective endeavour. The aspect of policy implementation of the norm for CCA can also be deconstructed in the Trump contestation practice of the Paris Agreement. With the contestation of the Paris Agreement, its implementation was refused and spoke against the norm, which is embodied in the Paris Agreement.

The legitimation engagement following the contestation speaks to the norm for CCA as collective endeavour. The UNFCCC and its community have adopted the norm and share the understanding that to successfully act on climate change, action needs to be taken collectively since it is a global issue that affects everyone. Here, most legitimation engagement came from member states, sub and non-state actors that reinforced their legitimacy belief in the norm for CCA by opposing Trump's contestation. The UNFCCC kept in the background and took on 'business as usual', which was a sensible choice, since the UNFCCC COPs and negotiations on global climate governance remain a member state-driven process. Not accepting the US's sovereign decision had the potential of dissatisfying other member states with the organization, which might have responded consequently with a withdrawal.

The UNFCCC has contributed to shaping the norm for CCA as well as building a community of climate change action, especially via previous non-state actor engagement. This way, the UNFCCC benefited from this network in 2017. Further, the UNFCCC expanded the relevant community for CCA. This network was then particularly influential in legitimation after the contestation. I identified several legitimation practices opposing Trump's contestation of the Paris Agreement, which show a clear pattern guided by the norm for CCA across the different actors. As I argue, these are expressions of both implicitly and explicitly recognizing and supporting the norm for CCA that guides this contestation–legitimation process.

5

Contestation Along the North–South Divide: The International Energy Agency Turning to Collective Action

As part of the global climate regime, not only the United Nations Framework Convention on Climate Change (UNFCCC), as analysed in the previous chapter, but also the International Energy Agency (IEA) alike is exposed to multiple pressures due to the variety of interests of the involved actors and the changing landscape in world politics and international cooperation (Biermann et al, 2009c, 2012; O'Neill, 2009; Pattberg and Biermann, 2012; Chasek et al, 2014). With the Yom Kippur War, several OPEC[1] countries cut their oil production and initiated an oil embargo on Israel-supporting countries in October 1973 (Türk, 2016). The following first oil crisis in 1974 hit Western countries that were 'unprepared' (IEA#1; IEA#3), leading to a severe oil shortage, years of inflation and economic stagnation (BMWK). To find ways to oppose this strong dependency on the oil-exporting countries,[2] 17 countries[3] founded the IEA. Established as an oil security organization within the OECD framework in 1974, the IEA pioneered in this regard to watch over the member countries' part-independency from the oil-producing countries (Van de Graaf, 2012; Türk, 2016). Here, the key strategy to remain resilient at least for a period of 90 days, if such embargos should be initiated again, is the emergency oil response system (Frøland and Ingulstad, 2020).

The IEA now aims to ensure and monitor the compliance of its member states with this response system. This key competence not only requires members to have 90 days of stockpiled supplies, but also demands solidarity of oil-sharing among members, and the development of an updated national oil security legislation, including regulations and a crisis response plan (IEA, 1974, 2018). The agency provided the framework for their member states and the link between the OECD countries to react to other future oil crises. However, with global changes, the rise of emerging powers, especially the

BRICS, climate change, the finite nature of oil and the IEA's focus on oil and fossil fuels, the growth of, and need for, new energy sources were not reflected by the IEA (Van de Graaf, 2012, p 234). The IEA could not keep up with the changing reality of the global landscape of emerging powers of the Global South as well as the demand for the energy transition and in turn transforming institutional formats, which enforced climate change action (CCA) as a guiding norm.

Due to its narrow exclusive focus on membership and oil, the IEA has been labelled as 'conservative', 'ineffective' or 'blind' and both national actors and scholars have questioned its existence and declared it almost obsolete in the past two decades (Van de Graaf and Lesage, 2009; Florini, 2010; Van de Graaf, 2012, 2013; Heubaum and Biermann, 2015; Carrington and Stephenson, 2018; Downie, 2020; Faude and Fuss, 2020). 'The perception of biased or unfair procedures and performances heightened over the years, leading to heated debates and mounting requests for programmatic reform' (Zelli, 2018, p 178). Not reflecting what was promised by the name of the IEA as the energy organization representing and reflecting the *international* realm turned out to be the IEA's Achilles' heel and gave way to major contestation.

Some of these claims within the contestation criticized its exclusive 'club' membership of OECD countries only. This non-universal frame meant a neglect of including rising powers, such as India and China, that have heavily increased their energy consumption over time (Van de Graaf, 2012, 2013). Because of this exclusion, the IEA was consequently lacking interlinked data access to the world's energy consumption. Moreover, with the rise of other sustainable energy resources, such as solar, hydrogen power and especially wind energy, the IEA's raison d'être as an oil crisis manager could not withstand the pressures of these upcoming, competing energy resources. The focus on oil did not reflect the changing reality of its member states and the demands of a changing world in light of finite energy resources, such as coal and oil, and climate change. Although the IEA's founding reason was to ensure oil security, the IEA's insistence on oil and not incorporating other resources no longer represented the changing reality of energy resources and consumption versus the IEA's aspired-to 'global role its name implies' (Van de Graaf, 2012, p 237). Table 5.1 shows the timeline of the IEA processes.

The two contestations manifested in the 2009 creation of International Renewable Energy Agency (IRENA) by three IEA members, which are also founders of the IEA. IRENA became a direct competitor to counter the IEA 'as an ambitious rival forum at the heart of an already complex institutional environment' (Zelli, 2018, p 178; see also Van de Graaf and Lesage, 2009; Van de Graaf, 2012, 2013; Faude and Fuss, 2020). The three founding members, Germany, Denmark and Spain, the latter two having special interests in wind and offshore renewables, created IRENA, as they regarded the IEA with great dissatisfaction due to its neglect of renewable

Table 5.1: Timeline milestones of processes IEA

Year	Event/Stage	Content
2009	Contestations Creation of IRENA	• by three member states (Denmark, Germany, Spain) • members discontent with IEA's performance • IEA criticized for non-universal membership and conservative energy policy portfolio and not incorporating renewables
2013	Modernization strategy	• strengthening and broadening commitment to energy security beyond oil, to natural gas and electricity • deepening the IEA's engagement with major emerging economies • providing a greater focus on clean energy technology, including energy efficiency
2013–2015	Association of non-OECD countries	• 'open door' policy to deepen the collaboration with eight associated countries
2015	Leadership Fathi Birol	• main figure to reach out and start cooperation with the non-OECD countries • promoter of connecting energy and climate action • one of the most 100 influential people in *Time* magazine 2021
2015	Cooperation with other IOs (UNFCCC and IRENA)	• cooperation with UNFCC especially compiling the Paris Agreement • IRENA and IEA share data base

energy (Van de Graaf, 2012, 2013; Faude and Fuss, 2020). IRENA catered to their contestation claims by (a) including universal membership, and (b) focusing on renewable energy resources, which the IEA until then had neglected to incorporate. In contrast to the OECD countries-only rule of the IEA with 30 members (IEA, nd [e]), 165 countries have joined IRENA to date. IRENA is not limited in terms of membership (IEA#7) and can have 'everybody around the table' (IEA#2).

The members' open contestation claimed that the IEA was not the 'appropriate venue' for reform (Van de Graaf and Lesage, 2009, p 303). This led the IEA into a dawning legitimacy crisis, with the possibility of further members following in these contestation claims of the IEA's inability to deal with the changing global reality appropriately (Van de Graaf and Lesage, 2009, p 309). Thus, it became an existential task for the IEA to not only rely on, or hope for, legitimation by outsiders or by their members, but moreover to become active in their self-legitimation. I identify both contestations as beginnings of the two processes for this case study, as the claims within these contestations, and more importantly the IEA's response to them, contribute to understanding why contestation can be followed by legitimation. The first is the contestation of the OECD-only membership, the second is the oil-only approach. In the following, I will analyse the contestation–legitimation processes of the IEA's OECD-only membership and how the norm for CCA guided these processes.

In this section, I analyse the contestation–legitimation process regarding the IEA's OECD-exclusive membership. After presenting the contestation, I will show how the IEA engaged in legitimation practices in two different ways to legitimate. On the one hand, the IEA aimed to meet the contestation claim and solve the legitimacy gap by adding the association of non-OECD countries as a new component. This institutional addition as a kind of self-legitimation is perceived as a necessary step to be able to portray and analyse the reality of energy consumption and thus energy scenarios. And in doing so, to legitimate against the contestation claims of blindness and obsolescence.

On the other hand, although it was a crucial point of the contestation, the exclusive OECD membership is also a source of legitimation for the IEA, as IEA members perceive this exclusivity and like-mindedness as a beneficial component for energy cooperation. This component is still perceived as a source of legitimacy for the member states. And in turn, this membership clause contributes to the legitimation, although it has been accused of being a weakness before. I will conclude by summarizing my findings, also regarding my argument of the norm for CCA as a guiding frame that frames the processes. Figure 5.1 illustrates the different stages of the contestation-legitimation process and its aspects.

The contestation: IEA OECD membership outdated

The contestation of the first process is the contestation of the IEA'S OECD-only membership, which manifested in the creation of IRENA as a form of institutional contestation. Only OECD countries can join the IEA as (full) members. Although IEA members generally see the 'healthy culture' for cooperation due to exclusivity (IEA#3; IEA#7), this exclusivity gave the IEA 'an image of a rich man's club' (Van de Graaf, 2012, p 240), which was a persistently discursively contested issue by non-members and academics, and some members alike (Van de Graaf, 2012; Heubaum and Biermann, 2015). The discrepancies of the OECD membership-only remained a pressing point of contestation, due to the changing reality of global power structures and energy consumption. At the same time, IEA member countries were 'concerned with ... China's foray into the African oil business' (Van de Graaf, 2012, p 234). This was a concern for the IEA as it meant a realistic loss of influence on global energy markets (Van de Graaf, 2012, p 235).

To exclude states such as India and China, that have heavily increased their energy consumption, would foster neither cooperation nor access to important energy-related data. Further, with this neglect, the risk of being

Figure 5.1: IEA: Process of OECD-only membership

Guiding frame
'Norm for climate change action'
Standard of appropriate behaviour

North–South divide

Contestation

OECD-only membership

Contestation: Challenge
- Contesting the IEA's non-inclusive membership for OECD countries only
- Struggle over legitimacy: non-representative neglecting inclusion of rising powers
- Indicating **legitimacy gap:** new major energy consumers, data and representation lack
- **Legitimation potential:** option for norm adoption and its translation through collective, global component

↓

Legitimation practices
Background: creation of IRENA

Practices: IEA
- *Association of non-OECD members (behavioural and institutional legitimation)*
- *Initiative leadership, actively approaching big players of non-OECD members, e.g. China, India (behavioural legitimation)*
- *Keeping 'club', 'healthy culture' to reassure IEA members (behavioural and institutional legitimation)*
- *Taking middle-ground approach by not discarding exclusive membership but including associated members in the dialogue and cooperation (discursive and behavioural legitimation)*

CCA norm and practices:
- *Norm adoption or norm is already adopted:*
  Norm not yet adopted, needs to be adopted
- *Explicit/implicit reference to core aspects of norm in the practices: including non-OECD members, association*
- *Practices are markers of core aspects of the norm: inclusive, family, all actors*

---

outrun by these emerging powers increased. Missing out on diplomatic ties with, and data access to, these countries was crucial, since it enabled diagnosis and prospects of the world's energy consumption. In fact, 'all of the additional energy-related CO2 emissions [by] 2030 are expected to come from countries outside of the IEA' (Van de Graaf, 2012, p 235). Also, within the IEA and among its members the realization manifested over the years that an exclusion of emerging powers denied the ability to globally cooperate on energy issues. Further, it hampered the ability to effectively find solutions for energy transition to act on climate change (IEA#2; IEA#3; IEA#9). Besides these IEA-specific micro-issues, the macro-issue of this contestation is the North–South divide. This divide as one of the major issues of conflict and struggle in the global climate regime manifests in this contestation and was catered to by IRENA due to their universal, inclusive full membership.

Since the norm for CCA includes the collective endeavour aspect, the IEA did not have the structures that speak to this aspect of the norm. The contestation can be aligned with the norm, indicating the legitimacy gap in its contestation claim. The contestation of the IEA OECD-only membership was aligned with the collective aspect of CCA, as actors need to cooperate collectively to succeed in energy transition and to tackle climate change. This shows that the norm for CCA is the core frame guiding the contestation that points to a legitimacy gap in the IEA's membership frame. By neglecting the inclusion of rising powers, and hence new major energy consumers, the IEA had a crucial lack of data access and representation.

This means that, on the one hand, the IEA was not in line with the norm at the time. At the same time, the legitimation potential was in overcoming this representation lack. Thus, it was necessary to have 'everybody around the table' (IEA#2) to collectively act on energy transition and to reflect the legitimacy belief of the norm for CCA. Norm adoption was thus a necessity in this IEA process, especially regarding the aspect of CCA as collective endeavour. In the case of the contestation–legitimation process of the IEA OECD-only membership, the aspect of the norm for CCA as collective endeavour is explicitly visible. To respond to the contestation of its exclusivity and to the change of the global energy market and its emerging, big consumers, such as China and India, the IEA initiated the so-called 'association of non-OECD countries', which is discussed in the next section of this chapter.

The middle ground: self-legitimation through member association

In the case of the IEA, the legitimation involves two aspects that the IEA could respond to. As I will show, the exclusive OECD membership of the IEA is, on the one hand, the essential part for the power transition contestation. On the other hand, it is also a source of legitimation for the IEA, as IEA members, over the years, came back to perceive this exclusivity and like-mindness as a beneficial component for energy cooperation. Yet, the reality of emerging powers in world politics, such as China and India, which are not only major energy consumers but moreover big CO_2 emitters. To overcome the conflict lines of the North–South divide, demanded some kind participation of these rising powers in the global energy discourse and decision-making. This will be discussed in the following.

The globally changing power structures struck IEA members and leadership in the emerging 2010s (IEA#2; IEA#9). Discussions about how to include non-OECD members without changing the whole legislation on IEA membership had been an issue for over 10 years as the 'role of the Western, of the OECD countries in the energy world has been shrinking for decades, so it's important to have a prominent organization that more or less represents, or at least counts in, its family many more countries than only OECD countries' (IEA#6). Further, the IEA has a special interest in not having only a conversation with these other high energy consumers, such as China and India, but impact and control, regarding its core competence of the emergency oil response system. Here, the IEA and its members face the dilemma of the global impact of possible oil crises.

> [It] is not really a matter of deciding whether it comes from the Middle East or from Africa or South America, if something is stuck somewhere then it will have worldwide impact. ... that is this dilemma for which there is no solution in the end and that is why they are always very interested in keeping in touch with the other countries – you know that in India and in China large oil inventories are built up and you don't know exactly how many and here one wishes for a better data exchange. (IEA#1)

Since the OECD countries are not the only large oil consumers anymore, they do not have the same influence on oil prices and supply in the case of a crisis. To remain in control and have an effective crisis response system, the incorporation of, and collaboration with, the now associated countries was a relevant step (IEA#4; IEA#6; IEA#7). Interviewees agreed that especially the inclusion of and exchange with China and India as big consumers was necessary in this regard, to have the data as well as an overview of the global oil market (IEA#1; IEA#3, IEA#9).

To overcome these shortcomings, also in regard to CCA as collective endeavour that can only be solved collectively and fill the legitimacy gap, IEA leadership started to meet the contestation after the creation of IRENA from 2013 onwards, with institutional and behavioural self-legitimation, and in the same breath discursive legitimation (von Billerbeck, 2020). IEA leadership, first with Maria van der Hoeven in 2013 and then with Fatih Birol from 2015, established and introduced the so-called 'association countries'. They did so in cooperation with the Turkish Minister of Energy and Natural Resources Taner Yildiz, who chaired the 2013 IEA ministerial meeting (IEA, 2013). With the possibility of future oil crises, the IEA members and the IEA saw the need 'to get these countries on board so that we can increase our resilience and our ability to cope with crises' (IEA#3).

To bridge the divide between this reality and the design of the IEA, with the incorporation of so-called 'associated countries' in 2015, the IEA created an 'open door' policy to deepen the collaboration with eight associated countries. These were Brazil, China, India, Indonesia, Morocco,

Thailand, Singapore and South Africa. Now 13 countries in total are associated: Argentina, Brazil, China, Egypt, India, Indonesia, Morocco, Thailand, Singapore, South Africa and Ukraine, which joined in 2022, and Kenya and Senegal, which joined in 2023. The creation of this policy can be counted as institutional legitimation practice. This attempt at association had already been initiated at the 2013 Ministerial Meeting with the 'Joint Declaration' by the IEA and six of seven 'partner countries' Brazil, China, India, Indonesia, Russia and South Africa expressing mutual interest in pursuing an association (IEA, 2013). Here, beside the 28 IEA members at that point, and more than 30 industry leaders from the IEA Energy Business Council, which included top companies active in energy or closely related fields, of Brazil, China, India, Indonesia, Mexico, Russia and South Africa also attended the meeting (IEA, 2013). After the joint statement of the IEA secretariat and seven of the eight countries, the IEA Executive Director Maria van der Hoeven concluded:

> Over the past year we have discussed with these key partner countries how we can build on our existing bilateral ties. The declaration we are unveiling today is a vital first step that can facilitate our shared consideration of new, broader approaches to cooperation, which better reflect today's global energy challenges and opportunities. (IEA, 2013)

The following Executive Director Fatih Birol played a special role in the finalization of this association. When he was elected in 2015, he had made calls before to the IEA members about his agenda to finally 'open the door' to non-OECD countries (IEA#9). This, then, 'was not something that has surprised our member countries' (IEA#9). In 2015, he emphasized this aspiration even more, by not following the regular protocol of visiting the US or Japan first after his election, but China:

> [His] first foreign trip was to China ... and he made it a point. I mean he didn't go by accident to China first, no, he made it a point ... because if we want to save the planet we need China on board already. [It] was the largest CO_2 emitter in the world, in volume, of course, not in capital, but because there are four times more Chinese people than US people ... . And then he engaged a lot with India, the same amount of people. (IEA#9)

Birol is regarded as the main figure to be able to reach out and effectively realize this cooperation with the non-OECD countries (IEA#9), which contributed to legitimation in a discursive and behavioural form. In fact, due to his outreach and vision on fortifying the global cooperation on energy and interconnected climate issue, he was selected as one of the most 100 influential people by *Time* magazine (Kerry, 2021). His recognition and close ties with non-OECD countries are also visible in the outreach by countries such as India, China, Indonesia and Colombia, which have asked him, and in turn the IEA, to chart road maps to expedite climate action and reach net-zero emissions in 2021. At the 2015 Ministerial Meeting, this association was finalized with the 'Joint Ministerial Declaration ... expressing the Activation of Association' (IEA, 2015). With this 'open door' policy the IEA seeks to deepen its collaboration with the eight associated countries, Brazil, China, India, Indonesia, Morocco, Thailand, Singapore and South Africa, so now the 'IEA family ... represents about 75% of global energy consumption, up from 40% in 2015' (IEA (nd) [a]). The association of non-OECD countries should provide:

> an efficient, voluntary means to work together on areas of mutual interest, including: increased information-sharing on common energy challenges and best practices; energy security; transparency and analysis of energy markets; energy technologies; energy efficiency and renewable energy. Association would also provide a common forum for regular dialogue between IEA member and partner countries via participation of partner countries in meetings of various IEA Standing Groups and Committees as well as this and future Ministerial Meetings. (IEA, 2013)

In 2017, the association of India was ratified by the Indian government and the IEA 'as a major milestone in the development of global energy governance, and another major step toward the IEA becoming a truly global energy organization' (Birol, 2017). Birol underlined the importance of the member association for the IEA 'family':

> It's a very important development in global energy governance. It is now impossible to talk about the future of global energy markets without talking about India. It's a country with a population now over 1.3 billion people. It is one of the brightest spots of the global economy. It is emerging as a major driving force in global energy trends with all modern fuels and technologies playing a part. India's new institutional ties with the IEA marked a critical addition to the IEA global outreach to our open-door policy. ... With India joining the family it means that the IEA is now more global, much stronger and much more representative. Once again I am proud to welcome India into the International Energy Agency. (Birol, 2017)

In the same year, China and the IEA signed a 'three-year work programme' to 'deepen ties', step up 'cooperation on energy security, capacity building, data and statistics' and 'expand their collaboration on a variety of key energy sector issues, including oil emergency management and preparedness, natural gas infrastructure, grid integration of variable renewables, energy efficiency, and technology innovation' (IEA, 2017).

To overcome the contestation, the IEA needed to engage in legitimation and adoption of the community norm with practices that reflect the norm and its aspects. By enforcing collective action and cooperation in a way that fits the IEA's structure, the organization moved towards adopting the norm for CCA. The association of non-OECD members and using symbolic language that refers to IEA cooperation with members and associated countries as 'family' reflects the legitimacy belief of the IEA-related community and speaks to the contestation. It also speaks to the shared understanding of the norm that to successfully act on climate change, this action needs to be taken collectively. Through the association, the IEA could enforce legitimation as working together on energy transition expertise to speak to the collective aspect of the norm to act on climate change.

The question of full membership instead of association of these non-OECD countries remains a recurring point of discussion (IEA#7). Full membership of non-OECD countries would require changing the legal framework and a renewed ratification of the treaty in many countries, which is regarded as an 'own goal' and the opening of 'Pandora's box', as with this legal change other demands for change, for example, change in the binding commitment to energy goals or the emergency oil response system, might come to the forefront (IEA#7). Not discarding the exclusive membership was a way to avoid this opening of 'Pandora's box'. Hence, it shows that keeping the exclusive full membership worked as a source of legitimation besides the association of non-OECD members, which will be discussed in the next section.

Exclusive at the core: self-legitimation by keeping the 'safe space'

While adding the strategy to incorporate non-OECD countries into the hub of the IEA in 2013/15, the IEA decided to keep the original membership clause as it is also a source of legitimation. Not following the example of its competitor IRENA by including universal membership but keeping the 'exclusivity' turns out to be a legitimation factor as IEA member states value this coherence and a consistent 'healthy culture' (IEA#7) in the IEA member community since the IEA is a 'member-driven organization'[4] (IEA#9). Thus, the IEA legitimated on a behavioural and institutional level by keeping this policy. National representatives perceive the 'relatively small circle of participants' at the IEA as 'healthy', which creates a common, consistent 'culture' for the negotiations, leading in turn to 'real' discussions rather than negotiations where participants do not interact but merely read out pre-prepared statements (IEA#7). Although IEA members regard universal membership with reservation, the association of non-OECD countries is seen as 'fruitful' and a necessity for the IEA to remain relevant and legitimate (IEA#6).

Full, universal membership, however, is still regarded with skepticism by both associated countries and IEA member states (IEA#3; IEA#4; IEA#6; IEA#7). The threshold of becoming an OECD member and in doing so giving up some autonomy is one factor that excludes membership for these countries (IEA#6). Another threshold is the obligations of the IEA emergency oil response system. The fulfilment of these obligations by the IEA members remains 'essential' (IEA#7), and the local structures in the respective country need to enable the implementation of these requirements, which some of the associated countries, such as Indonesia, might not be able to provide (Interviewee#5, #7).

Further, the structural transition that would be necessary to fulfil the obligations is too costly an endeavour for most of the associated countries, and the '90 days of storage requirements ... for countries like India and China is a very big step in the area of giving up a sacred part of their national autonomy' (IEA#7). Other factors in this regard are the periodic energy reviews of the IEA and the reciprocal reporting by the member countries (IEA#7). Thus, it remains 'an act of balance', since:

> [t]here is no country outside of the OECD that says, so we do it. We really take on the whole package in all of our obligations and then let us please join. So, there are a few that say '[w]e would like to join' but at the same time want to negotiate about the other criteria because they do not regard them as suitable. This, I think, will be a balancing act for the foreseeable future. (IEA#7)

At first sight, keeping the OECD-only clause for becoming an IEA member speaks against the collective aspect of the norm for CCA. However, for the IEA as an energy organization that was found to cover an oil-related mandate for energy security, the IEA's history and the relation to its members give a path dependency to keep an exclusive component. Negotiating and partnering on energy *security* carries concerns about the interests of others. Similar interests and longer paths of cooperation over time foster a sense of security and trust when it comes to energy *security* issues. Negotiations and cooperation are perceived as potentially more successful among IEA members (IEA#3). As can be seen in the successful legitimation of the IEA as it is now perceived as the most 'suitable' organization to organize the energy policy field (IEA#7), choosing the middle ground by the association of member states was enough to reflect the adoption of the norm for CCA regarding its collective aspect.

Having the association instead of opening up to universal membership caters to keeping the 'healthy culture' (IEA#3; IEA#7). The 'healthy culture' among IEA members is regarded as being related to the 'consistency' among, in particular, the European member states that are used to frequent direct 'neighbourhood policing', for example, in the European Union, and have the tendency to act as a 'conglomerate' against strong members such as the US (IEA#3). The US, as in many international forums, is a special driving force and has been allocated a leading role, including in the IEA. 'Whenever you talk about energy security at a global level, the US has been very present in that work over the decades' (IEA#2). The IEA 'is one of a few international organizations where the United States is active, actively involved and supporting' (IEA#6).

Further, the requirement of OECD membership is regarded as a practical, 'easy' solution that benefits the consistency and partnering among IEA members (IEA#3; IEA#7). The OECD membership contributes to a partial 'depoliticization' that works as a 'filter' and enables this 'healthy' discussion environment and consistent 'culture' for negotiations (IEA#7). Besides the formal stage, 'a lot of discussions take place not necessarily in the governing board but in the hallways' (IEA#4). This kind of informal engagement is not only quite common in negotiations, but for the IEA it can also be traced back to the consistency in the member 'club', because people 'know each other' (IEA#3; IEA#7).

Although the IEA is a largely member-driven organization, at the same time the member states rely on the technological and scientific expertise of the IEA, which in turn has a high impact on this agenda setting (IEA#7). There is a 'functioning, lively' discussion between the organization and its member states, the latter giving their own input on their position, to which the IEA adds, especially through its director Fatih Birol, who is very 'proactive' in this 'intense discussion process' (IEA#7). It is a two-way street as '[through] the IEA Ministerial, the Secretariat develops ideas for existing or new work programmes, which are then discussed with member countries in various IEA committees and ultimately presented to the Governing Board for approval' (IEA, nd [c]). Also, the member countries decide every two years on the budget and work scope of the IEA, which needs to be approved by the governing board (IEA, nd [c]).

Further, the IEA organizes working groups that consist of member state government officials several times a year. These working groups are divided into the standing groups of the 'Standing Group on Emergency Questions', 'Standing Group on Oil Market', 'Standing Group on Long-Term Cooperation' and 'Standing Group on Global Energy Dialogue', and the committees 'Committee on Energy Research and Technology' and

'Committee on Budget and Expenditure', in which the respective issues are discussed (IEA, nd [c]). As the different groups most of the time consist of the same representatives, 'you always see the same faces', which member state representatives perceive as a valuable aspect of these groups and participation at the IEA in general (IEA#1; IEA#3; IEA#7). These meetings are regarded as an important component. Also, meetings over 'wine and dinner' foster cooperation within the IEA.

> Ultimately the connections grow together and that actually fits very well when you meet three times a year so that you always come back to your own groups … . In this respect, it is always good to know who you can call on for individual questions and that is of course also very important in a crisis. (IEA#3)

By creating these different structures, the IEA has used different sources of legitimation that were able to speak to the contestation of exclusivity but at the same time reflect norm adoption towards the community. In this way, the IEA 'played a valuable role in bringing a group together' (IEA#2). But moreover, by speaking to the needs of different parts of the community, the IEA has managed successful behavioural- and institutional-level self-legitimation by adopting the collective aspect of the norm for CCA and being perceived as a 'valuable partner, one which is clearly extremely well placed in the global system' (IEA#2). Consequently, the IEA manifested its role in providing expertise for energy transition, and through this, acting on climate change.

Conclusion: Middle ground to act collectively on climate change

The IEA has been criticized for its exclusive 'club' membership of OECD countries only. The non-universal frame meant a neglect of including rising powers, such as India and China, that have greatly increased their energy consumption over time (Van de Graaf, 2012, 2013). Because of this exclusion, the IEA consequently lacked interlinked data access to the world's energy consumption. The contestation, which manifested even more through the creation of IRENA with universal membership, pointed towards a legitimacy gap in the IEA system. At the same time, it showed where the legitimation should come from. Thus, norm adoption was also a necessity regarding the aspect of CCA as collective endeavour.

To achieve this, the IEA opened the door and at the same time kept the 'Pandora's box' closed through a combination of discursive, behavioural and institutional legitimation. The IEA did not discard exclusive membership but included associated members in the dialogue and cooperation (IEA#7).

The IEA responded to this contestation via the association of non-OECD countries in 2015. In incorporating the reality of emerging powers in world politics, such as China and India, that are not only major energy consumers but moreover big greenhouse emitters, the IEA created an 'open door' policy to deepen the collaboration with now more than eight associated countries.[5] This fortification of cooperation contributed to the re-legitimation of the IEA as it found an effective way to bridge its exclusivity and at the same time did not have to discard its original framework.

In the next chapter, I will analyse the contestation–legitimation process of the IEA's oil-only approach. Similarly to the OECD-only membership, the contestation was in line with the aspects of the norm for CCA, especially regarding policy implementation. However, also here the IEA had two sources to legitimate, as they depend on each member state's concerns about energy security. On the one hand, the IEA legitimated by incorporating renewables in their energy portfolio. On the other hand, they kept their oil emergency security mechanism.

6

Frozen in Time: The International Energy Agency Moving Towards Climate Change Action

Here, I will examine the response of the International Energy Agency (IEA) to the contestation of its institutional format, the oil-only approach. Also, here in the process, the IEA could incorporate two ways to legitimate itself. First, I will examine the IEA's transition to incorporate an expertise change to renewable energy, by also widening its network to do so. This also led to the deepened recognition and reflection of the policy implementation aspect of the norm for CCA. Further, through developing close cooperation with other international organizations (IOs) in the intersected field, the IEA could reflect the adoption of the norm for CCA as collective endeavour. At the same time, the IEA kept its emergency oil response system, which at first sight speaks against the norm for climate action (CCA) but still benefits the IEA's legitimacy. This, like the Organisation for Economic Co-operation and Development (OECD)-only membership, is impacted by concerns over energy security. I will discuss this later. I will conclude by summarizing my findings. Figure 6.1 illustrates the different stages of the contestation–legitimation process and its aspects.

The contestation: 'frozen in time' without renewables

In 2009, the IEA and its institutional format did not reflect the reality of energy politics and the wider global climate regime. The worldwide energy consumption and threats from climate change demanded both action for further development and incorporation of other energy sources, especially renewables. The IEA seemed to be 'structurally frozen in time' (Colgan et al, 2012, p 126). In 2009, the claim of the IEA contesters was that 'for renewable energy there is no international governmental organization that focuses on

Figure 6.1: IEA: Process of oil-only approach

Guiding frame
'Norm for climate change action'
Standard of appropriate behaviour

Institutional format

Contestation

Oil-only approach

Contestation: Challenge
- Contesting the IEA's institutional format of the oil-only approach
- Struggle over legitimacy: neglecting new developments in energy realm and reality of climate change
- Indicating **legitimacy gap:** IEA 'blind' expertise
- **Legitimation potential:** opportunity to reorientate towards renewable energy source, energy transition and through this to CCA

↓

Legitimation practices
Background: creation of IRENA

Practices: IEA
- *Incorporating renewable energy expertise (behavioural and institutional legitimation)*
- *Vocal leadership on promoting energy transition and CCA (discursive legitimation)*
- *Expanding network and cooperation on energy and climate change (behavioural legitimation)*
- *Recruiting renewable energy staff (behavioural legitimation)*
- *Keeping raison d'être, emergency oil response system as a solidarity system for member states (institutional legitimation)*

CCA norm and practices:
- *Norm adoption or norm is already adopted:*
  Norm not yet adopted, needs to be adopted
- *Explicit/implicit reference to core aspects of norm in the practices: including renewable energy sources, build expertise*
- *Practices are markers to core aspects of the norm: adapt, transform, renewables, energy transition, climate change*

---

the global mobilization of renewable energy in a way that is increasingly urgent' (Scheer, 2008). The contestation by three IEA members, Spain, Denmark and Germany, which saw the costs of creating a new organization rather than reforming the existing one as being more effective, perceived the IEA as not the 'appropriate venue for reform at the time' (Van de Graaf and Lesage, 2009, p 303; Van de Graaf, 2012).

Hermann Scheer, for example, who as part of the German Parliament at the time was an advocate of renewable energy development and one of the driving forces in the creation of International Renewable Energy Agency (IRENA), criticized the IEA for leaving 'no stone unturned when it comes to emphasizing the long-term indispensability of nuclear and fossil energy' (Scheer, 2007, p 174; Van de Graaf, 2012, p 237; see also IEA#13). In his 2008 speech in the German Bundestag he promoted and justified his ambition for creating a counter institution:

> The fact to date is: for renewable energy there is no international governmental organization that focuses on the global mobilization of renewable energy in a way that is increasingly urgent. Today it is undisputed worldwide that there is no way around renewable energies on a large scale and ultimately to cover all energy needs. ...
>
> So, we not only have legitimacy and credibility based on our own work to take the initiative for the creation of IRENA, but also an ethically based international duty to act. ... But the objection was always the same, without an existing international forum ever taking on renewable energies in the form it deserves.
>
> This review proves that there is no alternative to IRENA. ... What is happening here is a big step, the global significance of which for overcoming energy problems may still be underestimated by many today, just as renewable energies were underestimated 30 years ago. (Scheer, 2008)

The creation of IRENA, which catered to the demand of IEA members to have energy cooperation on renewable energy, manifests in the contestation of the IEA's oil-only approach. The contestation was thus aligned with the norm for CCA regarding its aspect of policy implementation, which is necessary for a successful energy transition to act on climate change. Creating a counter organization that caters better to the demands of the member states and outclasses the IEA in representing the international realm of energy (Van de Graaf, 2012) had the risk of all IEA members moving over to IRENA and neglecting the IEA. Further, contestation by member states themselves is crucial since, as in the case of the IEA, they are the main actors responsible for funding and recognizing the organization's legitimacy. As the IEA is a member-driven organization and their main task is to deliver to the energy-related needs of their members, contestation by member states is a serious rupture that can cause a severe legitimacy crisis that can even lead to IO death. The contestation of policy implementation had serious potential for threatening the overall existence.

The universal mandate on energy and renewables that was constituted in IRENA represents the legitimacy belief in CCA as collective endeavour of most of the community. The community believed that finding ways to act on climate change through energy transition was necessary and adopted this as an appropriate standard of behaviour. Their creation of IRENA contesting the IEA was thus framed by the norm for CCA as a guiding frame. The contestation made clear that the behaviour must reflect the community's legitimacy belief. The indication of the legitimacy gap of the IEA's then 'blind' expertise shows the clear legitimacy belief of the community in CCA and the need for policies that reflect this norm.

Also, beyond member states, other parts of the community, such as practitioners and academics alike, brought forward a similar criticism (see, for example, Aleklett et al, 2010), especially on the IEA's conservative projections in its yearly report, the World Energy Outlook (WEO). For example, the United Nations Framework Convention on Climate Change (UNFCCC) pushed the IEA to engage beyond oil and to take 'a stronger climate perspective' (IEA#2).

> for a long time, they were a little bit stuck in a business-as-usual-type scenario, when there's a wonderful chance of IEA projections of how far renewable energy, ... wind or solar will develop, and then you see the next year ... that the projections have totally changed because reality has gone much faster than they were seeing. And I think many of us over the years have engaged with the IEA to try and bring them [to the point that] they are now thinking about true transformation scenarios ... and even starting to talk about 1.5 degrees, which I think has been difficult for them. But it's starting to come through. For a long time their climate action scenarios were still taking us above 2 degrees, so I think a lot of the debate that many of us have had with the IEA has been ... very useful. (IEA#2)

The struggle for legitimacy came from this neglect of new developments in the energy realm. The contestation pointing towards the legitimacy gap of missing policies for implementation of a timely energy transition to tackle climate change was also the case in the contestation–legitimation process of the IEA oil-only approach. And it also shows that transforming the IEA's institutional format was the (only) answer to fill this gap. Here, the legitimation potential was to re-orientate towards a renewable energy source and through this adopt the norm for CCA to successfully enforce energy transition in practice to tackle climate change, which will be discussed in the next section.

Legitimation: including renewable energy expertise

After the creation of IRENA, the IEA itself had not adopted the norm for CCA. Therefore, to be aligned with its community, the IEA needed to move towards a norm adoption that would be reflected in a policy that speaks to the implementation of the norm. It was thus necessary to legitimate to reflect the community's legitimacy belief, and, moreover, reflect this belief in practice. The IEA needed to satisfy members and gain relevance in the energy field. After a period of reluctance from the early 2000s to 2009 against opening to the emergence of renewable energy resources and the reality of climate change, the IEA initiated modernization to embrace and overcome these challenges (Heubaum and Biermann, 2015). The IEA re-oriented towards renewable energy sources, energy transition and through this to CCA by incorporating renewable energy expertise in different ways. These legitimation practices included the incorporation of renewable energy expertise (behavioural and institutional legitimation) and recruiting renewable energy staff (behavioural legitimation). Further, the IEA expanded its network and cooperation on energy and climate change (behavioural legitimation). Similarly, to the association of non-OECD countries IEA leadership was very vocal and promoted energy transition and climate change action (discursive legitimation).

By responding with this transition to incorporate an expertise change on renewables, the IEA could legitimate itself after the contestation. Now the IEA is perceived as an important knowledge producer, provider and adviser for renewable energy. Further, the IEA widened its network to do so (IEA#2; IEA#7). Since 2009, the IEA leadership has fortified the addition of expertise on the different layers of energy resources, technologies, consumption and prospects to this key competence. The IEA leadership has been very vocal on promoting energy transition and stressing the need to act on climate change. Also, the IEA has developed close cooperation with other international organizations in the intersected field, such as the UNFCCC and even with its competitor IRENA (Heubaum and Biermann, 2015; IEA#2) to exchange expertise. Here, especially with the UNFCCC, the cooperation is based on reciprocal exchange and consultation of expertise on data analysis, regarding issues such as energy efficiency and transformation, but also technology issues, climate change and collaborating on bringing state actors together in several fora (IEA#2).

Besides being pushed by the UNFCCC to move towards climate action, the IEA could benefit the UNFCCC as a 'valuable partner' in assisting and advising on technological and analytical questions, especially on compiling the Paris Agreement (IEA#2). When constructing the Paris Agreement particularly, the IEA assisted the UNFCCC as a technical expert. The IEA contributed 'intellectual backing to informal work' and provided 'technical solutions', and continued to do so beyond 2015, for example for further tailoring Article 6 of the Paris agreement (IEA#2). The IEA benefits from the UNFCCC's expertise on climate change, especially regarding CO_2 emission and the so-called 'carbon budget' it assesses, which the IEA needs to incorporate into their analysis (IEA#9). Further, they have a 'memorandum of understanding on coorporation' and a joint database on policies and measures of countries that both organizations maintain together (Heubaum and Biermann, 2015, p 234; IEA#9).

Moreover, the IEA and OECD initiated the Climate Change Expert Group that gives technical input to the UNFCCC process separately to the climate conferences, in which representatives from governments, industry and civil society meet twice a year (Heubaum and Biermann, 2015, p 234).

I remember being in the meeting in Brussels and then Fatih Birol came into the next session and was taking part in a debate with the ministers around the table around the energy transition, which is needed, that type of action, for the mobilization … with other players. I think the Green Climate Fund was there, and a number of other actors, while the IEA was one of the organizations, and it was invited to debate and to engage directly with ministers on that occasion. (IEA#2)

The IEA further widened its network in 2012 by signing 'an official partnership agreement, targeting the development and publication of the IEA/IRENA Global Renewable Energy Policies and Measures Database in technology and innovation, and the sharing of renewable energy statistics' (Heubaum and Biermann, 2015, p 234). Since then, the IEA and IRENA have had a reciprocal relationship, engaging in workshops and technology briefs. Through this collaborative approach, rather than falling into competitive hostility entirely, the IEA could overcome the contestation from the creation of IRENA and even benefit from it (Heubaum and Biermann, 2015). The IEA and IRENA also have a joint database of renewable energy policies and measures. Regarding statistics, the IEA is also a co-founder of the Joint Organisations Data Initiative (JODI), working alongside Asia-Pacific Economic Cooperation (APEC), the Statistical Office of the European Communities (EUROSTAT), the Gas Exporting Countries Forum (GECF), the Latin American Energy Organization (OLADE), the United Nations Statistics Division (UNSD), OPEC and the International Energy Forum (IEF).

Moreover, the IEA has a strong presence in formal political forums, such as the G7 and G20 (IEA#4; IEA#5; IEA#6; IEA#7), being consulted for energy-related issues. Further, on regional levels, the IEA also works with organizations such as the Asian Development Bank (ADB), the Association of Southeast Asian Nations (ASEAN), the Asia Pacific Economic Cooperation (APEC) forum and the African Union (AU) to promote regional energy cooperation (IEA, nd [f]). By enforcing this collective action in a way that fits the IEA's (legal) structure when incorporating renewables, the organization moved towards adopting the norm for CCA. Also, regarding the cooperation with the associated non-OECD countries, the IEA stressed 'work[ing] together on areas of mutual interest, including: … energy efficiency and renewable energy' (IEA, 2013). This cooperation speaks to the collective endeavour aspect of the norm for CCA.

Further, the incorporation of renewables speaks to the aspect of policy implementation of CCA. After the dawning legitimacy crisis with the creation of IRENA, the IEA leadership followed up on its shortcoming by adding expertise on renewable energy, technologies, and consumption. This also led to deepened recognition, incorporation, and relevant analysis of climate action. The IEA structured its modernization under three pillars: 'strengthening and broadening the IEA's commitment to energy security beyond oil, to natural gas and electricity; deepening the IEA's engagement with major emerging economies; and providing a greater focus on clean energy technology, including energy efficiency' (IEA, nd [a]).

Also, here, the current executive director Fatih Birol has played a special role since coming into office as the IEA director in 2015 (IEA#2; IEA#3). In 2015, Fatih Birol was no stranger to IEA members, as he previously worked at the IEA as chief economist and was known to be very 'knowledgeable' (IEA#9). He was not only key in emphasizing the cooperation with other international organizations in the intersected field, for example, as mentioned, with IRENA and the UNFCCC to exchange expertise (Heubaum and Biermann, 2015; IEA#2). But he has also had a strong discursive public engagement on social media, speaking out for working towards energy transition and acting on climate change. Here, he presents the IEA's expertise as an essential component in this regard, moreover underlining international cooperation even beyond the OECD members (IEA#2; IEA#3; IEA#4; IEA#5; IEA#6; IEA#7). There has been a 'cultural change', in which the IEA shifted to reflect the emerging reality of climate change, moving away from fossil fuels only (IEA#2; IEA#7), which marks the adoption of the norm for CCA.

Considering COP21 in 2015 when the Paris Agreement was ratified, the IEA itself acknowledged this need for a 'cultural change' and its responsibility for a successful energy transition to act on consequential climate change. For example, in the 2016 Insights report 'Energy, Climate Change and Environment', Birol stated in the report's foreword that:

> [g]reater ambition than is embodied in the NDCs is quickly needed to achieve the aims of Paris, and the Agreement itself provides a framework for increasingly ambitious measures. Stronger action beyond the level conveyed in the NDCs is realistic, cost-effective and essential – and is needed to achieve even a 2 °C goal, let alone the well-below-2 °C ambition of the Paris Agreement. ... As we advance further into a post-COP21 reality, the gap between the goals of the Paris Agreement and efforts on the ground looms large. Actions to both achieve and surpass the NDCs will require a sophisticated, detailed analysis of key policy areas, which can help break the overarching task down into manageable pieces. ... Transformation of the energy sector will play an outsized role in accomplishing this, as energy is the primary contributor to planet-warming gases, but with the energy transition also holding the key to a cleaner and more secure energy future. (Birol in IEA, 2016a, p 3)

Further, the report stresses that climate change 'poses clear challenges for the energy sector' and 'a serious threat to energy security', and demonstrates the need to 'enhance adaptive capacity, strengthen resilience, and reduce vulnerability' (IEA, 2016a, p 85). That year, the IEA moved towards COP22 with the motto: 'We can't act on climate change without acting on energy #COP22' (IEA, 2016b). Discursively embracing the responsibility to act on climate change and by incorporating renewables into their policy portfolio but also through collective cooperation, the IEA translated both aspects of the norm for CCA into practice. This way, the IEA could reflect this norm adoption to the community, which demanded this change with their impactful contestation that manifested in the creation of IRENA.

In practice, to succeed in this turnaround, and to be able to deliver this expertise, the IEA, on the one hand, expanded their staff in all other divisions except oil (Heubaum and Biermann, 2015; IEA#9). The division of renewable energy rose from five to 20-plus staff members (IEA#9). 'And also, if you look at the number of people at the IEA, it grew, doubled over the last 10 years or so. [The] number of people that are working on oil emergency is still the same' (IEA#9). In 2015, Heubaum and Biermann observed this 'high staff turnover' in their research, which brought in 'in-house expertise' of younger experts that have been more exposed to the connection of climate policies and energy policy-making (2015, p 233).

On the other hand, the IEA adapted towards more financial independence by initiating the sale of data and the aspect of voluntary contributions to the IEA budget. Since the mandatory contributions of IEA members have not been adapted since 2009 (IEA#9), in the early 2010s, the IEA's budget remained an Achilles' heel as it had not grown in previous years despite the rising demand for incorporating diverse energy analyses (Van de Graaf, 2012, p 238). Despite selling data next to the IEA's free publications, the voluntary contribution is not only a tool for the IEA to be able to deliver on their expert analysis but is also a sign of the legitimacy perception through this material recognition by member countries, non-member countries and companies alike.

> That is a kind of recognition, I think, of how countries and companies value our ... they like what we're doing. I think additional research, so easy access is important, additional work on climate change is important, additional work on helping India or China or South Africa is important, so they give money for those specific projects and then we are able to deliver on that. (IEA#9)

More than 10 years after IRENA's creation, and through the start of the modernization in 2015 to legitimate itself, the IEA is widely perceived as 'expert' (IEA#4; IEA#5; IEA#6; IEA#7; IEA#10). It shifted from an 'oil piling organization to a general energy organization and really a think tank' (IEA#6). In embracing diverse energy expertise,

> [the IEA guides] research on specific issues, day-to-day business is being done within the agency, so the experts of the agency do modelling, the experts of the agency gather data and make analysis, it helps experts in their discussion. ... second one is that to change from an oil and energy security organization into a more general energy think tank, [and] to move on the discussion in the 70s about oil security through gas security and now more and more about clients[1] and energy and how to live up to the goals of the Paris agreement. ... so, they're helping administrations, they're helping governments, they're helping businesses in their daily practice. (IEA#4)

Members perceive the IEA as being expert in giving out 'undisputed high-quality data, in-depth reviews [and] thematic reviews' (IEA#5) and 'the world's most authoritative and comprehensive source of global energy data' (IEA, nd [g]). Further, it is seen as 'a valuable partner, one that is clearly extremely well placed in the global system because climate policy in the end requires fundamental transformation of energy systems and ... that expertise they have has been valuable' (IEA#2). These perceptions further show the successful adoption of the norm for CCA. The IEA was able to incorporate the adoption in practice, which reflected the norm to their members and the wider community.

Thus, the IEA could not only transform in response to the contestation of its oil-only approach but moreover re-legitimate itself. The IEA adopted what the relevant community perceived as necessary and legitimate, namely finding ways of implementing measures towards energy transition and acting on climate change. This way, the norm for CCA guided this self-legitimating transformation of the IEA. The contestation, therefore, was followed by self-legitimation, with which the IEA could overcome its phase of a dawning legitimacy crisis. However, the IEA did not entirely discard its raison d'être energy security organization. The IEA kept its emergency oil response system as this turned out to be a necessary component for their members and thus remained a source of legitimacy. This will be discussed in the next section, also regarding the norm for CCA.

Legitimation: keeping the 'raison d'être'

The IEA's narrow focus on oil has been contested in the past, especially with the creation of IRENA. Considering the reality of climate change, finite energy resources, especially of oil, emerging sustainable resources and the demand for energy transition to act on climate change, the IEA was criticized for its conservative projections and its focus on oil. As shown in the previous section, the IEA responded to this contestation by expanding on its analysis and expertise on the variety of existing and developing energy resources. However, despite the rising importance of renewables, the consumption of oil is still widespread and at high levels around the globe and is thus perceived as a relevant source of energy (IEA#1; IEA#3; IEA#4; IEA#5; IEA#6; IEA#7).

This shows, for example, in the IEA's 2021 report that projects the global oil consumption to reach 104.1 mb/d (barrels per day), which is an increase of 4.4 mb/d from 2019 levels (IEA, 2021). This consequently translates into the remaining demand for oil. It also shows that the IEA's key competence of the emergency oil response system remains relevant, as it is a way of guaranteeing energy security (IEA#1). The emergency oil response system requires members to have 90 days' worth of oil stockpiling supplies, solidarity of oil-sharing among members, and to develop and update national oil security legislation, including regulations and a crisis response plan (IEA, 1974, 2018, 2020). The agency provides the framework for their member states and the link among the OECD countries to react to other future oil crises. In the following, I will show the prolonging perception that the necessity of the IEA's key competence of the emergency oil response system for energy security remains a source of legitimacy and a practice of institutional legitimation, although it speaks against the norm for CCA.

At first sight, keeping oil as a relevant source of energy and the emergency oil response system as a key competence speaks against the norm for CCA. Fossil fuels in general and related industry are responsible for high emissions of CO_2 and other greenhouse gases (see, for example, Frumhoff et al, 2015). However, as the IEA as an energy organization was found to cover an oil-related mandate for energy security, the IEA's history and the relation to its members give a path dependency to keep this component. Like the OECD-only membership clause, energy *security* and the experience of the 1974 oil crises bear concerns for future ruptures that would demand ways to remain resilient in an energy crisis.[2] It is a mechanism that will ensure solidarity in oil sharing and individual stockpile responses to these concerns over energy security and energy independence. The mechanism cannot guarantee but can foster a sense of security and trust when it comes to energy security issues. Thus, here too the IEA chose the middle ground by incorporating other energy sources in its expertise and promoting renewables but keeping its emergency oil response system that was its founding reason. Choosing this middle ground by including renewables next to fossil fuels was enough for the relevant community to reflect the adoption of the norm for CCA regarding its policy implementation aspect.

There have been discussions among member states as to whether there should be a re-designing of this system, which 'did not work out mainly because one … country refused to change something [but they] now have a new government so perhaps the discussion will be rekindled' (IEA#6).

Yet, although the scenarios of energy resources, distribution and use have changed, oil is still part of the contemporary reality of energy consumption and 'still plays a strong role ... because you can't estimate exactly, as it is already being done with the energy transition, but ... yes, you have to say, globally seen [oil] still plays an important role and you are dependent on certain regions of the world' (IEA#1). It is 'still a big share of our energy demand, especially for [Germany], so from our perspective for the next decades the crisis mechanism remains of utmost importance to have it and to involve other big countries in the oil market' (IEA#6).

Member states' representatives agree that the emergency oil response system therefore 'makes a lot of sense' (IEA#1), 'still [is] an important issue' (IEA#5), and 'as long as we have it, we can make use of it and we will have to make use of it if necessary ... . [It] started with the oil crisis but ... above all it is an energy security mechanism' (IEA#6). The IEA not only provides the frame for the emergency oil response system but is also responsible for monitoring the member states' compliance to oil stockpiling, their national oil security legislation, including regulations and their crisis response plan (IEA#1; IEA#3). Here, the IEA keeps continuous control over its members and the emergency oil response system. Not discarding its emergency oil response system but working ways around it that serve the perceptions and demands of the community and the legitimate norm by incorporating renewables into their portfolio reflects as legitimation after the contestation.

Conclusion: Finding the middle ground for energy expertise

By analysing the process after 2009, I showed how the IEA managed to legitimate itself as a 'valuable partner, one which is clearly extremely well placed in the global system' (IEA#2). Although the IEA is a member-driven organization that relies on the legitimation by its member states and its *international* responsibility to manage all issues on global energy, it is also dependent on the external perception and legitimation of state and non-state actors. The IEA's focus on oil did not reflect the changing realties of its member states and the demands of a changing world in the light of finite energy resources, such as coal and oil, and climate change. Also, here, the contestation involves two ways that the IEA could incorporate to legitimate.

On the one hand, the IEA legitimated on several levels: institutional, behavioural and discursive. The IEA started a vast transition to incorporate an expertise change for renewable energy and widened its network to do so. Since 2009, the IEA leadership has fortified the addition of this expertise on the different layers of energy resources, technologies, consumption and prospects. Further, the IEA has developed close cooperation with other international organizations in the intersected field, such as the UNFCCC, but also with its competitor IRENA (Heubaum and Biermann, 2015; IEA#2) to exchange expertise. Moreover, the IEA has a strong presence in formal political fora, such as the G7 and G20 (IEA#4; IEA#5, IEA#6; IEA#7), being consulted on energy-related issues.

On the other hand, the IEA did not discard its raison d'être expertise of the oil emergency response system. The IEA was founded as an energy organization to cover an oil-related mandate for energy security, like the OECD-only membership clause, energy security and the experience of the 1974 oil crises, which bear concerns of the IEA members over an energy crisis that would demand ways to remain resilient. IEA members still perceive this emergency system as necessary and as valuable too, not least due to the remaining importance of oil as an energy and production source (IEA#1, #8), despite acknowledging the importance of the energy transition to act on climate change. Also, here the IEA chose the middle ground by incorporating other energy sources in its expertise and promoting renewables and keeping its emergency oil response system. This middle ground was sufficient for the relevant community to reflect the adoption of the norm for CCA regarding its policy implementation aspect.

7

Comparing Cases: Climate Change Action Across the Climate–Energy Nexus

To answer this book's research question and show that climate change action (CCA) is the guiding norm in the processes analysed here, I conducted two case studies with two contestation–legitimation processes each. The previous chapters answered *How and why are IOs in the global climate regime able to self-legitimate despite contestation?*, while this chapter will deepen the answer to why contestation can be followed by (self-)legitimation and provide an analysis to deconstruct the guiding frame of the processes, the norm for CCA, further. Due to the objective, the refusing nature of contestation, we would expect rather negative consequences to this contestation, such as de-legitimation, which can even lead to a legitimacy crisis and pose an existential threat to IOs. However, in the previous analysis of the two cases, the United Nations Framework Convention on Climate Change (UNFCCC) and the International Energy Agency (IEA), I showed that the opposite can be the result, as here contestation was ultimately followed by legitimation. As I argue, this is conditioned by the guiding frame of the norm for CCA. This chapter provides empirical evidence from four contestation–legitimation processes in the global climate regime. In the following, I will compare these four processes, and I will be able to show why contestation can be followed by legitimation in the global climate regime and answer this book's research question.

The focus, to compare the UNFCCC's and the IEA's contestation–legitimation processes, will be twofold. On the one hand, I will order the cases by two bigger main issues in global climate governance that were contested. This way, the G77 walkout of the UNFCCC case and the IEA OECD-only membership can be allocated to the North–South divide in global climate governance. The other two processes, the US contestation of the Paris Agreement by former president Trump and the contestation of the

IEA's oil-only approach, are about the contestation and legitimation of an institutional format in the climate regime. When comparing the processes in this structure, it will be possible to clarify further which aspect of the norm becomes visible in the contestation and legitimation. As discussed previously, to show that the norm for CCA is the guiding frame of the contestation–legitimation processes, I argue that each process speaks to the core aspects of the norm. The core aspects of the norm for CCA relevant here are climate change action as a collective endeavour on the one hand, and climate change action as a guiding frame for policy implementation to achieve environmental goals, for instance the Paris Agreement or incorporation of renewables, on the other. Table 7.1 summarizes all the processes of the two cases and the status of adoption of the norm for CCA in the contestation and legitimation practices of processes per case and issue area.

To further carve out the norm and to show why contestation can be followed by legitimation in the global climate regime and answer the research question, I will compare the processes in regard to the norm adoption of the community in each process. To compare the cases, I will analyse at which stage of adoption the norm for CCA was in the processes. I will show that, in each process, the relevant majority of actors within a community had adopted the norm, as:

> [w]e only know what is appropriate by reference to the judgments of a community or society. We recognize norm-breaking behavior because it generates disapproval or stigma and norm-conforming behavior either because it produces praise or, in the case of a highly internalized norm, because it is so taken for granted that it provokes no reaction whatsoever. (Finnemore and Sikkink, 1998, p 892)

Norms are the key link to what is perceived as legitimate and guide the respective community. Contestation indicates a legitimacy gap that needs

Table 7.1: Norm for CCA in contestation and legitimation practices of processes by case and issue area

Issue	North–South divide		Institutional format			
IO	UNFCCC	IEA	UNFCCC		IEA	
Process/ Norm	G77 walkout	OECD-only membership	Trump contestation of Paris Agreement		Oil-only approach	
Norm for CCA Collective Endeavour, Policy Implementation	*Contestation* • aligned with norm	*Contestation* • aligned with norm	*Contestation* • against norm	*Legitimation* • reinforce adopted norm	*Contestation* • aligned with norm	*Legitimation* • adopt norm

to be filled by legitimation. Depending on who has adopted the norm, the contested party, which has not adopted the norm yet, needs to translate the norm into practice to reflect norm adoption to the community. Or the contester will be met with opposition if the contestation speaks against the adopted norm of the majority of the community. The two core aspects of the norm for CCA, the collective endeavour and policy implementation aspect, indicate the stage of norm adoption within the community.

This chapter proceeds as follows. To show that the norm for CCA is the guiding frame of the four processes I will start by comparing the processes that can be allocated to the North–South divide. Afterwards, I will move over to comparing the processes in which the institutional format was contested and legitimated. To successfully carve out the norm, I need to deconstruct these processes into their two main parts, which are the contestation and the legitimation. Here, I will also analyse the contestation and legitimation regarding the norm adoption within the community by deconstructing the practices to the core aspect of the norm. This way, I will be able to explain why contestation was followed by legitimation rather than the anticipated negative consequences due to the opposing nature of contestation, such as de-legitimation. I will summarize this chapter by reflecting on the norm for CCA and the implications of contestation–legitimation processes in the cases analysed here.

The norm for CCA and the North–South divide: contestation

Here, I will compare the contestations of the processes that can be allocated to the North–South divide. As I analyse the contestation and legitimation as an interlinked process, the framing norm can guide both the contestation and legitimation. The contestation of the G77 walkout and the contestation of the IEA OECD-only membership can be allocated to the North–South divide in global climate governance. The contestation by the G77 was due to the non-cooperative behaviour of Western parties in the negotiation of the loss and damage mechanism. This mechanism had been a long-time agenda item since 2010, since countries of the Global South are affected more by the consequences of climate change and the wealth required to sufficiently adapt and transition is unequally distributed. Thus, climate change demands collective action to bridge this divide along the lines of the Global North and South. The contestation of the IEA's OECD-only membership manifests along these global lines, since countries of the Global South were largely excluded, and the IEA did not represent international energy politics as its name implies.

In the case of the G77 walkout, over the years, the divide between the Global North and the G77, including other parties from the Global South, hardened and mistrust from the G77 towards Western parties manifested (Hermwille et al, 2017). The escalation of the walkout that contested this, in their perspective, non-solidaric behaviour of Western parties, indicated a legitimacy gap in the negotiation process on the loss and damage mechanism over the years. This legitimacy gap points towards the power play of Western states that speaks against the necessity of climate change to adapt and find solutions collectively to help out vulnerable countries that are more affected by climate change but do not have the means to adapt and transition on their own. The norm for CCA requires the community to collectively act against climate change. Thus, the contestation of the G77 parties in 2013 was in line with this aspect of the norm.

For the IEA, the contestation of their non-universal membership that manifested with the creation of International Renewable Energy Agency (IRENA) indicated the legitimacy gap in the IEA's system. The IEA was perceived as being biased along the North–South divide, with unfair procedures and performances (Zelli, 2018, p 178). The creation of an energy organization with universal membership that IEA members perceived as a more appropriate platform carried the risk of member withdrawal and IEA members investing in this new organization rather than in IEA reform (Van de Graaf and Lesage, 2009). By neglecting the inclusion of the rising powers and hence new major energy consumers, the IEA had a crucial lack of data access and representation. At the same time, the legitimation potential was in overcoming this lack of representation.

Like the G77 process, parts of the community of the IEA were contesters. However, in this case it was not a struggle over a negotiation item and a conflict between the negotiating member states but IEA member states that contested the organization itself. The universal mandate on energy and renewables that was constituted in IRENA represents the legitimacy belief in CCA as an appropriate standard as the collective endeavour of most of the community. Also, here, the community believed in abiding by the appropriate standard as necessary and their creation of IRENA contesting the IEA was framed by the norm for CCA as a guiding frame. The contestation made clear that the behaviour must reflect the community's legitimacy belief.

Also, in the G77 process, collective action was not only a wish but a processual requirement of the UNFCCC negotiations that decisions need to be made consensually. With their walkout, the G77 were contesting the non-solidarity behaviour of Western parties, which was contra to the aspect of CCA as a collective endeavour, and in this way made a consensual decision. The hardlining of many Western parties objecting 'to the creation of a new mechanism because of its political implications ... that loss and damage will imply blame or liability', or even 'culpability' (Busby, 2013), also reinforced the contestation of the G77 in regard to the aspect of policy implementation for CCA, as the contestation was precisely about the mechanism as a policy.

Without deciding on the loss and damage mechanism in Warsaw in 2013 after three previous Conferences of the Parties (COPs) that were unsuccessful in reaching consensus on this mechanism, COP19 could have potentially ended in a breakdown as COP15 did in 2009.

Further, there would have been no agreement that would guide and re-ensure policy implementation to assist developing countries that are particularly vulnerable to the effects of climate change and especially enhance '*action* and support, including finance, technology and capacity-building' (UN, nd [c]). The latter speaks to the crucial aspect of CCA that requires obligatory agreements about policy implementation for all parties. The contestation was thus in alignment with this aspect of the norm for CCA and indicated a legitimacy gap regarding the negotiation process on this particular mechanism. The legitimation potential here was clearly moving forward with the decision on the mechanism and reaching consensus on a just policy that would reflect the uneven effects climate change has on countries in the Global South. And that would also reflect the uneven distribution of means to tackle this issue to protect societies and prevent loss and damage.

Although the impacts that both contestations could have had within the respective processes differ, they do contain significant consequences for the processes and have the potential for de-legitimation as well as for a legitimacy crisis. For the G77 walkout, ending the conference in a breakdown due to a failure to reach consensus on the loss and damage mechanism, only four years after the legitimacy crisis of COP15 in Copenhagen, would have meant a repetition of this experience and potentially bringing the whole UNFCCC regime and global cooperation on climate change into question. The IEA, too, was brought into question with the contestation of the creation of IRENA, as the organization could not keep the promise suggested by its name to represent the *international* realm.

Both contestation–legitimation processes show that the norm had not been adopted by all parts of the community yet. The G77 walkout at COP19 shows that the norm for CCA had not been adopted by all parties and was overshadowed by the power play of the West before the contesting walkout proceeded. In 2013, the tipping point towards the legitimacy belief in CCA was reached. A major part of the community believed that abiding by the appropriate standard was necessary, and the norm for CCA guided the process to its turnaround. This can also be seen in the walkout of civil society as additional contestation in support of the G77 contestation. Through the contestation the norm cascaded. In this particular contestation–legitimation process, the legitimation potential of the breakdown after the G77 walkout was to bring forward and to decide on a just, differentiated agreement to collectively act on climate change. By consenting to the demands of the G77 and deciding on the loss and damage mechanism, Western parties adopted the idea that they would contribute according to their differentiated wealth for climate transition across the globe. In this way, the norm was finally reflected.

Missing norm adoption was also the case for the IEA. Similarly, to the contestation of the G77 walkout, contesting parties that created IRENA saw the need to have an energy organization that covers global energy consumers and accordingly have a universal membership contra to the IEA. Delivering successful energy monitoring and assistance to member states and helping them with their energy transition is a vital part of tackling climate change, and thus CCA. Due to its collective endeavour aspect, the IEA did not have the structures that spoke to this aspect of the norm. This means that the IEA was not in line with the norm at the time. The contestation of the IEA required the organization to bring forward an approach that would be in line with the norm. The collective aspect of CCA, in other words having 'everybody around the table' (IEA#2), was part of the contestation of the IEA non-OECD membership. The norm was at a similar stage in this process. Before it could cascade into adoption, the norm emerged from 2009 after the creation of IRENA until it was finally reflected in the ratification of the non-OECD country association in 2015.

To summarize, both contestation–legitimation processes show that the contestation was guided by the norm for CCA as the contestation spoke to the aspect of policy implementation (loss and damage), and especially the aspect of CCA as collective endeavour. CCA thus conditions the contestation and frames the overall contestation–legitimation processes. In the process of the G77 walkout, all parties needed to consent to a just and appropriate policy that would reflect collective action on climate change. For the IEA, collectively acting together on energy transition was a major part of implementing CCA and reaching implementation goals to fight climate change. The legitimation that followed the contestation in both processes will be discussed in the next section.

The norm for CCA and the North–South divide: legitimation

The contestation in the processes indicates a legitimacy gap in the contested target and this points to a legitimation potential. As the contestation–legitimation processes are framed by a specific guiding frame, I argue that the norm for CCA is guiding the processes analysed. This not only becomes visible in the contestations but also in the legitimation. Also here, aspects of the norm are addressed. In the following section, I will compare the legitimation within the process and highlight the aspects of CCA and show that it is the guiding norm of the whole process and not only within either the contestation or legitimation.

In the case of the G77 walkout, reaching consensus on the loss and damage mechanism was necessary to not only bring COP19 back on track but also to not repeat the breakdown of COP15 in 2009 in Copenhagen and the legitimacy crisis thereafter (see, for example, Walker and Biedenkopf, 2020). When deconstructing the legitimation in the process of the G77 walkout, the aspects of collective action and policy implementation become visible. The legitimation engagement of the UNFCCC reflects these aspects of the norm since reaching consensus on the policy of loss and damage was the mandatory result of the negotiation. This (re-)legitimation of the negotiations at COP19 was not only necessary to bring the process back on track but moreover reflects the legitimacy belief of the UNFCCC in line with the G77 contestation, which was aligned with the norm for CCA. The UNFCCC's perception of CCA as an appropriate standard and norm guides the legitimation as it frames the process.

As elaborated in Chapter 3, the UNFCCC has been key in pushing the norm for CCA in the global climate regime and is a promotor of the norm. The UNFCCC is intrinsically motivated by this effort towards CCA, which explains their legitimation response after the G77 contestation to move parties forward towards consensus in favour of global climate change action. The decision on the loss and damage mechanism and the need to re-legitimate the negotiation process to reach consensus was a necessary means that would not only reflect the legitimacy belief in the norm for CCA but the adoption of the norm by all parts of the community. In response to the G77 contestation, the UNFCCC engaged in several informal but also formal practices that involved discursive and behavioural legitimation, such as mediation. The re-engagement with the contesters, but also the contested counterpart, mediated these parties towards reaching consensus on the loss and damage mechanism that reflects the policy implementation aspect of CCA and as a mechanism for a just, collective policy to act on climate change, which speaks to the aspect of CCA as collective endeavour.

In contrast to this, the IEA itself was contested by a part of the community as the IEA had not adopted the norm yet. To legitimate and to not run into a severe legitimacy crisis and cease to exist, the legitimation demanded norm adoption and practices that reflect the norm and its aspects. As outlined in Chapter 5, the association was a way to find middle ground between universal and the OECD-only membership. The IEA opened the door and at the same time kept the 'Pandora's box' closed by not discarding exclusive membership but including associated members in the dialogue and cooperation (IEA#7). By finding a tool to embrace a collectivism and cooperate with non-OECD members, and further, by expanding its network to work on the renewable energy expertise and related output and cooperating with other organizations, for example, the UNFCCC and IRENA, the IEA not only underlined its liability and expertise in the diverse energy field, but also, through this, the IEA could enforce legitimation, as working together on energy transition expertise speaks to the collective aspect of the norm to act on climate change. By enforcing collective action in a way that fits the IEA's (legal) structure, the organization moved towards adopting the norm for CCA.

To summarize, both processes show that the legitimation engagement following the contestation speaks to the norm for CCA and reflects an adoption of the norm. Both the UNFCCC and the IEA-related community share the understanding that to successfully act on climate change, action needs to be taken collectively since it is a global issue that affects everyone. The legitimation of the processes discussed here differs regarding whether the norm for CCA had already been adopted and by whom. Also, the differences lie in who from the community contested and which target was contested. This also has consequences for who engaged in legitimation and in what way. In the next section, I will compare the contestations of the processes in which the institutional format was contested. For the UNFCCC, this is the US contestation by president Trump of the Paris Agreement. For the IEA, it is the contestation of its oil-only approach that manifested in the creation of IRENA.

The norm for CCA and the institutional format: contestation

In the following, I will compare the contestations of the processes in which the institutional format was contested. For the UNFCCC, the institutional format of the Paris Agreement was contested by US president Trump. In line with his protectionism and isolationism contra multilateralist cooperation, Trump's contestation spoke out against the 'unfair' procedures of the Paris Agreement and against collectively acting on climate change (UNFCCC#6; see also Betsill, 2017; Bomberg, 2017). He claimed that the Paris Agreement would handicap the US for the benefit of the other parties of the agreement and the wider community. In contrast to the US contestation, the IEA was contested for its oil-only approach and missing institutional format that would reflect the implementation of a timely energy transition to tackle climate change. This contestation manifested in the creation of IRENA in 2009 initiated by three IEA member states.

With his contestation of the Paris Agreement, Trump refused to further implement this agreement, which spoke against the norm for CCA that is embodied in the Paris Agreement. As mentioned in the previous chapters, due to the dual quality of norms as a stable and flexible guiding frame, I argue, it is also possible to carve out the guiding norm of a process if the contestation speaks against the community norm. Allegedly, they wanted 'to gain wealth' at the US's expense, which speaks out against the aspect of CCA as a collective endeavour. At the same time, this aspect of collectively acting on climate change is a clear condition of the contestation claim and thus is one aspect of the norm that guides this contestation–legitimation process.

From the protectionist perspective of US president Trump, the collective aspect and the policy aspect of the norm for CCA are a legitimacy gap in the Paris Agreement and the UNFCCC-facilitated regime. From this perspective, the constitution of the agreement puts the US at a disadvantage with unjust, unequal treatment compared to the other parties and hence is perceived as illegitimate. However, most of the community had adopted the norm when Trump contested the agreement in 2017. Like the other processes, the community played a significant role in this contestation–legitimation process. The legitimation potential lay in the reinforcement of and recommitment to the Paris Agreement and acting collectively on climate change.

Contrary to this, the manifestation of the contestation of the IEA's institutional format showed that the IEA did not reflect the demand of the community to incorporate the global energy reality at the time as well as the rising demand for renewable energy (Van de Graaf, 2012). The contestation against the IEA's oil-only approach also demanded a policy transition towards CCA. The contestation also revealed that the oil-only approach was a significant legitimacy gap in the institutional structure of the IEA. The struggle for legitimacy came from this neglect of new developments in the energy realm. In 2009, the claim of the IEA contesters was that 'for renewable energy there is no international governmental organization that focuses on the global mobilization of renewable energy in a way that is increasingly urgent' (Scheer, 2008). This contestation was thus aligned with the norm for CCA regarding its aspect of policy implementation, which is necessary for successful energy transition to act on climate change.

As the IEA is a member-driven organization and its main task is to meet the energy-related needs of its members, contestation by member states is a serious rupture that can cause a severe legitimacy crisis that can become an existential threat. The wider community, and, among this, the IEA member states that contested the IEA believed in abiding by the appropriate standard as necessary. The norm for CCA determines this standard, and IEA members saw that the IEA was not reflecting the norm. The indication of the legitimacy gap of the IEA's then 'blind' expertise shows the clear legitimacy belief of the community in CCA and the need for policies that reflect this norm. And it also shows that the transformation of the IEA's institutional format structure and move towards norm adoption was the answer to fill this gap. Here, the legitimation potential was to re-orientate towards a renewable energy source and through this adopt the norm for CCA to successfully enforce energy transition in practice to tackle climate change. Before the norm could be adopted, the modernization of the IEA towards renewables in 2015 from the contestation in 2009 after the creation of IRENA needed to be proceeded.

In contrast to the IEA, in the case of the US contestation of the Paris Agreement the policy already existed. Again here, like the aspect of CCA as collective endeavour, the contestation of Trump also spoke against the policy implementation aspect of the norm. While from the UNFCCC side the contestation was expected at the time, it was acknowledged that it was a crucial moment of contestation that needed to be taken seriously. By indicating that a legitimacy gap in the Paris Agreement was unfair to the US and declaring global warming a 'hoax' (Cheung, 2020), the Trump contestation was crucial as the US remained a major power. Also, like the case of the IEA contestation of the oil-only approach, member states' support of the organization's policy structure and regime is one of the most important components to stay legitimate. Also here, a legitimacy struggle, for example in the form of withdrawal by other member states, needed to be prevented. Yet, in contrast to the case of the IEA's oil-only approach, the agreement that reflected the norm for CCA already existed and was adopted in the community, including the UNFCCC. Thus, the legitimation potential lay in reinforcing the legitimacy belief in the importance of the Paris Agreement that embodies the norm for CCA.

Responding to a major power's contestation requires addressing the indicated legitimacy gap and engaging in legitimation practices. To stop a lingering persuasion by this contestation of other members that have a similar populist position to Trump and to prevent other member states from withdrawing, it was necessary to reinforce the legitimacy belief in CCA and insist that the behaviour must reflect this belief in the community. This can be observed in the extensive legitimation engagement in the process. For the IEA, the contestation was existential and thus needed to be responded to with the expected, appropriate behaviour and legitimation.

To summarize, the contestation of the institutional format could have had great potential for leading both the UNFCCC and the IEA into de-legitimation as well as a legitimacy crisis. Especially for the IEA, the contestation had high potential for threatening the overall existence of the organization as member states are the main drivers of the organization. Creating a counter organization that caters better to the demands of the member states and outclasses the IEA in representing the international realm of energy (Van de Graaf, 2012) bore the risk of all IEA members moving over to IRENA and neglecting the IEA.

For the UNFCCC, as the Paris Agreement is their flagship, the contestation of this main policy by a major power can result in de-legitimation (UNFCCC#2; UNFCCC#6; see also Jotzo et al, 2018). However, here, the community had already adopted the norm for CCA that the Paris Agreement embodies. Thus, breaking this legitimacy belief in the policy of CCA was a rather unlikely turn in the process. CCA thus conditions the contestation and frames the overall contestation–legitimation processes. In the next section, I will analyse the legitimation of both processes.

The norm for CCA and the institutional format: legitimation

The contestation in the processes indicates a legitimacy gap of the contested target and points to a legitimation potential. As the contestation–legitimation processes are framed by a specific guiding frame, the norm, this potential is in line with this guiding norm. As I argue, that CCA is the guiding norm of the processes analysed here. This becomes visible not only in the contestations but also in the legitimation. Also here, the aspects of the norm are addressed. In the following section, I will analyse the legitimation within the process to highlight the aspects of the norm and show that CCA is the guiding norm of the whole process and not only within either the contestation or legitimation.

When deconstructing the legitimation practices in the process after the US contestation of the institutional format, the Paris Agreement, the collective endeavour aspect of the norm for CCA can be observed in three ways (Betsill, 2017, p 190; UNFCCC#1; UNFCCC#4; UNFCCC#6). First, the UNFCCC itself engaged in legitimation by its non-state actor orchestration, especially from 2015. After the Trump contestation in 2017, the UNFCCC benefited from this network with which the UNFCCC enlarged the relevant community for CCA. Second, in 2017, this network was particularly influential in the legitimation after the contestation. As discussed in Chapter 4, especially US sub- and non-state actor-initiated events, movements, and coalitions, such as 'We're still in', engaged in legitimation (Betsill, 2017, p 190; UNFCCC#1; UNFCCC#4; UNFCCC#6). This was not only collective building, but moreover within building these groups and at their events it was stressed that the importance of the Paris Agreement and its implementation can only be successful when all global actors act collectively. Collective action, therefore, is part of the legitimacy belief of this community.

Third, member states, sub- and non-state actors, especially from the US, adopted an explicit and open opposition stance contra the Trump contestation. Further, they praised the Paris Agreement and displayed their belief in this policy implementation agreement for the norm for CCA as legitimate and the 'only global answer to climate change' (UNFCCC#5). By praising the Paris Agreement and initiating support in various ways for the implementation of the agreement, the legitimating actors underlined the collective aspect of CCA in a united collective themselves and opposed Trump. The legitimation engagement was also aligned with the policy implementation of the norm for CCA.

In contrast to this, as mentioned earlier for the case of the IEA, the IEA itself was still outside of the norm for CCA community, which contrasts with the UNFCCC processes. Thus, the IEA needed to move towards a norm adoption that would be reflected in a policy that would speak to the implementation of the norm. It was thus necessary to legitimate to reflect the community's legitimacy belief and, moreover, reflect this belief in practice. The IEA needed to satisfy members and gain back relevance in the energy field. Thus, the IEA had to legitimate its institutional format through transformation to reflect norm adoption to the community.

In 2015, the IEA re-orientated towards renewable energy, energy transition and through this to CCA by incorporating renewable energy expertise in different ways. To incorporate this expertise change, the IEA not only hired new staff, but developed close cooperation with other international organizations in the intersected field, such as the UNFCCC and even with its competitor IRENA, and moreover enforced international cooperation beyond the OECD members (Heubaum and Biermann, 2015; IEA#2). This was not necessary for the UNFCCC when Trump contested the Paris Agreement. In this case, he was the outsider to what the community perceived as an appropriate standard and legitimate behaviour. Accordingly, the UNFCCC could remain in the background. Contrarily, the IEA had to put in effort to reflect norm adoption in practice. Thus, the IEA leadership was very engaged in not only institutionally but also discursively legitimating itself by being very vocal in promoting energy transition and stressing the need to act on climate change.

To summarize, both processes show that the legitimation engagement following the contestation speaks to the norm for CCA and reflect an adoption of the norm. Both the UNFCCC and the IEA-related community share the understanding that to successfully act on climate change, action needs to be taken collectively since it is a global issue that affects everyone. The legitimation of the processes discussed here differs regarding whether the norm for CCA had already been adopted and by whom. The aspects of the policy implementation and CCA as collective endeavour become visible in the legitimation engagement of the two processes. CCA thus guides the legitimation and frames the overall contestation–legitimation processes. The different kinds of legitimation were necessary after the contestations to avoid de-legitimation and a legitimacy crisis for the UNFCCC and IEA.

Discussion: the norm for climate change action in contestation–legitimation processes of the UNFCCC and the IEA

For the case of the UNFCCC, I analysed the G77 walkout and the US contestation of the Paris Agreement, and for the IEA, the contestations of the OECD-only membership and the oil-only approach that manifested in the creation of the counter organization IRENA. I allocated these processes to two of the main issues in the global climate regime, namely the North–South divide and the institutional formats in climate governance. The G77 walkout and the IEA's OECD-only membership are issues along the North–South divide, while the US contestation of the Paris Agreement and the IEA's oil-only approach were processes about the IO's institutional format. By deconstructing the processes to carve out the guiding norm for CCA, I examined each process regarding the core aspects of the norm. The core aspects of the norm for CCA relevant here are the collective endeavour aspect on the one hand, and the policy implementation aspect to achieve environmental goals, for instance, the Paris Agreement or incorporation of renewables, on the other.

In the processes that can be allocated to the North–South divide, especially the collective endeavour aspect becomes visible. In the processes of the G77 walkout and the IEA OECD-only membership, parts of the community were contesters. For the G77 walkout, the contestation was due to the negotiation on the loss and damage mechanism and conflict among the negotiating member states. For the IEA, IEA member states contested the organization itself and its neither universal membership nor universal mandate on energy that led to the creation of IRENA. Through IRENA, most of the community could channel their legitimacy belief in CCA as an appropriate standard and as collective endeavour. Table 7.2 summarizes the contestation and legitimation practices by case and major key issue in global climate governance, the North–South divide.

For these processes the contestations manifested that the behaviour must reflect the community's legitimacy belief. The G77 contestation claim spoke to the need for a policy that would reflect and enable the implementation of CCA. The UNFCCC's legitimation response after the G77 contestation aimed to move parties forward to consensus aligned with global climate change action. Yet, in this case, the IEA itself was still outside of the norm for CCA community, which contrasts with the UNFCCC processes. Thus, the IEA needed to move towards norm adoption to legitimate to reflect the community's legitimacy belief and, moreover, reflect this belief in practice.

In the process of the US contestation of the Paris Agreement, Trump's contestation claimed that the institutional format, the Paris Agreement, would handicap the US for the benefit of the other parties of the agreement and the wider community, which speaks out against the aspect of CCA as collective endeavour. At the same time, the aspect of collectively acting on climate change is a clear condition of the contestation claim and thus is one aspect of the norm that triggered and guides this contestation–legitimation process. The contestation against the IEA's oil-only approach also demanded a policy transition towards CCA as the IEA itself was still outside of the

Table 7.2: Summary of contestation and legitimation practices by case and major key issue in global climate governance, North–South divide

Issue/IO	UNFCCC		IEA	
North–South divide	G77 walkout		OECD-only membership	
	Contestation	*Legitimation UNFCCC*	*Contestation*	*Legitimation IEA*
	G77	• Moderating, conflict-solving communication *(discursive legitimation)*	**Member states**	• Association of non-OECD members *(behavioural and institutional legitimation)*
	• Walkout *(behavioural contestation)*		• Open, vocal criticism *(discursive contestation)*	
	• Protest *(behavioural contestation)*	• Informal practices of fostering trust *(behavioural legitimation)*	• Creating counter institution *(institutional contestation)*	• Initiative leadership *(behavioural legitimation)*
	• Open, vocal criticism *(discursive contestation)*	• Convince negotiators *(behavioural legitimation)*	**Externals** *(academics, non-member states)*	• Including associated members in the dialogue and cooperation *(discursive and behavioural legitimation)*
	Civil society	• Mediation *(behavioural legitimation)*	• Open, vocal criticism *(discursive contestation)*	
	• Walkout *(behavioural contestation)*			• Keeping OECD-only full membership *(behavioural and institutional legitimation)*
	• Demonstration *(behavioural contestation)*			
	• Shaming and protest banners *(discursive contestation)*			

norm for CCA community, which contrasts with the UNFCCC processes. Thus, the IEA needed to move towards norm adoption that would be reflected in practice. It was thus necessary to legitimate to reflect the community's legitimacy belief. The US contestation of the Paris Agreement, however, rejected its implementation and spoke against the norm, which is embodied in the Paris Agreement. Table 7.3 summarizes the contestation and legitimation practices by case and major key issue in global climate governance, the institutional format.

Both the UNFCCC and the IEA-related community share the understanding that to successfully act on climate change, action needs to be taken collectively since it is a global issue that affects everyone. The legitimation of the processes discussed here differs regarding whether the norm for CCA had already been adopted and by whom. The IEA needed to adopt the norm to legitimate itself, which demanded institutional transformation. In the process after the US contestation of the Paris Agreement the UNFCCC kept in the background. Most explicit legitimation engagement came from the rest of the community, which reinforced their legitimacy belief in the norm for CCA by opposing Trump's contestation. In both IEA processes, legitimation practices towards norm adoption can be observed. For the UNFCCC, the G77 contestation claimed a policy that would demand a collective norm adoption represented by the loss and damage mechanism. In the case of the US contestation of the Paris Agreement, the community had already adopted the norm and engaged in further legitimation contra the contestation.

Conclusion: The norm for CCA in contestation–legitimation processes

In this comparative analysis, I showed that the norm for CCA is the guiding frame of the contestation–legitimation processes selected here. To do so, I compared four contestation–legitimation processes. The results of the two case studies and the four processes show that, first, contrary to the expectation of negative consequences of contestation such as a destructive rupture, contestation can in fact trigger legitimation. Second, they show that to really understand why contestation was followed by legitimation it is necessary to view contestation and legitimation as an interlinked process rather than being conceptually isolated. Third, through understanding contestation–legitimation in a process and the related norm adoption, these four cases unveil the broader frame in which they take place and, moreover, that they are conditioned by the frame. Further, as the four processes show, this frame conditions processes as the appropriate standard of behaviour, the norm, within the given community. Thus, this analysis demonstrates that the norm for CCA is one of the guiding frames in the global climate regime. In

Table 7.3: Summary of contestation and legitimation practices by case and major key issue in global climate governance, institutional format

Issue	UNFCCC		IEA	
	Trump contestation of Paris Agreement		Oil-only approach	
Institutional format	Contestation Trump	Legitimation UNFCCC	Contestation Member states	Legitimation IEA
	• Protest (*behavioural contestation*) • Refusal (*behavioural contestation*) • Open, vocal criticism (*discursive contestation*) • Withdrawal (*institutional contestation*)	• Non-state actor engagement (*behavioural and institutional legitimation*) • Moderating, neutral communication (*discursive legitimation*) • Filing exit in accordance with the Paris Agreement (*institutional legitimation*) **State and non-state actors** • Praise (*discursive legitimation*) • Taking leadership role (*discursive legitimation*) • Opposing statements contra contestation (*discursive legitimation*) • Financial compensation (*behavioural legitimation*) • Networks and events (*behavioural legitimation*)	• Open, vocal criticism (*discursive contestation*) • Creating counter institution (*institutional contestation*) **Externals** (academics, non-member states) • Open, vocal criticism (*discursive contestation*)	• Incorporating renewable energy expertise (*behavioural and institutional legitimation*) • Leadership vocal on promoting energy transition and CCA (*discursive legitimation*) • Expanding network and cooperation on energy and climate change (*behavioural legitimation*) • Recruiting renewable energy staff (*behavioural legitimation*) • Keeping emergency oil response system (*institutional legitimation*)

this comparative analysis, I showed how the different stages of norm adoption of the parts of the respective communities informed the contestation practice as well as legitimation engagement after the contestation.

As I argue, the norm as a guiding frame structures behaviour, determines the legitimacy belief of the community and conditions the process as a guiding frame. Due to the dual quality of norms, as they themselves can be both stable and flexible, they too can be reflexive within (social) processes. This means that in contestation–legitimation processes, they can present as a guiding frame of the contestation and/or of the legitimation. As a result, I was able to show why contestation can be followed by legitimation in the global climate regime and answer this book's research question.

8

Conclusion: Contestation and Legitimation of IOs in the Global Climate Regime

The global climate regime is at a crossroad, as recent events and the last years of global climate summits reveal. In 2025, Donald Trump moved back into the presidential office, and the US once more and immediately withdrew from the Paris Agreement (for example Hirji, 2025). The patch-up of the Biden administration in between the Trump presidencies could not last and could not be saved. While 'Trump's Climate Whiplash' (Hirji, 2025) was responded to also once again by, for example, the Bloomberg foundation, that stepped up to fund the US financial obligations to the convention and reassured that the coalition of city, state and corporate leaders will use 'its powers to uphold the US promise to lower its greenhouse gas emissions' (Mathiesen, 2025), the chances for climate action to prevail may not look as promising as they were 10 years ago, when the Paris Agreement had been signed.

Also, the global climate summits paint a picture of ups and downs. Although back in 2021, COP26 'marked the beginning of a possible turning point in international cooperation on fighting climate change and moving towards the goal of the 1.5 degrees stated in the Paris Agreement, and breaking 'new ground' (van Asselt and Green, 2022). Just one year later in 2022, COP27 brought mixed messages and feelings, for example about narratives of 'low emissions' instead of none or about non-state actor inclusion (Slavin, 2022; see also Kaplan, 2022). While this Conference of the Parties (COP) is not regarded as the most successful one, the place and time of its occurrence seemed to be just right (Ghosh et al, 2022). Besides the active hurricane season that autumn, the year 2022 had brought record heatwaves across the world in summer, a drought in Africa that meant the risk of starvation for 22 million people and floods in Pakistan that overran two-thirds of the country (Ghosh et al, 2022). The time was right to remind leaders of climate change realities. Next to criticism and disappointment about the organization of COP27 in Sharm El-Sheikh (see, for example, Slavin, 2022), negotiators, for example, reached 'a breakthrough agreement' on loss and damage (UNFCCC, 2022).

In 2023, COP28 in Dubai was closed with the 'historic' agreement that countries would transition away from fossil fuel. But at the same time, it 'lacked a balance between financial decisions and science-based decisions' as well as a 'concrete global targets for reduction of fossil fuel consumption [that] sounds more suggestive than decisive. Hence, although the decision marks the beginning of the end of the fossil fuel era, care will have to be taken so that loopholes are not taken an advantage of' (Arora, 2024). Afterwards in 2024, COP29 was on the one hand regarded as 'stepping stone to COP30, when updated national climate plans are expected to be presented, the bar was set high this year for hammering out a landmark climate finance deal' and on the other ended with frustration, disappointment and the question 'if the COP framework needs an overhaul, but rather what form that overhaul might take' (Kustova et al, 2024). Yet, what COP30 holds with a missing US and the world's leaders focus being on other crisis heat spots that threaten societies all around the globe – the escalation in the Middle East between Israel and Iran, the Gaza conflict, the Russian invasion of Ukraine, civilian suppression in the US, and populist and authoritarian backlash all around the world – may only be seen.

This short overview alone shows once more that international cooperation and collective action on climate change is an urgent yet complex endeavour. Climate governance is at the centre of global cooperation and world leaders are held accountable for their actions to fight climate change. For example, the timeline of the mechanism of loss and damage that was agreed upon and ratified at COP19 in 2013 in Warsaw and its successful improvement in 2022 almost 10 years later attests that climate change action guides the community in the global climate regime as the norm. However, as I show in this book, throughout these 10 years and before, there have been contestation struggles in this regime. For example, COP15 in Copenhagen in 2009 is regarded as a major flop and contestation to the cooperation on climate change. COP15 ended in a total breakdown and left the United Nations Framework Convention on Climate Change (UNFCCC) on the brink of a legitimacy crisis as parties could not come to any agreement. Beforehand, in 2007, preparations were made for a global agreement to be adopted in 2009 (Walker and Biedenkopf, 2020). The failure to agree and the related conflict was especially along the lines of this North–South divide (see, for example, Walker and Biedenkopf, 2020).

Revisiting the puzzle and the research question

The contestation struggles in the global climate, investigated in this book, move along the conflict lines of its two key issues, the North–South divide and the institutional formats. As explained earlier, the North–South divide encompasses conflicts and struggles among the various involved actors due to their different geopolitical needs and interests (Depledge, 2006; Biermann et al, 2009c, 2012; O' Neill, 2009; Pattberg and Biermann, 2012; Chasek et al, 2014). The collective action for climate governance that is required to conquer climate change, since it is a global crisis that affects everyone, is navigated through the institutional formats in this regime. These formats need to be negotiated, ratified and accepted as appropriate, legitimate formats. However, due to the changing reality of global governance that is in flux, these formats are often, too, the targets of conflict and contestation.

As I have illustrated in this book, contestation is widely understood as a social practice of disapproval, objection and refusal (Wiener, 2014, p 1). By default, these negative characteristics of contestation make negative consequences seem only logical. For international organization (IOs), negative consequences could be missing financial contributions that can cause a performance loss and gridlock (see, for example, Hale et al, 2013), or the creation of counter institutions (Urpelainen and Van de Graaf, 2015), or member withdrawal that can lead to a domino effect of other members cancelling their membership (Walter, 2021). All of these can work as de-legitimation and can lead to a loss and crisis of legitimacy. We would expect that, in particular, the more powerful the contester as part of the community is, the more likely we would see a negative, delegitimizing impact of that contestation (Zürn, 2018), which was for example the case of the World Trade Organization (WTO) Appellate Body (Zaccaria, 2022).

In fact, not too long ago in 2022, this has been the case with the Energy Charter Treaty (ECT) in the global climate regime. The ECT was found in 1998 to protect firms in the energy industry by giving them the right to 'sue governments on policies affecting their investments' (Abnett, 2022). However, its use has been critical in the past, as companies have challenged policies that would negatively affect or even lead to their shut down, which at the same time goes at a critical disadvantage for addressing climate change. Italy left the treaty in 2016. Further, 'the efforts to reform the treaty have been insufficient to support ambitious climate action' (IISD, 2022). In 2022, France, Germany, the Netherlands, Poland and Spain announced their intent to withdraw from the treaty. Further, they increasingly pressure the EU to coordinate an EU-wide withdrawal as the treaty undermines the EU's climate targets. And 'the European Commission said the "most adequate" option would be for the EU and its 27 member states to leave' which 'appears to be unavoidable' (Abnett, 2022). This process shows that the contestation set the ECT in a downward spiral of de-legitimation with more than half of the member states proclaiming to quit the ECT. This signals a deep legitimacy crisis. Yet, contrary to this logic, and as I have showed in this book, we can see that despite several, different instances of contestation, some IOs neither experience consequences of de-legitimation nor do they end in an existential crisis of legitimacy. In fact, there are a considerable number of cases in which contestation is followed by legitimation.

To explain this, I asked in this book: *How and why are IOs in the global climate regime able to self-legitimate despite contestation?* To answer this question, I analysed two influential cases of IOs in the global climate regime: the UNFCCC and the International Energy Agency (IEA). To understand the puzzling processes and the explicit connection between contestation and legitimation, my theoretical framework is based on connecting the knowledge of contestation and legitimation research alike. I engaged with the previous research of both scholarly fields that have, on the one hand, established a large body of literature legitimation of IOs (see, for example, Reus-Smit, 2007; Symons, 2011; Tallberg et al, 2018; Tallberg and Zürn, 2019), and on the other, of contestation as concept in relation to norms (see, for example, Wiener, 2014; Lantis and Wunderlich, 2018; Deitelhoff and Zimmermann, 2019). Once more, it is important to stress that this book's theoretical framework is about the contestation of IOs and their legitimation thereafter and how this is enabled by the adopted norm dynamics that work in global governance. It is about the role that norms play as guiding frames in distinct processes, or to put it differently, life episode, for the survival and development of IOs to counter contestation and self-legitimate.

Within the two cases I analysed two contestation–legitimation processes each. After analysing them individually, I compared these four processes. For the case of the UNFCCC, I analysed the G77 walkout and the US contestation of the Paris Agreement, and for the IEA, the contestations of the Organisation for Economic Co-operation and Development (OECD)-only membership and the oil-only approach that manifested in the creation of the counter organization International Renewable Energy Agency (IRENA). I allocated these processes to two of the main issues in the global climate regime, namely the North–South divide and the institutional formats in climate governance. The G77 walkout and the IEA's OECD-only membership are issues along the North–South divide, while the US contestation of the Paris Agreement and the IEA's oil-only approach were processes concerning the IOs' institutional format.

Findings: contestation, legitimation and the adoption of the norm for CCA

I was able to collect puzzling findings in these four processes of contestation and legitimation. For the case of the UNFCCC, the first process is the walkout of the G77 countries at the Warsaw COP19 in 2013. This instance is a prime example of the North–South divide. Also, the mechanism on 'loss and damage', which was debated at COP19, is key in politically addressing the damaging and existential threat of climate change that is for now unequally affecting the globe. The walkout of the G77 led to an abrupt break in COP19. I showed that this contestation was followed by legitimation. Further, I find in my research that this kind of contestation and subsequent legitimation practices trace back to COP15 in Copenhagen in 2009. The previous experience in Copenhagen and thereafter established practices that led to the rekindling of the conference and thus re-legitimized COP19 and its negotiations despite the contesting walkout. The norm for climate change action (CCA) frames the overall process and thus conditioned the legitimation after contestation. Establishing a collective mechanism to prevent loss and damage due to climate change is a vital part of the norm.

The second process is the US contestation with the announcement of its withdrawal from the Paris Agreement by former president Trump in 2017. With this contestation, it was anticipated that a domino effect of further contestation and withdrawal by other member states would follow. However, I demonstrated that contrary to these apprehensions and de-legitimation, legitimation followed this contestation. Several members of the UNFCCC as well as sub-state and non-state actors opposed Trump's position and engaged in different kinds of legitimation practices, supporting and emphasizing the importance of the Paris Agreement, the UNFCCC and climate change action. I showed that this process of legitimation, too, is conditioned by the frame of the norm for CCA.

For the IEA, I identified two processes of contestation and legitimation that manifested in the creation of IRENA by three IEA members as a direct competitor to counter the IEA in 2009. In the first process, the non-inclusivity of membership of the IEA's exclusive 'club' membership of OECD countries only was contested. This non-universal frame meant a neglect of including rising powers, such as India and China, that have greatly increased their energy consumption over time (Van de Graaf, 2012, 2013). This speaks to the unequal burden of the effects of climate change and related emissions and energy consumption by states. The second process contested the IEA's oil-only approach and the non-inclusion of the IEA's renewable energy. Yet, I found that, despite the dawning legitimacy crisis, the IEA engaged in self-legitimation practices. This legitimation, too, was conditioned by the frame of the norm for CCA. Here, the norm was the common understanding of the contesting actors and an adaptive response by the legitimating parties alike. The understanding of the norm implied the need to collectively change towards a more sustainable and inclusive political procedure. The IEA legitimated through the association membership of non-OECD countries as well as transitioning its expertise to all energy sources, beyond fossil energy only (Heubaum and Biermann, 2015).

The results of the two case studies and the four processes show that, first, contrary to the expectation of negative consequences of contestation such as a destructive rupture, contestation can in fact trigger legitimation. Second, they show that to really understand why contestation was followed by legitimation, it is necessary to view contestation and legitimation as an interlinked process rather than being conceptually isolated. Third, through understanding contestation–legitimation as an interlinked process and through focusing on the related norm adoption, these four cases unveil the broader frame that they are conditioned by. Further, as the four processes show, this frame guides processes as the norm is the appropriate standard of behaviour within the given community. I was able to deconstruct the norm for climate change action as a guiding frame in the processes' practices. At the same time, this book acknowledges that norm adoption is never final. In accordance with Wiener (2008; 2014) and Deitelhoff and Zimmermann (2020) norms are contestable and will find re-interpretation as change in global governance is constant and inevitable. However, in contestation–legitimation processes, norm adoption can tell us why contestation of a specific, empirical target is met with legitimation engagement and not de-legitimation.

I showed that CCA emerged as a guiding norm and standard of appropriate behaviour in the global climate regime. CCA is the guiding norm that frames the contestation–legitimation processes selected here. To demonstrate this, I examined each process regarding the core aspects of the norm and deconstructed the practices of contestation and legitimation. The core aspects of the norm for CCA relevant here, as previously introduced, are the collective endeavour aspect on the one hand, and climate change action as a guiding frame for policy implementation to achieve environmental goals, for example, the Paris Agreement or incorporation of renewables, on the other. To be able to understand the connection between contestation and legitimation in the processes, I traced the occurring practices of the contestation and its legitimation in an interlinked process. I engaged in an altered form of process tracing, namely 'practice tracing', which allows interpretive analysis (Pouliot, 2009; for process tracing see, for example, Bennett, 2010; Collier, 2011; Beach and Pedersen, 2013; Beach, 2016).

Via the deconstruction of the practices and through identifying the 'markers' for the norm aspects within them (see Table 2.1), I showed how the different stages of norm adoption of the parts of the respective communities informed the contestation practice as well as legitimation engagement after the contestation. The norm as a guiding frame structures behaviour, determines the legitimacy belief of the community and conditions the process as a guiding frame. In contestation–legitimation processes, norms can present as a guiding frame of the contestation and/or of the legitimation. Therefore, I was able to show why contestation can be followed by legitimation in the global climate regime and answer this book's research question.

When deconstructing the practices to the norm aspects, while both aspects were addressed, a connection to the major key issues of global climate governance could be seen. In the processes that can be allocated to the North–South divide, the aspect of CCA as collective endeavour became visible. In the processes of the North–South divide, the G77 walkout and the IEA OECD-only membership, parts of the community were contesters. For the G77 walkout, the contestation was due to the negotiation on the 'loss and damage' mechanism and conflict among the negotiating member states. For the IEA, IEA member states contested the organization itself and its neither universal membership nor universal mandate on energy that led to the creation of IRENA. Through IRENA, most of the community could channel their legitimacy belief in CCA as an appropriate standard and as collective endeavour.

For these processes the contestations manifested that the behaviour must reflect the community's legitimacy belief. The G77 contestation claim spoke to the need for a policy that would reflect and make possible the implementation of CCA. The UNFCCC's legitimation response after the G77 contestation aimed to move parties forward towards consensus in favour of global climate change action. Yet, in this case, the IEA itself was still outside of the norm for CCA community, which contrasts with the UNFCCC processes. Thus, the IEA needed to move towards norm adoption to legitimate to reflect the community's legitimacy belief and, moreover, reflect this belief in practice.

When the institutional format was contested, the aspect of policy implementation of the norm for CCA was most often addressed. In the process of the US contestation of the Paris Agreement, Trump's contestation claimed that the institutional format, the Paris Agreement, would handicap the US for the benefit of the other parties of the agreement and the wider community, which speaks out against the aspect of CCA as collective endeavour. At the same time, the aspect of collectively acting on climate change is a clear condition of the contestation claim and thus is one aspect of the norm that triggered and guides this contestation–legitimation process. The contestation against the IEA's oil-only approach also demanded a policy transition towards CCA as the IEA itself was still outside of the norm for CCA community, which contrasts with the UNFCCC processes. Thus, the IEA needed to move towards norm adoption that would be reflected in practice. It was therefore necessary to legitimate to reflect the community's legitimacy belief. The US contestation of the Paris Agreement, however, rejected its implementation and spoke against the norm, which is embodied in the Paris Agreement.

Both the UNFCCC and the IEA-related community shared the understanding that to successfully act on climate change, action needs to be taken collectively since it is a global issue that affects everyone. The legitimation of the processes discussed here differs regarding whether the norm for CCA had already been adopted and by whom. The IEA needed to adopt the norm to legitimate itself, which demanded institutional transformation. In the process after the US contestation of the Paris Agreement the UNFCCC kept in the background. Most explicit legitimation engagement came from the rest of the community that reinforced their legitimacy belief in CCA as the norm by opposing Trump's contestation.

As I argue, when it comes to contestation followed by legitimation, the legitimation is connected to the contestation in an interlinked process. Due to the reflexive quality of norms, the contestation can either be aligned with the norm, embodied in the contestation claim, which indicates a legitimacy gap, or the contestation cannot be in line with the norm of the community. When norms are not themselves the explicit target of contestation, they either lie in the contestation claim itself, which then influences possible legitimation in light of the norm, as could be seen in the processes of the IEA and the G77 walkout. The identified legitimacy gap in the contested target also signals a legitimation potential. This can be fulfilled through adoption of the norm and engaging in legitimation practices that reflect the norm towards the community. Or the norm is embodied in the contested target itself and reinforced through the community that believes in the standard of appropriate behaviour given by the norm and opposes the contestation, for example, in the process of the US contestation of the Paris Agreement.

In both IEA processes, legitimation practices towards norm adoption can be observed. For the UNFCCC, the G77 contestation claimed a policy that would demand a collective norm adoption represented by the 'loss and damage' mechanism. In the case of the US contestation of the Paris Agreement, the community had already adopted the norm and engaged in further legitimation contra the contestation. Norm adoption, however, does not equal missing recurrence of conflict or disagreement within IOs and among their communities. Norms guide behaviour and thus frame contestation–legitimation processes, yet they are not an absolute determinant.

Reflections: looking back and moving forward

When looking back on this book, its narrative and what it could show, juxtaposed to media coverage as well as the voices of climate activists on the streets and social media, it is not too much to use the saying, 'all that glitters is not gold'. What is happening on the ground when it comes to climate change action in global climate governance and in the domestic spheres of states is that there is a lot of talk but less walk. The interconnections among politics, economy and power leave a lot of promise and action lagging behind that are necessary to achieve the goals of the Paris Agreement. States are still reluctant to *really* get together to stand in for each other, as the ups and downs of the last years' COPs and the repeated US withdrawal from the Paris Agreement show.

With recent events discussed in the beginning of this conclusion, and revisiting the first version of this book that was written in 2023, the then written text of 'While acknowledging this part of reality, at the same time, it is equally true to say that the norm for CCA does still guide the community in the global climate regime', may not completely hold anymore. With the cases investigated in this book, it demonstrates a growing adoption of the CCA norm as a guiding frame; however, we are witnessing a reverse motion, with CCA being questioned. As illustrated, fighting climate change and moving towards a successful energy transition is not the top priority of many, which can be seen with the COPs from 2022 onwards, and the overall crisis of the liberal international order with the second Trump term, populist backlash, but also powerful countries lowering their ambitions for climate action. For example, Germany with the Ministry of Economy just turned their back on their climate goals and re-invited fossil fuels (Stehle, 2025). So, is the role of the CCA norm as a guiding frame (still) robust? What will it be?

As for the investigated cases but also looking into the recent status of 2025, the Paris Agreement, the UNFCCC and promotion for climate action of the IEA are not dead. Yet, norms as a guiding frame cannot be a cure-all as further research has shown (see, for example, Wiener, 2014; Schmidt and Sikkink, 2019). Also, vowing to adopt the appropriate standard of behaviour that the norm prescribes does not equal action. Considering the findings of this book, as mentioned, I do not assume a priori that contestation being followed by legitimation is always the case and the new normal. But this connection does exist and is puzzling, especially when the contestation comes from a major actor or from most of the respective community in the regime. The legitimation after contestation is framed by the norm as a guiding frame. Norms do constitute behaviour and have a part in structuring the governance within the regime. There are, of course, other theoretical voices that would explain the course of action in the processes and the following legitimation after contestation differently.

Some may argue that in the cases analysed here, legitimation after contestation is the result of the interest of states that remain the only relevant actors when it comes to IOs and their development (see, for example, Krasner, 1999). Surely, norms as a guiding frame that set the appropriate standard and structure behaviour are not the sole factor in why action is taken and in what way. Global governance regimes are complex environments, in which different constellations of actors and their networks, as well as different local and trans-global adoption of norms and sense of best practices, can lead to different outcomes. Empirics and their connections are complex, and the continuous interaction in the global governance regime impacts norm robustness, interpretation and its legitimacy.

So, what has been learned from this book, what knowledge can be gained? The aim of this book was to understand how IOs self-legitimate amid contestation and what informs the processes of contestation and legitimation, what guides actors to act within the global climate regime. Certainly, this book gives us new empirical insights into global climate governance and the cooperation on environmental and energy-related issues within it. By combining the two cases of the large IOs in the field, the UNFCCC and the IEA, a broader view and at the same time a deeper connection of the two issue areas, environment and energy, in the global climate regime have been achieved. Through this, I could not only ask why contestation was followed by legitimation in the four processes in this regime, but I could in fact show that there is an overarching norm that guides these processes and ties the two issue areas together.

Also, after reading this book, readers will have gained new insights into the connection between contestation and legitimation. Thinking about contestation and legitimation together and zooming in on the different targets that can be contested can help us deconstruct the norm that guides action in processes. With this book I have stressed the importance of understanding what contestation–legitimation processes are about; it is important to not only concentrate on norm contestation per se, but on the contestation of other targets that are constituting parts of the analysed IOs. When analysing de-legitimation or legitimation, not including contestation as a concept in this analysis closes the door to fully understanding why de-legitimation or legitimation occurs. As contestation triggers a critical engagement about the contested objects and the underlying guiding norm, this points to the object's legitimacy and potential legitimacy gaps. As I have shown, these in turn leave room for de-legitimation or legitimation. In a nutshell, this book encourages connecting concepts and working together to gain a deeper knowledge of why processes might turn out to be contrary to the prescribed logics, for example of contestation.

This has important implications for other issue areas in global governance. When researching other international regimes, norms and the contestation as well as legitimation of other targets should not be considered separately. Norms research has shown in the past that a variety of norms exists in, for example, the global security regime (see, for example, Welsh, 2019). But the focus had rather been on how the norm is contested or robust itself. However, if a norm, such as the responsibility to protect, exists with all its implications, interventions into conflict areas, including civil or interstate wars, by the international community will be considered through the lens of the understanding that the norm provides.

In the example of the responsibility to protect, this means the responsibility of the state to protect its populations and of the international community to prevent and protect populations when the state fails to do so, thereby breaching the state's sovereignty, a procedure that has been highly contested. Actions, agreements or coalitions by states to protect civil society that are not 'theirs' may be contested by non-state or state actors alike. We can only fully understand these contestations and subsequent de-legitimation or legitimation through the interpretation of the norm that guides the action and manifests the belief of what is legitimate. Thus, this book emphasizes the scope of how to think about the connection of norms as a guiding frame with contestation and legitimation processes not only of IOs in the global climate regime, but also of other fields.

Henceforth, this book opens a variety of possibilities for future research. For research of IOs but also of norms in the global climate regime, I have shown with this book that it is worthwhile combining cases from the energy and environmental field to learn more about contestation and legitimation and guiding norms in this regime. In this way, I do contribute to new knowledge about which norms structure the behaviour in the global climate regime. And I could already contribute to more understanding and knowledge of what this norm for CCA is about. When it comes to IOs and norms in the global climate regime, future research can move into different angles to explore more, for example, which norms guide action, where they come from and who recognizes them and how, as well as which IOs as entrepreneurs contribute to the emergence of certain norms. To be more certain about which norms are at play, future research should move up and down the ladder of place and time and select other cases in a comparative manner or single cases to examine the emergence and influence of norms in the regime.

Moreover, the research of other IOs that are not mandate specific but have a broader scope, such as the EU, will be relevant to gain more knowledge about norms and IOs in climate governance. As this book shows, climate change action is a collective endeavour that needs joint policies for implementation. In broad, non-task-specific IOs, the interrelation between climate governance and other sectors, for example the economic or infrastructure sector, is complex and difficult to unite. Thus, it is necessary to understand how broad IOs that encompass different fields and related tasks for whole regions relate to climate norms, such as CCA, and how they facilitate these norms in practice.

Additionally, research should also move beyond Western-centric regions and include regional IOs from the Global South to gain more insights into the different interpretations of climate norms, how they guide action and how they inform contestation. This is necessary as successful action on climate change can only be achieved by collectively working together, as this book has underlined. Climate change is a global crisis that demands a common understanding of the problems and needs of the diverse regions and their societies. This common understanding can only be achieved if there is a consensus on the meanings of these problems and needs and the norms that inform the necessary, appropriate behaviour.

Further, this book adds to previous research by showing that the community in the global climate regime is much wider than just the state. The interpretation of the norm for CCA of non-state actors who constantly contest governance practices in the climate regime matters for understanding not only contestation–legitimation processes but also the emergence of the norm itself. Further, this book provides an opening for future research on the norm for CCA itself. Consequently, by engaging in the analysis of the birth, development and possible different interpretations of the norm for CCA, and through understanding the roots of the norm, this book can in turn gain more depth and vice versa. This, too, will be an endeavour for future research.

This book shall encourage future research to move (back) into the field and engage with all different sectors of the community. So, international relations (IR) research and broader science can not only gain a deeper understanding of the interpretation as well as impact of norms in the global climate regime and why actors think and act in the way they do, but also, scholars who research this regime are themselves part of the community and contributors to the understanding and interpretation of norms and action within this regime. Climate change influences us and the future that we hold through our existence. This counts for all of us. This book thus also encourages scholars to reflect on their own positionality and, moreover, the impact they can have themselves in global climate governance and for climate change action.

To think back to the opening of this book and the insistent plea of Mia Mottley at COP26, 'what must we say to our people …? Will we act in the interest of our people who are depending on us or will we allow the path of greed and selfishness to sow the seeds of our common destruction?' (Mottley, 2021). So, what must we say to *our* people? To our friends, the family that we have and might have in the future, and to our colleagues, neighbours, our closer and broader community? The steps we take, the words we say, the questions we ask, the notes we take in the field and the words we put together as our research output can only happen because we are on this earth, from which we take our energy, get our nourishment and breathe our air. It is worthwhile thinking about what our research can do for it in return.

APPENDIX A

List of Interviews

IEA

IEA#1, national oil association, date: 19-04-2021.
IEA#2, UNFCCC negotiator IEA relations, date: 21-04-2021.
IEA#3, national IEA member state representative, date: 11-05-2021.
IEA#4, national IEA member state representative (group interview), date: 17-05-2021.
IEA#5, national IEA member state representative (group interview), date: 17-05-2021.
IEA#6, national IEA member state representative (group interview), date: 17-05-2021.
IEA#7, national IEA member state representative, date: 27-05-2021.
IEA#8, national IEA member state representative, date: 02-07-2019.
IEA#9, IEA staff, date: 21-09-2021.
IEA#10, IEA staff, date: 13-10-2021.
IEA#11, IRENA staff, date: 03-11-2021.
IEA#12, IRENA staff, date: 11-11-2021.
IEA#13, former IRENA staff, date: 02-12-2021.
IEA#14, IRENA staff (group interview), date: 01-02-2022.
IEA#15, IRENA staff (group interview), date: 01-02-2022.
IEA#16, IRENA staff (group interview), date: 01-02-2022.
IEA#17, IRENA staff (follow-up), date: 13-06-2022.

UNFCCC

UNFCCC#1, former UNFCCC staff, date: 30-03-2020.
UNFCCC#2, UNFCCC staff, date: 31-03-2020.
UNFCCC#3, UNFCCC staff, date: 03-04-2020, 09-04-2020.
UNFCCC#4, UNFCCC staff, date: 07-04-2020.
UNFCCC#5, UNFCCC staff, date: 09-04-2020.
UNFCCC#6, negotiator (Global North), date: 12-05-2020.
UNFCCC#7, negotiator and adviser (Global South), date: 04-06-2020.

UNFCCC#8, non-state actor COP participator (Global South), date: 07-07-2020.
UNFCCC#9, GCF staff, date: 20-08-2020.
UNFCCC#10, former UNFCCC staff, date: 25-08-2020.
UNFCCC#11, former UNFCCC staff, date: 28-09-2020.
UNFCCC#12, UNFCCC adviser (Global South), date: 08-10-2020.
UNFCCC#13, negotiator (Global North), date: 21-10-2020.
UNFCCC#14, negotiator (Global North), date: 21-10-2020.
UNFCCC#15, negotiator (Global North), date: 29-10-2020.
UNFCCC#16, negotiator (Global North), date: 30-10-2020.
UNFCCC#17, UNFCCC adviser (Global South), date: 15.02.2021.
UNFCCC#18, negotiator (Global North), date: 18-02-2021.
UNFCCC#19, negotiator (Global North), date: 18-02-2021.
UNFCCC#20, former negotiator (Global North), date: 24-02-2021.
UNFCCC#21, negotiator (Global North), date 04-03-2021.
UNFCCC#22, negotiator (Global North), date: 04-03-2021.
UNFCCC#23, negotiator (Global South), date: 04-03-2021.
UNFCCC#24, negotiator (Global North), date: 09-03-2021.
UNFCCC#25, negotiator (Global North), date: 25-03-2021.
UNFCCC#26, negotiator (Global South), date: 20-04-2021.

APPENDIX B

Questions to the Interviewees

UNFCCC: Interview questions 1st draft

- First, how can I imagine what your daily work is like in your section for you?
- So, what did you think when Trump announced that the US would leave the Paris Agreement?
- What did your unit/organization do?
- What were the reactions?
- Were new actions set in motion right away in your day-to-day work then? What did you think about this?
- What do you think about the reasoning behind the withdrawal? (Note: 'As noted in his 1 June 2017 remarks, President Trump made the decision to withdraw from the Paris Agreement because of the unfair economic burden imposed on American workers, businesses, and taxpayers by U.S. pledges made under the Agreement.')
- Also, I would like to know what you think about the events at the 2013 Warsaw conference.
- I mean, the mechanism established there is an essential part of the Paris Agreement.
- However, during its negotiation at the conference it was strongly opposed, including physically, when 132 countries walked out during the conference. What do you think about this? What were the reactions?
- What about the walkout of several organizations on the last day of the conference?
- How was this perceived within your organization, and how do you think it was perceived from the outside?
- Were there any actions taken for the future so that these kinds of walkouts will not happen again?
- Follow-up: Which?/Why not?

UNFCCC: Interview questions 2nd draft

- First, how can I imagine what your daily work is like in your section?
- When the Trump administration announced its intent to exit the Paris Agreement, what did your unit/organization do?
- What were the reactions?
- Were new actions set in motion right away? What did you think about this?
- What about the contribution cuts?
- Also, what about the 'We're still in' movement by sub-actors and non-actors after the announcement? Did the UNFCCC actively partake in its creation?
- Also, I would like to know what you think about the walkout of the G77 countries at the 2013 Warsaw conference.
- What happened?
- How was this perceived?
- What did your organization do?
- What mechanisms were set in place?
- What about the walkout of civil society on the last day of the conference?
- What was their role in this?
- Were there any actions taken for the future so that these kinds of walkouts will not happen again?
- Which?/Why not?

UNFCC: Interview questions 3rd draft

- First, how can I imagine your work in general and your role as a negotiator at the UNFCCC COPs?
- So, what did you think when the Trump administration announced its intent to exit the Paris Agreement?
- What were the reactions?
- What were your tasks then in the related COPs?
- Were new actions set in motion right away? What did you think about this?
- What do you think of the reasoning behind the withdrawal?
- (Note: 'As noted in his 1 June 2017 remarks, President Trump made the decision to withdraw from the Paris Agreement because of the unfair economic burden imposed on American workers, businesses, and taxpayers by U.S. pledges made under the Agreement.')
- Also, I would like to know what you think about the events at the 2013 Warsaw conference when 132 countries walked out during the conference.
- What did you think about this?
- How were you involved exactly?
- What about the walkout of several organizations on the last day of the conference?
- How was this perceived?

- Were there any actions taken for the future so that these kinds of walkouts will not happen again?
- Follow-up: Which?/Why not?

IEA: Interview questions 1st draft in German

- Meine Fragen in unserem Gespräch würden sich zum Einen auf die generelle Kommunikationspraktik und kooperierende Praktiken der Zusammenarbeit auf internationaler Ebene sowie der IEA beziehen, zum Anderen würde ich gerne ein tieferes Verständnis für die Geschichte und Implementierung des Erdölbevorratungssystems auf nationalen Ebenen entwickeln.
- Ich würde heute gerne mit Ihnen über das Erdölbevorratungssystem sprechen und was dahinter steckt.
- Können Sie mir erzählen was die Implikationen des Systems auf nationaler ebene sind?
- Und wie ist die die Verbindung zwischen Ihnen und unter anderem der IEA in diesem Zusammenhang auf internationaler Ebene?
- Der Erdölbevorratungsverband wurde 1978, also 4 Jahre nach der IEA, gegründet – gab es seitdem eine Veränderung im System der Erdölbevorratung?
- Gab es Veränderung in der internationalen Zusammenarbeit?
- Falls noch Zeit ist: was ist ihr blick auf das Erdölbevorratungssystem im Angesicht der starken Diskussion und auch Förderung von erneuerbaren Energien?

IEA: Interview questions 2nd draft in English

- My questions in our conversation would relate, on the one hand, to the general communication practice and cooperative practices at the international level and especially with the IEA; on the other hand, I would like to develop a deeper understanding of the history and implementation of the crisis mechanisms and the oil storage system on a national level.
- What about …
- Cooperation with IRENA
- Association
- Expertise
- Fatih Birol?
- G7/G20?
- Why not discard emergency response?
- Universal membership?

IRENA: Questions

- As part of my research, I specifically analyse the processes occurring in international organizations in the field of environmental and energy politics, in this case IRENA and the IEA. I would like to explore the period from 2009 to the present day and what has happened with the relationship between IRENA and the IEA since. Also, I would like to learn more about IRENA's impact on international cooperation and its expertise.

- Since the creation of IRENA in 2009, as a counter to the then claimed inability of the IEA to deal with the issue of renewable energy, how has the relationship between IRENA and the IEA developed and changed over time?
- What is the cooperation between IRENA and the IEA like?
- Now, 12 years since the IEA underwent modernization to add other layers of expertise enabling it to provide analysis and expertise on all kinds of energy resources, are there overlaps in the mandates? Is there some kind of tension or competition?
- What is the cooperation with IRENA's member countries like? Are there differences between those that are IEA members and those that are not?
- What is your perspective on IRENA's development since its creation? Have there been changes since, compared to the expectations when the agency was created?

APPENDIX C

Ethics – Consensual and Safe Research with Participants and Data

This section explains the selection process and ethical standard of this book. Its ethics clearance is in accordance with the ethics of the overall project NestIOr 'Who gets to live forever? The decline and death of international organizations'. This project has received clearance from the ERC Review Board and the Maastricht ERCIC Ethics Board.[1] By mandatory principle, the participation in interviews of policy makers, civil servants, diplomats and other humans was voluntary and interviewees were assured that they would take place based on informed consent and confidentiality. Interviewees were identified and recruited based on their expertise and functions. This way, I tried to ensure that interviewees were not, in any way, discriminated between based on nationality, sex, and the like. Non-discrimination, of course, is the highest ethical standard to commit to not only in research but in social life itself.

The approach used for finding interviewees was diverse. First, I asked the organization for relevant contacts through formal channels (for example, the press office) or by asking the current office holder. Also, I asked local academics and think tank experts for referrals. All were contacted via email. Further, I searched on the social media platform LinkedIn for further names to get in touch with more people. Also, once I had been in the field, I made use of a custom method in interviewing and asked interviewees at the end of the interview whether they could recommend other colleagues to talk to, which is referred to as the 'snowballing' technique. Of course, all techniques can include different degrees of bias, as I was not able to ask everyone at the end, due to time issues or discomfort. Bias may also have occurred as interviewees might have referred me to potential other interviewees not only due to competence but also personal preference and sympathy. Bias is always included and implicit in qualitative research as, regarding responses, some interviewees may respond to interview requests, while other potential interviewees ignore requests. I hence tried to reach out to interviewees twice or three times, and sometimes even more often.

Making contact, however, was overall a limiting factor. Not only did language barriers exclude me from getting in touch with more practitioners from the southern regions, but also the lack of access to contact information on countries' ministries' website. Contact details were often also outdated and front-offices have most of the time neither forwarded them to me nor responded to my inquiries. Once an interviewee had consented to participating in the interview, the participant received an information sheet and a consent form before the interview via email. This ensured that the participant was fully informed and was partaking voluntarily and with their consent. This needed to be signed by them. Due to the COVID-19 pandemic, all interviews except one were conducted online via the video-call app Zoom, provided by the university, so all consent forms are saved in electronic format.

Because interview data might contain sensitive information about the operation of IOs or the interviewees' personal views, the project and this research treated the data carefully on different levels of confidentiality. On their consent form, interviewees stated whether they would agree to (1) a recorded interview and/or (2) written notes. If they did not agree to a recording or notes, the interview data cannot be shared and used among project staff and only serve as background information for the relevant researcher. Finally, all quotes and/or attributions required the explicit additional written consent of the interviewees. The interviewees were informed, via the information sheet and by my introductory words in the interview, that they could withdraw the disclosed data at any point during or after the interview. The information sheet lists the contacts of the Principal Investigator and the Maastricht University Data Protection Officer. Any request to remove an interview from the record was immediately granted. The pseudonymity clause implies that while the identity of interviewees is known to the project (and safely stored on SURFdrive, in a separate folder, linked through a confidential key, see previous section), it is not disclosed in any publication or other document. The interviewees give their informed consent to a pseudonymized source, for instance 'Interview IEA#12'. A confidential key with metadata, linking the interview numbers with the interview transcripts, will be kept on SURFDrive, in a separate folder, to allow for the verification of the data source. I furthermore ensure that the data revealed by interviewees in the (public) deliverables do not allow for the interviewees to be indirectly identified.

In line with Dutch regulations on research integrity and so the university's ethical guidelines, all interviewee data will be kept, in the case of their informed consent, for a maximum of 10 years after the end of the project.

Data are pseudonymized: the contact information and the signed consent form are kept separate from the interview transcript. They are linked through a key (for example, IO#1 … #100). All data were finally kept on SURFDrive. This is a cloud-based system (cf. Dropbox) developed by Dutch universities with high security and privacy levels. Only the project's Principal Investigator and I have access to the data. While the interview transcript and/or recording includes rich data with the interviewees answering questions, I removed disclosed data from the record that involve special categories of data (data revealing racial or ethnic origin, political opinions, religious or philosophical beliefs, or trade union membership, and the processing of genetic data or biometric data for the purpose of uniquely identifying a natural person, data concerning health or data concerning a natural person's sex life or sexual orientation). I also removed disclosed data that project researchers believe are classified.

Notes

Chapter 1
1. Or university classes or work, since the movement not only includes school students but spans several ages of children and adolescents, or even adults aged over 30 (see, for example, de Moor et al, 2020).
2. In the following referred to climate change action (CCA) for consistency reasons with previous publication. Please note that climate action and climate change action can be used simultaneously.
3. Please note that in the following CCA always stands for the norm for climate change action. So, if referred to for example, 'CCA as guiding frame' read, 'the norm for CCA as guiding frame'.

Chapter 2
1. The complete quote ends with 'of norms' (Wiener, 2014, p 1).
2. Oxford dictionary: 'the group of people who have gathered to watch or listen to something'. See: Oxford Learner's Dictionaries (nd) 'Audience', *Oxford Learner's Dictionaries*, [online], Available from: www.oxfordlearnersdictionaries.com/definition/american_english/audience#:~:text=audience,noun,%2C%20someone%20speaking%2C%20etc. [Accessed 2 February 2022].
3. Gronau and Schmidtke use the term 'strategies'.

Chapter 3
1. By indicating once here terms such as 'developing' countries with '...', I want to express my concerns about these labels, which divide countries of the world into such development hierarchies as 'underachieved' and 'achieved'.

Chapter 4
1. Several responses to Paris Agreement withdrawal: Walsh, A. (2017) 'World reacts to US withdrawal from Paris pact', *DW*, [online] 6 January 2017, Available from: www.dw.com/en/world-reacts-to-us-withdrawal-from-paris-agreement/a-39088295 [Accessed 17 August 2020]. Also, an instance that shows the framing of disapproval towards Trump among nation state leaders is the NATO summit in December 2019, in which the Canadian prime minister, among others, sounded off about Trump: No Author (2019) 'Nato summit: Trump calls Trudeau 'two-faced' over video', *BBC*, [online] 4 December 2019, Available from: www.bbc.com/news/world-europe-50653597 [Accessed 18 August 2020].
2. This was immediately the case after President Joe Biden was elected into office in 2020/21; see, for example, Milman, O. (2021) 'Biden returns US to Paris climate accord hours

after becoming president', *The Guardian*, [online] 20 January 2021, Available from: www.theguardian.com/environment/2021/jan/20/paris-climate-accord-joe-biden-returns-us [Accessed 12 March 2024]. Yet, in 2025 Trump exited the Paris Agreement again after his re-election in November 2024; see, for example, the statement by the White House from 20 January 2025: The White House (2025) 'Putting America First in International Environmental Agreements', *The White House*, [online] 20 January 2025, Available from: www.whitehouse.gov/presidential-actions/2025/01/putting-america-first-in-international-environmental-agreements/ [Accessed 24 February 2025].

Chapter 5
1. Organization of the Petroleum Exporting Countries.
2. 'Weg vom Nahostöl!' (≈ 'Get away from Middle Eastern oil!') (Türk, 2016, p 60).
3. Austria, Belgium, Canada, Denmark, Germany, Ireland, Italy, Japan, Luxembourg, the Netherlands, Norway (under a special agreement), Spain, Sweden, Switzerland, Turkey, the United Kingdom, and the United States.
4. '[A]nd they basically are our bosses' (IEA#9).
5. Brazil, China, India, Indonesia, Morocco, Thailand, Singapore and South Africa.

Chapter 6
1. = member states.
2. As experienced in 2022, energy security and independence are ever more present since the Russian invasion of Ukraine, related EU sanctions against Russia and gas cuts from Russia to the EU.

Appendix C
1. Approval by Maastricht University Ethical Review Committee Inner City Faculties (ERCIC) on 18 October 2018 and 19 December 2019 (reference: ERCIC_098_01_10_2018). Approval by European Research Council (ERC) Ethics Review on 25 October 2018 (reference: Ares (2018) 5481894) and 24 March 2020 (reference: Ares (2020) 1725290).

References

Abbott, K.W. (2014) 'Strengthening the transnational regime complex for climate change', *Transnational Environmental Law*, 3(1): 57–88.

Abbott, K.W. and Bernstein, S. (2015) 'The high-level political forum on sustainable development: Orchestration by default and design', *Global Policy*, 6(3): 222–33.

Abbott, K.W. and Snidal, D. (2009) 'Strengthening international regulation through transnational new governance: Overcoming the orchestration deficit', *Vanderbilt Journal of Transnational Law*, 42(2): 501–78.

Abbott, K.W., Genschel, P., Snidal, D. and Zangl, B. (eds) (2015) *International Organizations as Orchestrators*, Cambridge University Press.

Abnett, K. (2022) 'Brussels says EU exit from Energy Charter Treaty 'unavoidable'', *Reuters*, [online] 7 February 2023, Available from: www.reuters.com/world/europe/brussels-says-eu-exit-energy-charter-treaty-unavoidable-2023-02-07/#:~:text=France%2C%20Germany%2C%20the%20Netherlands%2C,Italy%20left%20in%202016 [Accessed 27 March 2023].

Adler, E. and Pouliot, V. (eds) (2011a) 'International practices: introduction and framework', in E. Adler and V. Pouliot (eds) *International Practices*, Cambridge University Press (Cambridge Studies in International Relations), pp 3–35.

Adler, E. and Pouliot, V. (2011b) 'International practices', *International Theory*, 3(1): 1–36.

Aleklett, K., Höök, M., Jakobsson, K., Lardelli, M., Snowden, S. and Soderbergh, B. (2010) 'The peak of the oil age-analyzing the world oil production reference scenario in World Energy Outlook 2008', *Energy Policy*, 38(3): 1398–414.

Arora, P. (2024) 'COP28: ambitions, realities, and future', *Environmental Sustainability*, 7: 107–13.

Aykut, S.C. and Maertens, L. (2021) 'The climatization of global politics: introduction to the special issue', *International Politics*, 58: 501–18. https://doi.org/10.1057/s41311-021-00325-0

Bäckstrand, K. and Söderbaum, F. (2018) 'Legitimation and delegitimation in global governance discursive, institutional, and behavioral practices', in J. Tallberg, K. Bäckstrand and J. Scholte (eds) *Legitimacy in Global Governance: Sources, Processes, and Consequences*, Oxford University Press, pp 101–18.

Bäckstrand, K., Kuyper, J.W., Linnér, B.-O. and Lövbrand, E. (2017) 'Non-state actors in global climate governance: From Copenhagen to Paris and beyond', *Environmental Politics*, 26(4): 561–79. doi: 10.1080/09644016.2017.1327485

Barker, R. (2001) *Legitimating Identities: The Self-Presentation of Rulers and Subjects*, Cambridge University Press.

Barnett, M. and Finnemore, M. (2004) *Rules for the World: International Organizations in Global Politics*, Cornell University Press.

Barnett, M. and Coleman, L. (2005) 'Designing police: Interpol and the study of change in international organizations', *International Studies Quarterly*, 49(4): 593–619.

BBC (2019) 'Paris climate accords: US notifies UN of intention to withdraw', *BBC*, [online] 5 November 2019, Available from: www.bbc.com/news/world-us-canada-50297029 [Accessed 14 August 2020].

BBC (2022) 'Gen Z: How young people are changing activism', *BBC*, [online] 8 August 2022, Available from: www.bbc.com/worklife/article/20220803-gen-z-how-young-people-are-changing-activism [Accessed 19 February 2025].

Beach, D. (2016) 'It's all about mechanisms: What process tracing case studies should be tracing?', *New Political Economy*, 21(5): 463–72.

Beach, D. and Pedersen, R.B. (2013) *Process-tracing Methods: Foundations and Guidelines*, University of Michigan Press.

Beetham, D. (2013) *The Legitimation of Power* (2nd edn), Palgrave Macmillan.

Bennett, A. (2010) 'Process tracing and causal inference', in H.E. Brady and D. Collier (eds) *Rethinking Social Inquiry: Diverse Tools, Shared Standards* (2nd edn), Rowman and Littlefield, pp 207–19.

Benson, M.H. and Craig, R.K. (2014) 'The end of sustainability', *Society & Natural Resources*, 27(7): 777–82. doi: 10.1080/08941920.2014.901467.

Bernauer, T. and Gampfer, R. (2013) 'Effects of civil society involvement on popular legitimacy of global environmental governance', *Global Environmental Change*, 23(2): 439–49.

Bernstein, S. (2001) *The Compromise of Liberal Environmentalism*, Columbia University Press.

Bernstein, S. (2011) 'Legitimacy in intergovernmental and non-state global governance', *Review of International Political Economy*, 18(1): 17–51.

Bernstein, S. (2018) 'Challenges in the empirical study of global governance legitimacy', in J. Tallberg, K. Bäckstrand and J. Scholte (eds) *Legitimacy in Global Governance: Sources, Processes, and Consequences*, Oxford University Press, pp 189–200.

Bernstein, S. and Hoffmann, M. (2018) 'Decarbonisation: The Politics of Transformation', in A. Jordan, D. Huitema, H. van Asselt and J. Forster (eds) *Governing Climate Change: Polycentricity in Action?*, Cambridge University Press, pp 248–65.

Bes, B.J., Sommerer, T. and Agné, H. (2019) 'On legitimacy crises and the resources of global governance institutions: A surprisingly weak relationship?', *Global Policy Volume*, 10(3): 313–26.

Betsill, M.M. (2017) 'Trump's Paris withdrawal and the reconfiguration of global climate change governance', *Chinese Journal of Population Resources and Environment*, 15(3): 189–91. doi: 10.1080/10042857.2017.1343908

Betsill, M.M. and Corell, E. (2008) *NGO Diplomacy: The Influence of Nongovernmental Organizations in International Environmental Negotiations*, The MIT Press.

Bexell M. and Jönsson, K. (2018) 'Audiences of (de)legitimation', in J. Tallberg, K. Bäckstrand, and J. Scholte (eds) *Legitimacy in Global Governance: Sources, Processes, and Consequences*, Oxford University Press, pp 119–33.

Bexell, M., Jönsson, K. and Stappert, N. (2020) 'Whose legitimacy beliefs count? Targeted audiences in global governance legitimation processes', *Journal of International Relations and Development*, Copy at: ISSN 1408-6980 N orcid.org/0000-0002-7396-2927

Biermann, F. (2014) *Earth System Governance: World Politics in the Anthropocene*, The MIT Press.

Biermann, F. and Pattberg, P. (eds) (2012) *Global Environmental Governance Reconsidered*, The MIT Press.

Biermann, F. and Kim, R.E. (eds) (2020) *Architectures of Earth System Governance: Institutional Complexity and Structural Transformation*, Cambridge University Press.

Biermann, F., Betsill, M. M., Gupta, J., Kanie, N., Lebel, L., Liverman, D., et al (2009a) *Earth system governance: People, places and the planet. Science and implementation plan of the Earth System Governance Project*, Earth System Governance Project.

Biermann, F., Pattberg, P., van Asselt, H. and Zelli, F. (2009b) 'The fragmentation of global governance architectures: A framework for analysis', *Global Environmental Politics*, 9(4): 14–40.

Biermann, F., Siebenhüner, B. and Schreyögg, A. (eds) (2009c) *International Organisations in Global Environmental Governance*, Routledge.

Birol, F. (2017) 'Statement, Dr. Fatih Birol, Executive Director of the International Energy Agency, "welcomes India as an Association country"', *International Energy Agency* [YouTube-Video] 5 April 2017, Available from: www.youtube.com/watch?v=qmG9GeIyvx0 [Accessed 5 October 2022].

Björkdahl, A. (2002) 'Norms in international relations: Some conceptual and methodological reflections', *Cambridge Review of International Affairs*, 15(1): 9–23.

Bomberg, E. (2017) 'Environmental politics in the Trump era: An early assessment', *Environmental Politics*, 26(5): 956–63.

Bourdieu, P. (1990) *The Logic of Practice*, Stanford University Press.

Bourdieu, P. (1998) *Practical Reason: On the Theory of Action*, Stanford University Press.

BMWK (nd) 'Zwischen Ölkrise und Mitbestimmung 1972–1982', *Bundesministerium für Wirtschaft und Klimaschutz*, [online], Available from: www.bmwi.de/Redaktion/DE/Artikel/Ministerium/72-82.html [Accessed 20 June 2021].

Bremberg, N., Mobjörk, M. and Krampe, F. (2022) 'Global Responses to Climate Security: Discourses, Institutions and Actions', *Journal of Peacebuilding & Development*, 17(3): 341–56.

Brunnée, J. and Toope, S.J. (2019) 'Norm robustness and contestation in international law: Self-defence against non-state actors', *Journal of Global Security Studies*, 4(1): 73–87.

Buchanan, A. and Keohane, R. (2006) 'The legitimacy of global governance institutions', *Ethics and International Affairs*, 20(4): 405–37.

Bueger, C. (2014) 'Pathways to practice: Praxiography and international politics', *European Political Science Review*, 6(3): 383–406.

Bueger, C. and Gadinger, F. (2018) *International Practice Theory*, Palgrave Macmillan.

Busby, J. (2013) 'Equity in Global Climate Governance: An update from Warsaw', *The Duck of Minerva*, [online] 22 November 2013, Available from: www.duckofminerva.com/2013/11/equity-in-global-climate-governance-an-update-from-warsaw.html [Accessed 20 September 2022].

Carr, E.H. (1946) *The Twenty Years' Crisis 1919–1939* (2nd edn), Macmillan.

Carrington, G. and Stephenson, J. (2018) 'The politics of energy scenarios: Are International Energy Agency and other conservative projections hampering the renewable energy transition?', *Energy Research & Social Science*, 46: 103–13.

Chasek, P.S. (2000) *The Global Environment in the Twenty-first century: Prospects for International Cooperation*, The United Nations University Press.

Chasek, P.S., Downie, D.L. and Welsh Brown, J. (2014) *Global Environmental Politics. Boulder*, Westview Press.

Cheung, H. (2020) 'What does Trump actually believe on climate change?', *BBC News*, [online] 23 January 2020, Available from: www.maxineu.com/uploads/2/4/5/6/24568078/trump_and_climate_change.pdf [Accessed 30 May 2022].

Clark, I. (2005) *Legitimacy in International Society*, Oxford University Press.

Clark, I. (2007) *International Legitimacy and World Society*, Oxford University Press.

Clark, I. and Reus-Smit, C. (eds) (2007) 'Resolving international crises of legitimacy', Special issue, *International Politics*, 44(2/3): 157–74.

Claude, I.L. (1966) 'Collective legitimization as a political function of the United Nations', *International Organization*, 20(3): 367–79.

Climate Mayors (2016) 'Open Letter to President-elect Donald J. Trump on Climate Action', *Climate Mayors*, [online] 22 November 2016, Available from: https://medium.com/@ClimateMayors/open-letter-to-president-elect-donald-trump-on-climate-policy-and-action-33e10dcdcf85 [Accessed 6 March 2025].

Climate Mayors (2017) 'WE ARE STILL IN: Open letter to the international community and parties to the Paris Agreement from U.S. state, local, and business leaders', *Tumblr*, [online] 5 June 2017, Available from: https://climatemayors.tumblr.com [Accessed 24 February 2021].

Colgan, J.D., Keohane, R.O. and Van de Graaf, T. (2012) 'Punctuated equilibrium in the energy regime complex', *Review of International Organizations*, 7(2): 117–43.

Collier, D. (2011) 'Understanding process tracing', *PS: Political Science and Politics*, 44(4): 823–30.

Cornut, J. (2015) 'The practice turn in international relations theory', in R.A. Denemark, and R. Marlin-Bennett (eds) *The International Studies Encyclopedia*, Blackwell Publishing, Oxford Reference Online.

Cottrell, P. (2016) *The Evolution and Legitimacy of International Security Institutions*, Cambridge University Press.

C2ES (nd) 'Business support for the Paris Agreement', *C2ES*, [online], Available from: www.c2es.org/content/business-support-for-the-paris-agreement/ [Accessed 29 September 2021].

Dalby, S. (2024) 'Reframing climate security: The "planetary" as policy context', *Geoforum*, 155: 104102.

de Boer, Y. (2009) 'Statement by Yvo de Boer, Executive Secretary, opening of the fifteenth session of the Conference of the Parties (COP 15)', *United Nations Climate Change*, [online] 7 December 2009, Available from: https://unfccc.int/news/statement-at-the-opening-ceremony-of-cop-15-and-cmp-5 [Accessed 19 September 2022].

de Moor, J., Wahlström, K.U., Wennerhag, M. and De Vydt, M. (eds) (2020) 'Protest for a future II: Composition, mobilization and motives of the participants in Fridays For Future climate protests on 20–27 September, 2019, in 19 cities around the world', *Södertörns Högskola*, Available from: http://sh.diva-portal.org/smash/record.jsf?pid=diva2%3A1397070&dswid=92 [Accessed 23 October 2022].

Deitelhoff, N. (2020) 'What's in a name? Contestation and backlash against international norms and institutions', *The British Journal of Politics and International Relations*, 22(4): 715–27.

Deitelhoff, N. and Zimmermann, L. (2019) 'Norms under challenge: Unpacking the dynamics of norm robustness', *Journal of Global Security Studies*, 4(1): 2–17.

Deitelhoff, N. and Zimmermann, L. (2020) 'Things We Lost in the Fire: How Different Types of Contestation Affect the Robustness of International Norms', *International Studies Review*, 22(1): 51–76. https://doi.org/10.1093/isr/viy080

Democracy Now! (2013) 'Interview Democracy Now! with Claudia Salerno, the lead climate negotiator for Venezuela', *Democracy Now!* [Video] 20 November 2013, Available from: www.democracynow.org/2013/11/20/as_poor_countries_walk_out_of [Accessed 1 November 2022].

Depledge, J. (2005) *The Organization of Global Negotiations: Constructing the Climate Change Regime*, Earthscan.

Depledge, J. (2006) 'The opposite of learning: Ossification in the climate change regime', *Global Environmental Politics*, 6(1): 1–22.

Derman, B.B. (2014) 'Climate governance, justice, and transnational civil society', *Climate Policy*, 14(1): 23–41.

Dijkstra, H., von Allwörden, L., Schuette, L. and Zaccaria, G. (2022) 'Donald Trump and the survival strategies of international organizations: When can institutional actors counter existential challenges?', *Cambridge Review of International Affairs*, 37(2): 182–205.

Dingwerth, K., Schmidtke, H. and Weise, T. (2020) 'The rise of democratic legitimation: Why international organizations speak the language of democracy', *European Journal of International Relations*, 26(3): 714–41.

Dingwerth, K., Witt, A., Lehmann, I., Reichel, E. and Weise, T. (2019) *International Organizations under Pressure: Legitimating Global Governance in Challenging Times*, Oxford University Press.

Downie, C. (2020) 'Strategies for survival: The International Energy Agency's response to a new world', *Energy Policy*, 141: 111452.

Ecker-Ehrhardt, M. (2012) 'Cosmopolitan politicization: How perceptions of interdependence foster citizens' expectations in international institutions', *European Journal of International Relations*, 18(3): 481–508.

Ecker-Ehrhardt, M. (2018) 'Self-legitimation in the face of politicization: Why International organizations centralized public communication', *Review of International Organization*, 13(4): 519–46.

Espinosa, P. (2020) 'Address to the mainly young audience at the College of Europe, Warsaw Campus today', *UN Climate Change News*, [online] 5 March 2020, Available from: https://unfccc.int/news/climate-crisis-needs-truly-collective-response-un-climate-chief [Accessed 23 October 2022].

Faude, B. and Fuss, J. (2020) 'Coordination or conflict? The causes and consequences of institutional overlap in a disaggregated world order', *Global Constitutionalism*, 9(2): 268–89.

Finnemore, M. and Sikkink, K. (1998) 'International norm dynamics and political change', *International Organization*, 52(4): 887–917.

Florini, A. (2010) 'The International Energy Agency in global energy governance', *Global Policy*, 2(S1): 40–50.

Fridays For Future (nd) 'Homepage', *Fridays For Future*, [online], Available from: https://fridaysforfuture.org [Accessed 21 November 2022].

Frøland, H.O. and Ingulstad, M. (2020) 'Be prepared! Emergency stockpiles of oil among Western consumer countries prior to the International Energy Agency system', in D.H. Claes and G. Garavini (eds) *Handbook of OPEC and the Global Energy Order: Past, Present and Future Challenges* (1st edn), Routledge.

Frumhoff, P.C., Heede, R. and Oreskes, N. (2015) 'The climate responsibilities of industrial carbon producers', *Climatic Change*, 132: 157–71. https://doi.org/10.1007/s10584-015-1472-5

Gadinger, F. and Niemann, H. (2025) 'Normativity in practice: Ordering through enactment, learning, and contestation in global protests', *Review of International Studies*, 1–20. doi:10.1017/S0260210525000142

Geertz, C. (1973) 'Thick description: Toward an interpretive theory of culture', in C. Geertz (ed) *The Interpretation of Cultures*, Basic Books, pp 3–30.

Gerring, J. (2004) 'What is a case study and what is it good for?', *The American Political Science Review*, 98(2): 341–54.

Gerring, J. (2006) 'What is a case study?: The problem of definition', in J. Gerring (ed) *Case Study Research: Principles and Practices*, Cambridge University Press, pp 17–36. doi:10.1017/CBO9780511803123.004

Gerring, J. and Cojocaru, L. (2016) 'Selecting cases for intensive analysis: A diversity of goals and methods', *Sociological Methods & Research*, 45(3): 392–423. https://doi.org/10.1177/0049124116631692

Ghosh, A., Runge-Metzger, A., Victor, D.G. and Zou, J. (2022) 'The new way to fight climate change – small-scale cooperation can succeed where global diplomacy has failed', *Foreign Affairs*, [online] 4 November 2022, Available from: www.foreignaffairs.com/world/new-way-fight-climate-change?check_logged_in=1&utm_medium=promo_email&utm_source=lo_flows&utm_campaign=registered_user_welcome&utm_term=email_1&utm_content=20221129 [Accessed 29 November 2022].

Global Climate Action UNFCCC (nd) 'Climate Action Summit', Global Climate Action *NAZCA*, [online] nd, Available from: https://climateaction.unfccc.int/Events/ClimateActionSummit [Accessed 6 March 2025].

Green Climate Fund (nd) 'About GCF', *Green Climate Fund*, [online], Available from: www.greenclimate.fund/about [Accessed 25 August 2020].

Gregoratti, C. and Uhlin, A. (2018) 'Civil society protest and the (de)legitimation of global governance institutions', in J. Tallberg, K. Bäckstrand and J. Scholte (eds) *Legitimacy in Global Governance: Sources, Processes, and Consequences*, Oxford University Press, pp 134–54.

Gronau, J. (2016) 'Signaling legitimacy: Self-legitimation by the G8 and the G20 in times of competitive multilateralism', *World Political Science*, 12(1): 107–45.

Gronau, J. and Schmidtke, H. (2016) 'The quest for legitimacy in world politics – international institutions' legitimation strategies', *Review of International Studies*, 42(3): 535–57.

Guzzini, S. (2013) *The Return of Geopolitics in Europe? Social Mechanisms and Foreign Policy Identity Crises*, Cambridge University Press.

Habermas, J. (1996) *Between Facts and Norms: Contributions to a Discourse Theory of Law and Democracy*, MIT Press.

Hackmann, B. (2012) 'Analysis of the governance architecture to regulate GHG emissions from international shipping', *International Environmental Agreements*, 12(1): 85–103.

Hale, T., Held, D. and Young, K. (2013) 'Gridlock: From self-reinforcing interdependence to second-order cooperation problems', *Global Policy*, 4(3): 223–35. https://doi.org/10.1111/1758-5899.12068

Halliday, T.C., Block-Lieb, S. and Carruthers, B.G. (2010) 'Rhetorical legitimation: Global scripts as strategic devices of international organizations', *Socio-Economic Review*, 8(1): 77–112.

Heinkelmann-Wild, T. and Jankauskas, V. (2022) 'To yield or shield? Comparing international public administrations' responses to member states' policy contestation', *Journal of Comparative Policy Analysis: Research and Practice*, 24(3): 296–312. https://doi.org/10.1080/13876988.2020.1822144

Hermwille, L. (2018) 'Making initiatives resonate: How can non-state initiatives advance national contributions under the UNFCCC?', *International Environmental Agreements*, 18: 447–66. https://doi.org/10.1007/s10784-018-9398-9

Hermwille, L., Obergassel, W., Ott, Hermann E. and Beuermann, C. (2017) 'UNFCCC before and after Paris: What's necessary for an effective climate regime?', *Climate Policy*, 17(2): 150–70.

Heubaum, H. and Biermann, F. (2015) 'Integrating global energy and climate governance: The changing role of the International Energy Agency', *Energy Policy*, 87: 229–39.

Hickmann, T. and Elsässer, J.P. (2020) 'New alliances in global environmental governance: How intergovernmental treaty secretariats interact with non-state actors to address transboundary environmental problems', *International Environmental Agreements*, 20(2): 450–81. https://doi.org/10.1007/s10784-020-09493-5.

Hickmann, T., Widerberg, O., Lederer, M. and Pattberg, P. (2019) 'The United Nations framework convention on climate change secretariat as an orchestrator in global climate policymaking', *International Review of Administrative Sciences*, 1–18 (Online First).

Hirji, Z. (2025) 'Trump's Climate Whiplash', *Bloomberg*, [online] 25 January 2025, Available from: www.bloomberg.com/news/newsletters/2025-01-25/trump-s-climate-whiplash [Accessed 4 July 2025].

Hirschmann, G. (2021) 'International organizations' responses to member state contestation: from inertia to resilience', *International Affairs*, 97(6): 1963–81.

Höhne, C., Kahmann, C., Lohaus, M. (2024) 'Continuity and Change in Norm Translations After the Paris Agreement: From First to Second Nationally Determined Contributions', *Global Environmental Politics*, 24(2): 69–97. doi: https://doi.org/10.1162/glep_a_00743

Holzscheiter, A., Bahr, T. and Pantzerhielm, L. (2016) 'Emerging governance architectures in global health: Do metagovernance norms explain inter-organisational convergence?', *Politics and Governance*, 4(3): 5–19.

Hurrelmann, A. and Schneider S. (eds) (2014) *The Legitimacy of Regional Integration in Europe and the Americas*, Palgrave.

IEA (nd [a]) 'History: From oil security to steering the world toward secure and sustainable energy transitions', *IEA*, [online], Available from: www.iea.org/about/history [Accessed 22 June 2021].

IEA (nd [b]) 'International Energy Agency', *LinkedIn*, [online], Available from: https://tz.linkedin.com/company/international-energy-agency?trk=ppro_cprof#:~:text=View%20all%20782%20employees,Economic%20growth%2C%20and%20Engagement%20worldwide[Accessed 5 June 2025].

IEA (nd [c]) 'Structure', *IEA*, [online], Available from: www.iea.org/about/structure [Accessed 22 June 2022].

IEA (nd [d]) 'International collaborations', *IEA*, [online], Available from: www.iea.org/about/international-collaborations [Accessed 6 March 2025].

IEA (nd [e]) 'Membership', *IEA*, [online], Available from: www.iea.org/about/membership [Accessed 25 September 2021].

IEA (nd [f]) 'Areas of Work', *IEA*, [online], Available from: www.iea.org/areas-of-work [Accessed 23 November 2022].

IEA (nd [g]) 'Data and statistics', *IEA*, [online], Available from: www.iea.org/data-and-statistics [Accessed 24 June 2021].

IEA (1974) 'Decision of the Council. Establishing an International Energy Agency of the Organisation', *IEA*, [online] 16 April 1999, Available from: https://iea.blob.core.windows.net/assets/ba8c3ef8-f5b3-45db-86d2-719502e8d4ef/decesionofthecouncil.pdf [Accessed 2 September 2021].

IEA (2013) 'IEA, key emerging economies announce mutual interest to pursue enhanced co-operation', *IEA*, [online] 20 November 2013, Available from: www.iea.org/news/iea-key-emerging-economies-announce-mutual-interest-to-pursue-enhanced-co-operation [Accessed 27 September 2021].

IEA (2015) 'Joint Ministerial Declaration on the occasion of the 2015 IEA Ministerial meeting expressing the Activation of Association', *IEA*, [online] 18 November 2015, Available from: https://iea.blob.core.windows.net/assets/9e4b932e-b553-4f2c-86c3-d677eddbae72/IEA_Association.pdf [Accessed 22 June 2021].

REFERENCES

IEA (2016a) 'Energy, climate change and environment: 2016 Insights, prepared by the Environment and Climate Change Unit (ECC), in the Energy Environment Division (EED) of the International Energy Agency (IEA)', *IEA*, [online] November 2016, Available from: https://iea.blob.core.windows.net/assets/6b2eaf11-d479-4ab2-b92f-a8832cda61e8/ECCE2016.pdf [Accessed 9 October 2022].

IEA (2016b) 'We can't act on climate change without acting on energy #COP22', *International Energy Agency*, [YouTube-Video] 8 November 2016, Available from: www.youtube.com/watch?v=tNsVWZybsJk [Accessed 10 October 2022].

IEA (2017) 'IEA and China deepen ties with extensive three-year work programme IEA statement on work programme with China', *IEA*, [online] 16 February 2017, Available from: www.iea.org/news/iea-and-china-deepen-ties-with-extensive-three-year-work-programme [Accessed 5 October 2022].

IEA (2018) 'Agreement on an International Energy Program', *IEA*, [online] 17 February 2018, Available from: https://iea.blob.core.windows.net/assets/c6be6d60-1ca8-4b99-b8c7-7ac508ec157c/IEP.pdf [Accessed 2 September 2021].

IEA (2021) 'Oil 2021: Analysis and forecast to 2026', *IEA*, [online] March 2021, Available from: www.iea.org/reports/oil-2021 [Accessed 27 September 2022].

IISD (2022) 'Energy Charter Treaty Withdrawal Announcements Reflect Reform Outcome is Insufficient for Climate Ambition', [Statement] 7 November 2022, Available from: www.iisd.org/articles/statement/energy-charter-treaty-withdrawal-announcements [Accessed 27 March 2023].

IPCC (2022) 'Climate change: A threat to human wellbeing and health of the planet. Taking action now can secure our future', *IPCC*, [online] 28 February 2022, Available from: www.ipcc.ch/2022/02/28/pr-wgii-ar6/ [Accessed 21 June 2022].

Ivanova, M. (2007) 'Designing the United Nations Environment Programme: a story of compromise and confrontation', *Int Environ Agreements*, 7(4): 337–61. https://doi.org/10.1007/s10784-007-9052-4

Jackson, P.T. (2002) 'Rethinking Weber: Towards a non-individualist sociology of world politics', *International Review of Sociology*, 12(3): 439–68.

Jackson, P.T. and Nexon, D.H. (1999) 'Relations before states: Substance, process and the study of world politics', *European Journal of International Relations*, 5(3): 291–332.

Jepsen, H., Lundgren, M., Monheim, K. and Walker, H. (eds) (2021) *Negotiating the Paris Agreement: The Insider Stories*, Cambridge University Press. doi:10.1017/9781108886246.019

Johnson, T. (2011) 'Guilt by association: The link between states' influence and the legitimacy of intergovernmental organizations', *Review of International Organizations*, 6(1): 57–84.

Jordan, A., Huitema, D., van Asselt, H. and Forster, J. (eds) (2018) *Governing Climate Change: Polycentricity in Action?*, Cambridge University Press.

Jotzo, F., Depledge, J. and Winkler, H. (2018) 'US and international climate policy under President Trump', *Climate Policy*, 18(7): 813–17.

Kanie, N., Nishimoto, H., Hijioka, Y. and Kameyama, Y. (2010) 'Allocation and architecture in climate governance beyond Kyoto: lessons from interdisciplinary research on target Setting', *International Environmental Agreements*, 10(4): 299–315.

Kaplan, S. (2022) 'COP27 leaves world on dangerous warming path despite historic climate fund', *Washington Post*, [online] 20 November 2022, Available from: www.washingtonpost.com/climate-environment/2022/11/20/cop27-climate-conference-deal-fund/ [Accessed 23 October 2022].

Keck, M.E. and Sikkink, K. (1998) *Activists beyond Borders: Advocacy Networks in International Politics*, Cornell University Press.

Kemp, L. (2017) 'US-proofing the Paris Climate Agreement', *Climate Policy*, 17(1): 86–101.

Keohane, R.O. (2006) 'The contingent legitimacy of multilateralism', in E. Newman, R. Thakur and J. Tirman (eds) *Multilateralism under Challenge? Power, Institutional Order, and Structural Change*, United Nations University Press, pp 56–76.

Kerry, J. (2021) 'Fatih Birol', *Time Magazine*, [online] 15 September 2021, Available from: https://time.com/collection/100-most-influential-people-2021/6095810/fatih-birol/ [Accessed 23 November 2022].

Krasner, S. D. (1999) *Sovereignty: Organized Hypocrisy*, Princeton University Press.

Krook, M.L. and True, J. (2012) 'Rethinking the life cycles of international norms: The United Nations and the global promotion of gender equality', *European Journal of International Relations*, 18(1): 103–27.

Kustova, I., Dietz, C. and van Hoof, R. (2024) '"COP29 Was a Mixed Bag": Highs and Lows of the 2024 UN Climate Change Conference', ENSURED, [online], Available from: www.ensuredeurope.eu/blog/cop29-was-a-mixed-bag [Accessed 12 March 2025].

Kwong, T.G. (2013) 'Statement by Honorable Minister Mr. Tiarite George Kwong Minister of Environment, Lands and Agriculture Development of the Republic of Kiribati High Level Segment, UNFCCC COP 19th Meeting', *United Nations Climate Change*, [Statement] November 2013, Available from: https://unfccc.int/files/meetings/warsaw_nov_2013/statements/application/pdf/cop19_hls_kiribati.pdf [Accessed 7 January 2023].

Lantis, J.S. and Wunderlich, C. (2018) 'Resiliency dynamics of norm clusters: Norm contestation and international cooperation', *Review of International Studies*, 44(3): 570–93.

Lechner, F.J. and Boli, J. (2005) *World Culture: Origins and Consequences*, Blackwell.

Lechner, S. and Frost, M. (2018) *Practice Theory and International Relations*, Cambridge University Press.

Lefstad, L. and Paavola, J. (2023) 'The evolution of climate justice claims in global climate change negotiations under the UNFCCC', *Critical Policy Studies*, 18(3): 363–88. https://doi.org/10.1080/19460171.2023.2235405

Lenz, T. and Burilkov, A. (2017) 'Institutional pioneers in world politics: Regional institution building and the influence of the European Union', *European Journal of International Relations*, 23(3): 654–80.

Lenz, T. and Viola, L.A. (2017) 'Legitimacy and institutional change in international organisations: A cognitive approach', *Review of International Studies*, 43(5): 939–61.

Lenz, T., Bezuijen, J., Hooghe, L. and Marks, G. (2015) 'Patterns of international authority: Task specific vs. general purpose', Special issue, *Politische Vierteljahresschrift*, 49: 131–56.

Loges, B. (2021) 'Zwischen Einheit und Vielfalt – Zum Verhältnis von Normenforschung und Metatheorie', in K. Glaab, A. Graf and S. Engelkamp (eds) *Kritische Normenforschung als Metatheorie und politische Praxis. Neue Wege in den Internationalen Beziehungen*, Nomos, pp 33–67.

MacKay, J. (2019) 'Legitimation strategies in international hierarchies', *International Studies Quarterly*, 63: 717–25.

Mathiesen, K. (2025) 'Bloomberg offers climate cash to UN amid Trump cutbacks', *Politico*, [online] 23 January, Available from: www.politico.eu/article/bloomberg-offers-climate-cash-to-un-amid-trump-cutbacks/ [Accessed 4 July 2025].

Mattern, J.B. (2011) 'A practice theory of emotion for international relations', in E. Adler and V. Pouliot (eds) *International Practices*, Cambridge University Press, pp 63–86.

McDonald, M. (2024) 'Climate change, security and the institutional prospects for ecological security', *Geoforum*, 155: 104096.

McGrath, M. (2018) 'Climate change: "Trump effect" threatens Paris pact' *BBC*, [online] 3 December 2018, Available from: www.bbc.com/news/science-environment-46384828 [Accessed 14 August 2020].

Morgenthau, H.J. (1948) *Politics among Nations: The Struggle for Power and Peace*, Alfred A. Knopf.

Mottley, M.A. (2021) 'Opening Ceremony at the "Conference of the Parties"/COP26', *United Nations Climate Change*, [Remarks] 1 November 2021, Available from: https://unfccc.int/sites/default/files/resource/Her_Excellency_Ms._Mia_Mottley_Prime_Minister_of_Barbados.pdf [Accessed 30 May 2022].

Nelson, S.C. and Weaver, C. (2016) 'Organizational culture', in J. Katz Cogan, I. Hurd and I. Johnstone (eds) *Oxford Handbook of International Organizations*, Oxford University Press, pp 920–38.

Niemann, H. and Schillinger, H. (2017) 'Contestation "All the Way down"? The Grammar of Contestation in Norm Research', *Review of International Studies*, 1(43): 29–49. doi:10.1017/S0260210516000188

Norman, L. (2015) 'Interpretive process tracing and causal explanations', *Newsletter of the American Political Science Association Organized Section for Qualitative and Multi-Methods Research*, 13(2): 4–9.

Norman, L. (2016) 'Explaining institutional change: The role of interpretive process tracing', in L. Norman (ed) *The Mechanisms of Institutional Conflict in the European Union* (1st edn), London, pp 35–40. https://doi.org/10.4324/9781315658995

NPR (2017) 'Fact Check – Trump's Speech on Paris Climate Agreement Withdrawal, Annotated', *NPR*, [online] 1 June 2017, Available from: www.npr.org/2017/06/01/531090243/trumps-speech-on-paris-climate-agreement-withdrawal-annotated?t=1659611746767 [Accessed 4 August 2022].

Nunez, C. (2019) 'Global warming: Is it real? Get the facts', *National Geographic*, [online] 31 January 2019, Available from: www.nationalgeographic.com/environment/article/global-warming-real [Accessed 30 May 2022].

Obergassel, W., Arens, C., Hermwille, L., Kreibich, N., Mersmann, F., Ott, H.E. and Wang-Helmreich, H. (2017) *Setting Sails for Troubled Waters. An Assessment of the Marrakech Climate Conference*, Wuppertal Institut für Klima, Umwelt, Energie (gGmbH).

Okereke, C. (2018) 'Equity and Justice in Polycentric Climate Governance', in A. Jordan, D. Huitema, H. van Asselt and J. Forster (eds) *Governing Climate Change: Polycentricity in Action?*, Cambridge University Press, pp 320–37.

O'Neill, K. (2009) *The Environment and International Relations Themes in International Relations*, Cambridge University Press.

Orchard, P. and Wiener, A (eds) (2024) *Contesting the World: Norm Research in Theory and Practice*, Cambridge University Press.

Orr, S. (2016) 'Institutional control and climate change activism at COP21 in Paris', *Global Environmental Politics*, 16(3): 23–30.

Partzsch, L. (2023) 'Introduction: The Integration of Development and Environmental Agendas', in L. Partzsch (ed) *Environment in Global Sustainability Governance. Perceptions, Actors, Innovations*, Bristol University Press, pp 1–18.

Pattberg, P.H. and Biermann, F. (eds) (2012) *Public–Private Partnerships for Sustainable Development: Emergence, Influence and Legitimacy*, Edward Elgar.

Pevehouse, J. and Nordstrom, T. and Warnke, K. (2004) 'The correlates of War 2 international governmental organizations data version 2.0', *Conflict Management and Peace Science*, 21(2): 101–19.

Pickering, J., McGee, J.S., Stephens, T. and Karlsson-Vinkhuyzen, S.I. (2018) 'The impact of the US retreat from the Paris Agreement: Kyoto revisited?', *Climate Policy*, 18(7): 818–27. doi: 10.1080/14693062.2017.1412934

Pouliot, V. (2007) "Subjectivism': Towards a constructivist methodology', *International Studies Quarterly*, 51(2): 359–84.

Pouliot, V. (2009) 'Practice tracing', in A. Bennett and J.T. Checkel (eds) *Process Tracing*, Cambridge University Press, pp 237–59.

Pouliot, V. (2014) 'Practice tracing', in A. Bennett and J.T. Checkel (eds) *Process Tracing in the Social Sciences: From Metaphor to Analytical Tool*, Cambridge University Press, pp 237–59.

Pouliot, V. (2015) 'Practice Tracing', in A. Bennett and J.T. Checkel (eds) *Process Tracing: From Metaphor to Analytical Tool*, Cambridge University Press, pp 237–59.

Reus-Smit, C. (2007) 'International crises of legitimacy', *International Politics*, 44: 157–74. https://doi.org/10.1057/palgrave.ip.8800182

Risse, T. and Sikkink, K. (2016) 'The socialization of international human rights norms into domestic practices, Introduction 1999', in T. Risse (ed) *Domestic Politics and Norm Diffusion in International Relations*, Routledge, pp 117–49.

Rittberger, B. and Schroeder, P. (2016) 'The legitimacy of regional institutions', in Börzel, T. and T. Risse (2016) *Oxford Handbook of Comparative Regionalism*, Oxford University Press, pp 579–99.

Rittberger, V., Zangl, B. and Kruck, A. (2012) *International Organization* (2nd edn), Palgrave.

Rittberger, V., Zangl, B., Kruck, A. and Dijkstra, H. (2019) *International Organization* (3rd edn), Red Globe Press.

Roberts, E. and Huq, S. (2015) 'Coming full circle: The history of loss and damage under the UNFCCC', *Int. J. Global Warming*, 8(2): 141–57.

Rousseau, D.M., Sitkin, S.B., Burt, R.S. and Colin, C. (1998) 'Not so different after all: A cross-discipline view of trust', *Academy of Management Review*, 22(3): 393–404.

Sandholtz, W. (2019) 'Norm contestation, robustness, and replacement', *Journal of Global Security Studies*, 4(1): 139–46.

Schatzki, T.R. (1996) *Social Practices: A Wittgensteinian Approach to Human Activity and the Social*, Cambridge University Press.

Schatzki, T.R., Knorr Cetina, K. and von Savigny, E. (eds) (2001) *The Practice Turn in Contemporary Theory*, Routledge.

Scheer, H. (2007) *Energy Autonomy: The Economic, Social and Technological Case for Renewable Energy*, Earthscan.

Scheer, H. (2008) 'Bundestagsrede zur IRENA', *Hermann Scheer*, [online], Available from: www.hermannscheer.de/de/index.php/presse-mainmenu-112/reden-mainmenu-108/612-bundestagsrede-hermann-scheer-zur-irena?tmpl=component&print=1&layout=default [Accessed 7 September 2022].

Schillinger, H. and Niemann, H. (2021) 'Die unsichtbare Verfassung der Umstrittenheit. Zur Rolle von Umstrittenheit in der Normenforschung', in K. Glaab, A. Graf and S. Engelkamp (eds) *Kritische Normenforschung als Metatheorie und politische Praxis. Neue Wege in den Internationalen Beziehungen*, Nomos, pp 143–66. https://doi.org/10.5771/9783748923312-143

Schmidt, A. and Sikkink, K. (2019) 'Breaking the ban? The heterogeneous impact of US contestation of the torture norm', *Journal of Global Security*, 4(1): 105–22.

Schneider, S., Nullmeier, F. and Hurrelmann, A. (2007) 'Exploring the communicative dimension of legitimacy: Text analytical approaches', in A. Hurrelmann, S. Schneider and J. Steffek (eds) *Legitimacy in an Age of Globalization*, Palgrave Macmillan, pp 126–54.

Scholte, J.A. (ed) (2011) *Building Global Democracy? Civil Society and Accountable Global Governance*, Cambridge University Press.

Scholte, J.A. (2018) 'Social structure and global governance legitimacy', in J. Tallberg, K. Bäckstrand and J. Scholte (eds) *Legitimacy in Global Governance: Sources, Processes, and Consequences*, Oxford University Press, pp 75–100.

Scholte, J.A. and Tallberg, J. (2018) 'Theorizing the institutional sources of global governance legitimacy', in J. Tallberg, K. Bäckstrand and J. Scholte (eds) *Legitimacy in Global Governance: Sources, Processes, and Consequences*, Oxford University Press, pp 56–74.

Schuette, L. (2021) 'Why NATO survived Trump: The neglected role of Secretary-General Stoltenberg', *International Affairs*, 97(6): 1863–81.

Schwandt, T.A. (1999) 'On understanding understanding', *Qualitative Inquiry*, 5(4): 451–64.

Scobie, M. (2019) *Global Environmental Governance and Small States: Architectures and Agency in the Caribbean*, Edward Elgar.

Seabrooke, L. (2007) 'Legitimacy gaps in the world economy: Explaining the sources of IMF's legitimacy crisis', *International Politics*, 44(2): 250–68.

Seawright, J. and Gerring, J. (2008) 'Case selection techniques in case study research: A menu of qualitative and quantitative options', *Political Research Quarterly*, 61(2): 294–308. doi:10.1177/1065912907313077

Simmons, B.A. and Jo, H. (2019) 'Measuring norms and normative contestation: The case of international criminal law', *Journal of Global Security Studies*, 4(1): 18–36. doi: 10.1093/jogss/ogy043

Slavin, T. (2022) 'After "disappointing" COP27, calls grow for new approach to fighting climate change', *Reuters*, [online] 28 November 2022, Available from: www.reuters.com/business/sustainable-business/after-disappointing-cop27-calls-grow-new-approach-fighting-climate-change-2022-11-28/ [Accessed 29 November 2022].

Steffek, J. (2003) 'The legitimation of international governance: A discourse approach', *European Journal of International Relations*, 9(2): 249–75.

Stehle, K. (2025) 'Gas ist ihr Antrieb', *Die Zeit*, [online] 26 June 2025, Available from: www.zeit.de/wirtschaft/2025-06/katherina-reiche-wirtschaftsministerin-klimaziele-stromsteuer-gaskraftwerke [Accessed 7 July 2025].

Stein, J.G. (2011) 'Background knowledge in the foreground: conversations about competent practice in "sacred space"', in E. Adler and V. Pouliot (eds) *International Practices,* Cambridge University Press (Cambridge Studies in International Relations), pp 87–107.

Suchman, M.C. (1995) 'Managing legitimacy: strategic and institutional approaches', *Academy of Management Review*, 20(3): 571–610.

Symons, J. (2011) 'The legitimation of international organizations: Examining the identity of the communities that grant legitimacy', *Review of International Studies*, 37(5): 2557–83.

Tallberg, J. and Zürn, M. (2019) 'The legitimacy and legitimation of international organisations: Introduction and framework', *The Review of International Organisations*, 14: 581–606.

Tallberg, J., Bäckstrand, K. and Scholte, J. (eds) (2018) *Legitimacy in Global Governance: Sources, Processes, and Consequences*, Oxford University Press.

Türk, H. (2016) 'Kooperation in der Krise? Die Ölkrise von 1973/74 und die multilaterale Zusammenarbeit der westlichen Industrieländer in der Energiepolitik', *Journal of European Integration History*, 22(1): 47–65.

The White House (nd) 'Statement President Trump', *The White House*, [online], Available from: www.whitehouse.gov/briefings-statements/statement-president-trump-paris-climate-accord/ [Accessed 20 September 2020].

Tussie, D. (2018) 'Bringing power and markets', in J. Tallberg, K. Bäckstrand and J. Scholte (eds) *Legitimacy in Global Governance: Sources, Processes, and Consequences*, Oxford University Press, pp 201–12.

UN (nd [a]) 'About the secretariat', *United Nations Climate Change*, [online], Available from: https://unfccc.int/about-us/about-the-secretariat#:~:text=Around%20450%20staff%20are%20employed,of%20Grenada%20since%20August%202022 [Accessed 21 October 2022].

UN (nd [b]) 'Adaptions and Resilience', *United Nations Climate Change*, [online], Available from: https://unfccc.int/topics/adaptation-and-resilience/workstreams/approaches-to-address-loss-and-damage-associated-with-climate-change-impacts-in-'developing'-countries [Accessed 3 August 2022].

UN (nd [c]) 'Approaches to address Loss and Damage associated with Climate Change impacts in developing countries', *United Nations Climate Change*, [online], Available from: https://unfccc.int/topics/adaptation-and-resilience/workstreams/approaches-to-address-loss-and-damage-associated-with-climate-change-impacts-in-developing-countries [Accessed 3 August 2022].

UN (1992) 'United Nations Conference on Environment and Development, Rio de Janeiro, Brazil, 3-14 June 1992', *United Nations*, [online] June 1992, Available from: www.un.org/en/conferences/environment/rio1992 [Accessed 24 October 2022].

UN (2015) 'The Paris Agreement', *United Nations*, [online], Available from: https://unfccc.int/sites/default/files/english_paris_agreement.pdf [Accessed 7 January 2023].

UNEP (2018) 'Global Climate Action Summit brings surge of new commitments and calls for increased government action', *United Nations*, [Press Release] 14 September 2018, Available from: www.unep.org/news-and-stories/press-release/global-climate-action-summit-brings-surge-new-commitments-and-calls [Accessed 1 March 2021].

UNEP (2019) 'The UN Environment Programme and the climate emergency official position note', *United Nations*, [Position Note] September 2021, Available from: www.unep.org/unga/our-position/unep-and-climate-emergency [Accessed 21 June 2022].

UNFCCC (nd [a]) 'The Paris Agreement', *United Nations Climate Change*, [online], Available from: https://unfccc.int/process-and-meetings/the-paris-agreement/the-paris-agreement [Accessed 20 June 2021].

UNFCCC (nd [b]) 'Introduction to Climate Action', *United Nations Climate Change*, [online], Available from: https://unfccc.int/climate-action/introduction-climate-action [Accessed 30 May 2022].

UNFCCC (nd [c]) 'Introduction: Global Climate Action', *United Nations Climate Change*, [online], Available from: https://unfccc.int/climate-action [Accessed 19 February 2025].

UNFCCC (nd [d]) 'Pre-2020 action by countries', *United Nations Climate Change*, [online], Available from: https://unfccc.int/resource/climateaction2020/ [Accessed 19 February 2025].

UNFCCC (2002) 'A guide to the climate change convention process', *United Nations Climate Change*, [online], Available from: https://unfccc.int/resource/process/guideprocess-p.pdf [Accessed 21 October 2022].

UNFCCC (2017) 'On the possibility to withdraw from the Paris Agreement: A short overview', *United Nations Climate Change*, [online] 14 June 2017, Available from: https://unfccc.int/news/on-the-possibility-to-withdraw-from-the-paris-agreement-a-short-overview [Accessed 14 June 2020].

UNFCCC (2022) 'COP27 reaches breakthrough agreement on new "loss and damage" fund for vulnerable countries', *United Nations Climate Change*, [online] 20 November 2022, Available from: https://unfccc.int/news/cop27-reaches-breakthrough-agreement-on-new-loss-and-damage-fund-for-vulnerable-countries [Accessed 29 November 2022].

Urpelainen, J. and Van de Graaf, T. (2015) 'Your place or mine? Institutional capture and the creation of overlapping international institutions', *British Journal of Political Science*, 45(4): 799–827.

Urpelainen, J. and Van de Graaf, T. (2018) 'United States non-cooperation and the Paris Agreement', *Climate Policy*, 18(7): 839–51.

van Asselt, H. and Zelli, F. (2018) 'International governance: polycentric governing by and beyond the UNFCCC', in A. Jordan, D. Huitema, H. van Asselt and J. Forster (eds) *Governing Climate Change: Polycentricity in Action?*, Cambridge University Press, pp 29–46.

van Asselt, H. and Green, F. (2022) 'COP26 and the dynamics of anti-fossil fuel norms', *WIREs Climate Change*, 14(3): e816.

Van de Graaf, T. (2012) 'Obsolete or resurgent? The International Energy Agency in a changing global landscape', *Energy Policy*, 48: 233–41.

Van de Graaf, T. (2013) 'Fragmentation in global energy governance: Explaining the creation of IRENA', *Global Environmental Politics*, 13(3): 14–33.

Van de Graaf, T. (2015) 'The IEA, the new energy order and the future of global energy governance', in D. Lesage and T. Van de Graaf (eds) *Rising Powers and Multilateral Institutions*, Palgrave Macmillan, pp 79–95.

Van de Graaf, T. and Lesage, D. (2009) 'The International Energy Agency after 35 years: Reform needs and institutional adaptability', *Review of International Organizations*, 4(3): 293–317. https://doi.org/10.1007/s11558-009-9063-8

Vandamme, D. (2021) 'Bringing researchers back In: Debating the Role of Interpretive Epistemology in Global IR', *International Studies Review*, 23(2): 370–90.

van Driel, M., Biermann, F., Kim, R.E. and Vijge, M.J. (2022) 'International organisations as 'custodians' of the sustainable development goals? Fragmentation and coordination in sustainability governance', *Global Policy*, 13(5): 669–82. Available from: https://doi.org/10.1111/1758-5899.13114

Vidal, J. (2013) 'Poor countries walk out of UN climate talks as compensation row rumbles on', *The Guardian*, [online] 20 November 2013, Available from: www.theguardian.com/global-development/2013/nov/20/climate-talks-walk-out-compensation-un-warsaw [Accessed 1 November 2022].

von Allwörden, L. (2025) 'When contestation legitimizes: the norm of climate change action and the US contesting the Paris Agreement', *International Relations*, 39(1): 52–75. https://doi.org/10.1177/00471178231222874

von Billerbeck, S. (2020) '"Mirror, mirror on the wall:" Self-legitimation by international organizations', *International Studies Quarterly*, 64(1): 207–19.

von Uexkull, N. and Buhaug, H. (2021) 'Security implications of climate change: A decade of scientific progress', *Journal of Peace Research*, 58(1): 3–17.

Walker, H. and Biedenkopf, K. (2020) 'Why do only some chairs act as successful mediators? Trust in chairs of global climate negotiations', *International Studies Quarterly*, 64(2): 440–52. https://doi.org/10.1093/isq/sqaa018

Walsh, A. (2017) 'World reacts to US withdrawal from Paris pact', *DW*, [online] 6 January 2017, Available from: www.dw.com/en/world-reacts-to-us-withdrawal-from-paris-agreement/a-39088295 [Accessed 17 August 2020].

Walter, S. (2021) 'Brexit domino? The political contagion effects of voter-endorsed withdrawals from international institutions', *Comparative Political Studies*, 54(13): 2382–415.

We Are Still In (nd) 'Climate Contributions', *We Are Still In*, [online], Available from: www.wearestillin.com/contributions [Accessed 21 February 2021].

Well, M., Saerbeck, B., Jörgens, H. and Kolleck, N. (2020) 'Between Mandate and Motivation: Bureaucratic Behavior in Global Climate Governance', *Global Governance: A Review of Multilateralism and International Organizations*, 26(1): 99–120.

Welsh, J.M. (2019) 'Norm robustness and the responsibility to protect', *Journal of Global Security Studies*, 4(1): 53–72.

White House (2017) 'Statement President Trump Paris Climate Accord', *The White House Government*, [online], Available from: www.whitehouse.gov/briefings-statements/statement-president-trump-paris-climate-accord/ [Accessed 1 June 2020].

Wiener, A. (2008) *The Invisible Constitution of Politics: Contested Norms and International Encounters*, Cambridge University Press. doi:10.1017/CBO9780511490408

Wiener, A. (2014) *A Theory of Contestation*, Springer.

Wiener, A. (2017) 'A theory of contestation: A concise summary of its argument and concepts', *Polity*, 49(1): 109–25. Available from: SSRN: https://ssrn.com/abstract=2946151

Wiener, A. (2018) *Contestation and Constitution of Norms in Global International Relations*, Cambridge University Press. doi:10.1017/9781316718599.003

Wiener, A. and Puetter, U. (2009) 'The quality of norms is what actors make of it: Critical constructivist research on norms', *Journal of International Law and International Relations*, 5(1): 1–16.

Yamin, F. and Depledge, J. (2004) *The International Climate Change Regime: A Guide to Rules, Institutions and Procedures*, Cambridge University Press.

Yanow, D. (2000) *Conducting Interpretive Policy Analysis*, SAGE Publications.

Yanow, D. (2003) 'Interpretive empirical political science: What makes this not a subfield of qualitative methods?', *Qualitative Methods*, 1(2): 9–13.

Yanow, D. and Schwartz-Shea, P. (2015) *Interpretation and Method: Empirical Research Method and the Interpretive Turn*, Routledge.

Zaccaria, G. (2022) 'You're fired! International courts, re-contracting, and the WTO Appellate Body during the Trump presidency', *Global Policy*, 13(3): 322–33. https://doi.org/10.1111/1758-5899.13032

Zaum, D. (ed) (2013) *Legitimating International Organizations*, Oxford University Press.

Zaum, D. (2016) 'Legitimacy', in J. Katz Cogan, I. Hurd and I. Johnstone (eds) *Oxford Handbook of International Organizations*, Oxford University Press, pp 1107–26.

Zelli, F. (2011) 'The fragmentation of the global climate governance architecture', *Wiley Interdisciplinary Reviews: Climate Change*, 2(2): 255–70.

Zelli, F. (2018) 'Effects of legitimacy crises in complex global in global governance discursive, institutional, and behavioral practices', in J. Tallberg, K. Bäckstrand and J. Scholte (eds) *Legitimacy in Global Governance: Sources, Processes, and Consequences*, Oxford University Press, pp 189–200.

Zelli, F. and van Asselt, H. (2013) 'The institutional fragmentation of global environmental governance: Causes, consequences, and responses', *Global Environmental Politics*, 13(3): 1–13.

Zhang, Y.-X., Chao, Q.-C., Zheng, Q.-H. and Huang, L. (2017) 'The withdrawal of the U.S. from the Paris Agreement and its impact on global climate change governance', *Climate Change Research*, 8(4): 213–19.

Zimmermann, L., Deitelhoff, N., Lesch, M., Arcudi, A. and Peez, A. (2023) *International Norm Disputes. The Link Between Contestation and Norm Robustness*, Oxford University Press.

Zürn, M. (2018) *A Theory of Global Governance: Authority, Legitimacy, and Contestation*, Oxford University Press.

Zürn, M. (2020) 'On the role of contestations, the power of reflexive authority, and legitimation problems in the global political system', *International Theory*, 13(1): 192–204.

Index

References to figures appear in *italic* type; those in **bold** type refer to tables.

A

Adler, E. 39
African Union (AU) 97
America's Pledge 75–6
Appellate Body of WTO 4, 123
Asia Pacific Economic Cooperation (APEC) forum 97
Asian Development Bank (ADB) 97
Asia-Pacific Economic Cooperation (APEC) 97
Association of Southeast Asian Nations (ASEAN) 97
Australia
  and COP19 55
  non-ratification of Kyoto Protocol 63
Aykut, S.C. 6

B

behavioural contestation 21, 52, 56, 67
behavioural legitimation 21, 36, 37, 44
  after G77 walkout at COP19 57–9, 110
  of IEA 84, 85, 87, 90, 96
  and Paris Agreement 70, 73, 74–6
Biden, Joe 121
Biermann, F. 6, 99
Birol, Fatih 84, 85–6, 89, 97, 98
Bloomberg Foundation 75–6, 121
Bolsonaro, Jair 68
Bourdieu, P. 39
Brazil, and Paris Agreement 68
Brown, Jerry 73, 75
Bush, George W. 63

C

China 50
  and IEA 79, 81, 83, 84, 85, 86–7, 88, 125
  support to Paris Agreement 70, 73
civil society 2
  and legitimation 37, 60
  walkout, at COP19 49, 56–7, 108

Clean Development Mechanism, Kyoto Protocol 65
Climate Action Mayors 74–5
climate change action (CCA), norm for 2, 7–8, 10, 12, 13–14, 16, 38, 41–4, 104, 105, 125, 126, 127–8
  adoption of 52, 58, 77, 83, 87, 89, 90, 95, 97, 98, 99, 100, 105, 106, 108–9, 110, 111, 112, 113, 115, 116, 118, 127–8, 129
  collective endeavour aspect *see* collective endeavour aspect of CCA
  and contestation–legitimation processes 115–16, **117**, 118, **119**
  and energy approach of IEA 94, 95, 97, 98, 99, 100, 101, 111, 112–13, 115
  future research on 132
  and G77 walkout at COP19 48, 49, 52–6, 57, 58, 60, 106–10, 111
  and IEA membership 83, 84, 87, 88–9, 90, 106, 107, 108, 109, 110–11
  policy implementation aspect *see* policy implementation aspect of CCA
  and US contestation of Paris Agreement 65, 67, 72, 73, 74, 76–7, 111–12, 113–14, 115
Climate Change Expert Group 96
climatization of global politics 6
Clinton, Bill 63
collective endeavour aspect of CCA 41, 42, **44**, 94, 105, 107, 126, 127
  and energy approach of IEA 97
  and G77 walkout at COP19 52, 54, 56, 58, 107, 109, 110, 116
  and IEA membership 83, 84, 87, 88–9, 90, 107, 109, 111–12, 116
  and US contestation of Paris Agreement 67, 72, 75, 76, 77, 111, 114
Conferences of the Parties (COPs) 65, 69, 129
  COP15 4, 11–12, 49, 50–1, 56, 57, 108, 110, 122, 125

164

INDEX

COP16 49, 50, 51
COP17 51–2
COP18 52
COP19 *see* G77 walkout at COP19 (2013)
COP20 60
COP21 98
COP22 65, 99
COP26 121
COP27 121–2
COP28 122
COP29 122
COP30 122
 and informal practices 54, 57, 58–9
 presiding officers 59
 and trust building 59
consent, practice of 37, 108–9
contestation 3–4, 10–11, 17–18, 19, 20, 22–7, 45, 105–6
 and authority 23
 behavioural 21, 52, 56, 67
 discursive 21, 67
 institutional 21, 67, 81
 legitimation scholars of international institutions 23–4
 norm contestation 22–3, 31–2
 as a social practice 25, 27, 123
 strengthening effect of 20, 22–3, 27
 weakening effect of 26
contestation–legitimation processes 4–5, 9, 11, 17–18, 19, 45–6, 104, 124–8, 130–1
 CCA norm 5, 10, 12, 13–14, 16
 community in 29, 30–1, 41, 112, 132
 conceptual connection 21
 contestation 19, 20, 22–7, 45
 legitimacy 27–30
 legitimacy beliefs 33–4, 35, 43, 46
 legitimation practices 21–2, 24
 norm adoption 13–14, 20–1, 22, 25–6, 29, 31–128, 32, 40, 41, 45, 124, 126, 127
 norms as guiding frames of 20, 21, 24, 25, 26, 30–3, 41, 43, 45–6, 118, 120, 124, 126, 129
 practice tracing in 5, 17, 37–45, 126
 stages of 19–22
 target of contestation 22, 23, 25–6, 41
 see also climate change action (CCA), norm for; G77 walkout at COP19 (2013); International Energy Agency (IEA); OECD-exclusive membership of IEA; oil-only approach of IEA; Paris Agreement, US contestation of
counter-institutionalization 23, 94, 113, 124
 see also International Renewable Energy Agency (IRENA)

D

de Boer, Yvo 58
decarbonization 6

Deitelhoff, N. 25, 26–7, 31, 126
de-legitimation 3–4, 17, 18, 19, 20, 22, 23, 24, 26, 45, 108, 113
 Energy Charter Treaty 123
 politicization 23
 practices 33, 34–7, 43
Denmark, and IRENA 9, 79, 93
Depledge, Joanna 49
discursive contestation 21, 67
discursive legitimation 21–2, 36, 37, 43, 55
 after G77 walkout at COP19 57, 58, 110
 of IEA 84, 85, 96, 99, 115
 and Paris Agreement 70, 72–3, 74–6

E

emergency oil response system, of IEA 78, 84, 88, 100, 101–2, 103
Energy Charter Treaty (ECT) 123
energy security 88, 89, 101–2
 see also International Energy Agency (IEA)
Espinosa, Patricia 42
European Union (EU) 73, 89, 123
explicit/implicit reference to norms 20, 44, 46

F

Finnemore, M. 30, 31
France, support to Paris Agreement 73
Fridays for Future movement 2
Frost, M. 39

G

G77 walkout at COP19 (2013) 9, 11–12, 47–9, *53*, 60, 116, **117**, 118, 124–5, 127
 background of 49–52
 and civil society walkout 49, 56–7, 108
 contestation for loss and damage and CCA 52–6
 legitimation by UNFCCC 57–60, 109–10, 111, 127
 and norm for CCA 48, 49, 52–6, 57, 58, 60, 106–10, 111, 116
 proposal of G77 55
 timeline of 50–2, **51**
Gas Exporting Countries Forum (GECF) 97
Germany
 funding to UNFCCC 74
 and IRENA 9, 79, 93, 94
 support to Paris Agreement 73
Global Climate Action Summit 75
Global South *see* North–South divide
Green Climate Fund 68
Gronau, J. 35

H

Heubaum, H. 99
Howard, John 63

I

IEA/IRENA Global Renewable Energy Policies and Measures Database 97
India 79, 81, 83, 84, 85, 86, 88, 125
institutional contestation 21, 67, 81
institutional format in climate governance 9, **10**, 11, 16, 42–3, 105, 116, 118, **119**, 123, 127
   and norm for CCA, contestation 111–14
   and norm for CCA, legitimation 114–15
   see also oil-only approach of IEA; Paris Agreement, US contestation of
institutional legitimation 21, 37, 44
   after G77 walkout at COP19 60
   of IEA 84–5, 87, 90, 96, 115
   and Paris Agreement 70, 71
Intergovernmental Panel on Climate Change (IPCC) 1
International Energy Agency (IEA) 5, 8–9, **10**, 11, 78–9, 90–1, 102–3, 104, 124
   cooperation with international organizations 96–7, 115
   criticism toward 79
   cultural change in 98
   emergency oil response system of 78, 84, 88, 100, 101–2, 103
   establishment of 78
   membership of non-OECD countries 13, 83–7, 90–1, 110
   norm adoption by 14
   open door policy of 84–5, 86, 91
   presence in formal political forums 97
   processes, timeline of **80**
   sale of data and voluntary contributions 99
   technological and scientific expertise of 89
   working groups of 89–90
   World Energy Outlook 95
   see also OECD-exclusive membership of IEA; oil-only approach of IEA
International Energy Forum (IEF) 97
International Renewable Energy Agency (IRENA) 9, 12, 79–80, 81, 83, 84, 90, 94, 96, 97, 99, 107, 109, 110, 111, 112, 115, 116, 125, 127
interpretivism 38, 40
Italy, support to Paris Agreement 73

J

Joint Organisations Data Initiative (JODI) 97

K

Kim, R.E. 6
Kwong, Tiarite George 48
Kyoto Protocol 43, 50, 57
   set up of 65
   US non-ratification of (2001) 4, 12, 63–4

L

Lantis, J.S. 27
Latin American Energy Organization (OLADE) 97
Lechner, S. 39
legitimacy 18, 26, 27–30
   beliefs 19–20, 24, 26, 30, 33–4, 35, 43, 46, 58, 87, 94, 107, 108, 110, 112, 113, 114, 115, 116, 118, 126, 127
   crisis 3, 4, 17, 19, 22, 37, 56, 80, 94, 108, 112, 122, 123
   social embeddedness of 28
legitimacy gap 19, 21, 22, 26, 29, 31, 41, 45, 105–6, 128
   in IEA membership 83, 84, 107
   in loss and damage mechanism negotiation 49, 54, 56, 107, 108
   and oil-only approach of IEA 94, 95, 112
   in Paris Agreement 67, 70, 112, 113
legitimation audiences 28–9, 36
legitimation potential 19, 21, 26, 29, 31, 41, 45, 128
   and energy approach of IEA 96, 112
   and G77 walkout at COP19 54, 108
   and OECD-exclusive membership of IEA 83, 107
   and US contestation of Paris Agreement 67, 70, 112, 113
legitimation practices 21–2, 24, 33, 34–7, 41, 43–4, 128
   after US contestation of Paris Agreement 70–6, 114, 127
   of IEA, related to energy approach 95–102, 115, 127
   of IEA, related to membership 83–90, 110–11, 127
   UNFCCC, after COP15 breakdown 50, 56
   UNFCCC, after G77 walkout at COP19 57–60, 109–10, 111, 127
   see also norm(s)
life cycle of norms 30
loss and damage mechanism 11, 47–9, 109–10, 122, 124–5
   contestation for 52–6, 106, 107–9, 116
   debate, timeline of 50–2, **51**
   UNFCCC mediation 59

M

Maertens, L. 6
Mottley, Mia Amor 1, 132

N

Nationally Determined Contributions (NDCs) 9, 69, 98
non-OECD countries, IEA membership of 13, 83–7, 90–1, 110
Non-state Actor Zone for Climate Action (NAZCA) 60

INDEX

norm entrepreneurs 30
norm(s) 5, 11, 18, 19, 28, 40, 105–6, 130–1
  adoption of 13–14, 20–1, 22, 25–6, 29, 31, 32, 40, 41, 45, 124, 126
  cascade stage of 30
  contestation of 22–3, 31–2
  dual quality of 32, 76, 111, 120
  emergence of 30
  essentialist understanding of 25
  explicit/implicit reference to 20, 44, 46
  future research on 131
  in global climate regime 7, 41, 131, 132
  as guiding frames of contestation–legitimation processes 20, 21, 24, 25, 26, 30–3, 41, 43, 45–6, 118, 120, 124, 126, 129
  internalization of 25, 30, 31
  interpretation of 25, 31–2, 126
  and legitimacy beliefs 33, 34, 43
  and legitimation practices 21–2
  life cycle of 30
  tipping point of 30
  see also climate change action (CCA), norm for
North Atlantic Treaty Organization (NATO) 3
North–South divide 6, **10**, 11, 16, 50, 60, 82–3, 104, 116, **117**, 123, 124–5, 127
  COP15 breakdown 4, 11–12, 49, 50–1, 56, 57, 108, 110, 122, 125
  and norm for CCA, contestation 106–9
  and norm for CCA, legitimation 109–11
  and US contestation of Paris Agreement 67, 68
  see also G77 walkout at COP19 (2013); OECD-exclusive membership of IEA

O

Obama, Barack 64, 66
OECD-exclusive membership of IEA 9, 12–13, 79, *82*, 116, **117**, 125, 127
  consistency and partnering 89
  contestation of 81–3
  exclusion of emerging powers 81–2
  healthy culture among members 89
  inclusion of non-OECD countries 13, 83–7, 90–1, 110
  maintaining exclusivity 87–90, 110
  and norm for CCA 83, 84, 87, 88–9, 90, 106, 107, 108, 109, 110–11
  see also International Energy Agency (IEA)
oil crisis (1974) 78
oil-only approach of IEA 9, 13, 92, *93*, 116, 118, **119**, 125, 127
  contestation of 92–5
  incorporation of renewable energy expertise 95–100, 115
  and norm for CCA 94, 95, 97, 98, 99, 100, 101, 111, 112–13, 115
  see also International Energy Agency (IEA)
open door policy of IEA 84–5, 86, 91
Organization of the Petroleum Exporting Countries (OPEC) 97

P

Paris Agreement 2, 4, 7, 41, 42–3, 48, 55, 56, 60, 128
  design of 64
  exit process 71
  Nationally Determined Contributions 9, 69, 98
  non-state actor engagement in 65–6, 70, 72, 74, 114
  role of IEA in compiling 96
Paris Agreement, US contestation of 4, 9, 12, 14, 62–3, *66*, 116, 118, **119**, 125, 127, 128
  legitimation practices of member states, sub- and non-state actors 72–6, 114
  neutral status of UNFCCC 71
  and norm for CCA 65, 67, 72, 73, 74, 76–7, 111–12, 113–14, 115
  and obstructionism 69
  timeline of **64**
  Trump election (2016) 65
  UNFCCC legitimation practices 70–2
  withdrawal 67–70
policy implementation aspect of CCA 41, 42, **44**, 105, 116, 126, 127
  and energy approach of IEA 94, 95, 97–8, 101, 112
  and G77 walkout at COP19 52, 56, 107–8, 109, 110
  and US contestation of Paris Agreement 67, 77, 113, 114
Pouliot, V. 39
practice tracing 5, 17, 37–45, 126
practice turn 39
principle of common but differentiated responsibility 50
protectionism 60, 62, 67, 69, 111, 112
Pulgar-Vidal, Manuel 60

R

renewable energy 12, 13, 75, 92–3, 107, 112
  expertise, incorporation in IEA 95–100, 115
  IRENA 9, 12, 79–80, 81, 83, 84, 90, 94, 96, 97, 99, 107, 109, 110, 111, 112, 115, 116, 125, 127
  see also International Energy Agency (IEA)
responsibility to protect 130–1
Rio Convention (1992) 7, 42, 43

S

Salerno, Claudia 55
Saño, Yeb 47, 48

Scheer, Hermann 93–4
Schmidtke, H. 35
Sikkink, K. 30, 31
Spain, and IRENA 9, 79, 93
Statistical Office of the European Communities (EUROSTAT) 97

T

Trump, Donald 2, 121
  contestation of Paris Agreement 67–70, 72, 73, 74–5, 76, 111–12, 113, 114, 115, 125
  contestation of WTO Appellate Body 4
  election (2016) 65
  see also Paris Agreement, US contestation of
trust building 57, 59, 60

U

United Nations Environment Programme (UNEP) 1–2
United Nations Framework Convention on Climate Change (UNFCCC) 1, 4, 5, 8–9, **10**, 11, 14, 24, 63, 65, 95, 104, 113, 124
  breakdown of COP15 4, 11–12, 49, 50–1, 56, 57, 108, 110, 122, 125
  cooperation of IEA with 96, 115
  funding for 68, 74
  legitimation practices, after G77 walkout at COP19 57–60, 109–10, 111, 127
  legitimation practices, after US contestation of Paris Agreement 70–2
  non-state actor engagement of 65–6, 70, 72, 74, 114
  and North–South divide 50
  see also Conference of the Parties (COPs); Paris Agreement, US contestation of
United Nations Statistics Division (UNSD) 97
United States
  non-ratification of Kyoto Protocol (2001) 4, 12, 63–4
  role in IEA 89
  states/corporations, support to Paris Agreement 73, 75–6
  see also Paris Agreement, US contestation of

V

Van der Hoeven, Maria 84, 85

W

Warsaw International Mechanism (WIM) 54
We Are Still In 76
Wiener, A. 25, 26, 32, 126
World Bank 3
World Energy Outlook (WEO) 95
World Trade Organization (WTO) 3, 4, 123
Wunderlich, C. 27

X

Xi Jinping 73

Y

Yildiz, Taner 84

Z

Zaccaria, G. 4
Zimmermann, L. 25, 26–7, 31, 126
Zürn, M. 23, 24, 27

www.ingramcontent.com/pod-product-compliance
Lightning Source LLC
Chambersburg PA
CBHW071708020426
42333CB00017B/2188